4 ⁵

Passports to Life

Passports to Life

Journeys into Many Worlds

Harry Llewellyn

Arranged in conjunction
with Pat Lucas

Hutchinson/Stanley Paul
London Melbourne Sydney Auckland Johannesburg

Hutchinson/Stanley Paul & Co. Ltd

An imprint of the Hutchinson Publishing Group

3 Fitzroy Square, London W1P 6JD

Hutchinson Group (Australia) Pty Ltd
30–32 Cremorne Street, Richmond South, Victoria 3121
PO Box 151, Broadway, New South Wales 2007

Hutchinson Group (NZ) Ltd
32–34 View Road, PO Box 40–086, Glenfield, Auckland 10

Hutchinson Group (SA) Pty Ltd
PO Box 337, Bergvlei 2012, South Africa

First published 1980

© Harry Llewellyn 1980

Set in Linotron Baskerville

Printed in Great Britain by The Anchor Press Ltd,
and bound by Wm Brendon & Son Ltd,
both of Tiptree, Essex

British Library Cataloguing in Publication Data

Llewellyn, Harry
    Passports to life.
    1. Llewellyn, Harry
    2. Horsemen and horsewomen – Great Britain – Biography
    I. Title
    798'.092'4   SF284.58.L/

ISBN 0 09 143360 6

Copyright photographs are acknowledged as follows:
E G Malindine; *Western Daily Press* and *Bristol Observer*;
Associated Press Ltd; Associated Newspapers Ltd; London
and County Press; *The Times*; Kemsley Newspapers Ltd;
Evening Standard; Topical Press Agency; *Daily Express*; Norman
Webber; Lichfield; Swaebe; *Western Mail and Echo*; Romley
Marney; Sport and General

Contents

*For those friends, particularly of recent years,
whom I have not mentioned in this book*

Preface

I have always been a chronicler by nature, but a diarist only in relation to a particular activity or a visit abroad. I kept a record of every race in which I rode; this was analytical and self-critical in order to help me improve myself as a steeplechase rider, and I did the same for show jumping until Foxhunter retired. Having been a keen photographer since 1930 I filled album upon album after visiting places like Russia, Africa, the Near East, and the Far West of Canada, as well as keeping full diaries; but it never occurred to me to write a book, especially one about myself as it has worried me that most autobiographies become so egoistic.

This record is not therefore intended as an autobiography in the true sense; it is mainly concerned with events in a number of different spheres of a fairly active life. I have used comparatively little material, and the result can be regarded as a précis of experiences which I hope will interest my readers. My publishers have, understandably, reduced the original to about half its length; they therefore take responsibility for the unavoidable omission of references to certain people whose friendships I have greatly valued.

As well as my articles for the *Field* and *Horse and Hound*, I also wrote technical articles for the *Western Mail* before the war, and after visiting foreign coalfields made numerous contributions on the classification and preparation of coal for the market. For a couple of years I enjoyed writing for the *Sunday Times* on show jumping. When Pat Landsberg produced his good book on Foxhunter I countered with *Foxhunter in Pictures* in 1952. In forty-eight hours I selected a number of photographs and added captions reflecting Foxhunter's views of his show jumping activities; it was really his book, not mine.

I am particularly grateful to Pat Lucas who suggested that I should record my experiences and then played a vital part in arranging them in a comprehensible order.

I have been lucky in having a zest for life, and more than my fair share of fun – never I hope at anyone else's expense. I shall be rewarded if people can enjoy reading my experiences as much as I have enjoyed recalling them.

Basically I believe that you can only reap what you have sown, and that complete dedication to any job is essential to achieve success. However, I have not set out to write anything but a light-hearted account, much of it dealing with scenes into which I have been introduced by various horses – my Passports to Life.

Part One
Road to Aintree

From Golden Bell to Silver Step

I lay on my bed, staring desperately at the white wall of my room and repeating over and over again, 'I must go to sleep – I must go to sleep.' And, eventually, I slept.

A few hours later I rode out of the Helsinki Stadium knowing that with Foxhunter's final effortless clear round the British team had won my country's only gold medal at the Summer Olympics of 1952. Somehow Foxhunter understood my elation as, with ears pricked, he trotted gaily from the arena.

For our disastrous first round in the morning we had incurred the alarming penalty of 16¾ faults – and all because I had failed to warm up Foxhunter adequately. By 1952 the British show jumping team had proved itself the best in the world. Yet after each horse had jumped his first round in this contest we were lying only sixth in the Grand Prix des Nations – and it was all my fault. I was shattered. The kindly sympathy of our supporters only added to my sense of failure as I followed Mike Ansell into the Olympic canteen for lunch.

I knew that Foxhunter would be having his midday nap – sighing peacefully as he did so. Though near to emotional collapse, as my wife Teeny took me back to the spotless white Finnish villa where we were staying, I was determined to follow Foxhunter's example. I knew that in order to play my full part in the vital last round I would have to calm my nerves by going to sleep.

That sleep was indeed my greatest achievement.

Both sides of my family are Welsh, claiming descent from such men of legend as the great lawmaker Hywel Dda; the last – and reputedly childless – Prince Llewelyn; and Sir Dafydd Gam, who protected his sovereign at Agincourt but received an arrow in the eye – hence

Gam, for 'gammy eye', perhaps. There was no central registration until 1837, so for our history before that date we have to rely on tombstones and the full entries in family Bibles. These contained not only records of births, marriages and deaths, but also the pedigrees of the family's horses, hounds and sheepdogs.

My family's roots are firmly set in Breconshire. Rees Llewellyn, my paternal grandfather, was High Sheriff in 1912, and chairman of the Bwllfa Steam Coal Company, the largest colliery of the day. His family owned tracts of land bordering the Brecon Beacons; and my father was to take his Bardic title as Dafydd o'er Parc, since his mother's family held land south of Brecon. No title came our way until my father was created a baronet in 1922, so my own baronetcy is rather 'new'.

On my mother's side, my grandfather was Dr Henry Hiley-Harries. He was 'the grand old man' of the Baptist ministry, a Greek scholar, the bard Afanwy and son of a captain in the Mercantile Marine.

So, through my veins flows the blood of men of the plough, the pit and the pulpit – and it is all Welsh.

There were eight of us in the family. Rhys, who died in 1978, was the eldest. I came next, followed by Elaine, Betty, David, Joyce, Rhidian and Claire. We all adored our very kind parents and our childhood was marvellously happy. Our lives have since taken different paths and we do not see as much of each other as we should, but we are just as affectionately bound as ever we were. However critical one member of that family might be of another, woe betide the outsider who criticizes one of us.

My mother was a fantastic organizer and strict, but this efficiency was combined with an affectionate warmth that spread to all of those whom we later married. She demanded a high standard of behaviour and we were never allowed to say unkind things about other people. She obeyed her own rules by setting a splendid example herself.

My father was equally firm. Once, when I was learning to drive, I waved my fist at another car. Quietly, he told me to pull up. When I asked why we were stopping he replied, 'For that other chap to come back and beat the hell out of you for being so rude.' Luckily for me, the other driver had already disappeared – but it was nevertheless a salutory lesson. I am a critical person by nature, and I can only be thankful that my early upbringing has deterred me from making unnecessary enemies by running people down.

A tremendously active man, my father was a Master of Hounds, as well as a fine fisherman, a superb shot and a brilliant engineer. He had a brain that absorbed everything and a prodigious memory. I think his only real fault was impatience, from which I suffer myself. Nothing irritated him more than other people's lateness and, in that respect, I am afraid I was one of the chief offenders.

As the chairman of many companies, including Lysaghts Steel, Welsh Associated Collieries, Graigola Merthyr and North's Navigation, GKN and Powell Duffryn, much of his time was spent in his offices. Amongst these was a London office based on a flat in Whitehall Court. These flats were to become well known to all the family a little later in life, as the focal point of many of our social activities.

Through his association with companies reputed to produce over half the output of coal in South Wales, my father felt he had a tremendous responsibility towards the coal trade, particularly towards his employees by whom he was held in high regard and of whom he was very fond. Often he would delay closing a pit because of the hardship it would have caused. This meant that he found himself leaning heavily upon the banks to maintain companies that had little prospect of profitability. He used to say, 'Coal stood by my family and I will stand by coal.' Time and again I have heard people say that if all employers had treated their workers as my father's family had, there would not have been so great a degree of industrial unrest in South Wales.

It amazes me that he remained so sane amidst all his business worries and the demands of an energetic young family. Although he was an impatient man, I found him a wonderful companion – but I was lucky because I grew up sharing his interests to a greater extent than did any of my brothers and sisters.

It is to him that I owe the early discipline and opportunities that helped me so much. Yet our mutual love of horses and racing might never have come to fruition, for I was nearly 'a goner' a couple of times at the age of three. I am told that I suffered from blood-poisoning as a result of having sucked my father's chain of office when he held the honorary appointment of High Constable of Upper Miskin.

Dr Banks, who had brought me into the world at Fairfield, my father's house near Aberdare, on 18 July 1911, later suggested that I should be given a pony to ride. I was then five, a thin and mingy little person who so far had shown little interest in anything except

'Uncle Oojah' in the *Daily Sketch*, caterpillars, butterflies, birds and birds' nests.

So it was a big moment in my early life when my father lifted me on to Fairy's back and held me there as I sat on a soft pad saddle and clutched a strap tied across the front of it. He told me later that the first thing I did was to give the pony a tremendous kick but, fortunately, the peaceful little Fairy stood still. This supremely quiet little mare, who knew she had a young child aboard, from then on always treated me with gentleness.

Fairy was a small, eleven-hands Welsh Mountain pony, light bay in colour with four white socks. She had come to us from the nearby Gurnos Farm (now Tom Parry's famous Gurnos Stud) and the affection I formed for her inspired me to start riding. So Fairy was the first of the various ponies and horses that were to become my passports to life.

I contracted double pneumonia when I was seven and therefore went to live with my Aunt Maud at Porthcawl for two years because it was thought that the sea air would do me good. My brother Rhys joined me and we both went to kindergarten school at Arlington House which was nearby. Rhys always defended his little brother against all the types of torture that young children delight in perpetrating upon those who cannot defend themselves. At that time a protective big brother was invaluable and he remained a kind man all his life.

Asthma and general ill-health precluded me from school sports at both Arlington House and St Christopher's in Bath, where I was sent at the age of nine. But it was loss of nerve rather than doctor's orders that stopped me riding for the best part of two years.

I had been keen to continue my riding when I started at St Christopher's and it was therefore arranged that I should go out twice a week with other small boys. We were mounted on hirelings from a local riding-school and I was continually put on ponies that were so big and strong for me that I had no control over them. After a couple of outings, I was completely terrified and I decided to hang up my boots.

A trip to North Africa at the age of eleven did nothing to improve my nerve as a rider. My parents had sent me there on a six-weeks' holiday with a charming 'eyes, nose and throat' specialist called Dr Ivor Davies. During our travels I was persuaded to ride a relatively quiet mule but, sensing my nervousness, he bucked me off after a few strides. You cannot sit 'into' mules as they have no withers, and I do not recommend them for nervous riders.

In all other respects, the trip to North Africa was a marvellous experience and one that was to give me an undying lust for travel. I was fascinated by the wildlife, from the soaring eagles in the Atlas Mountains to the myriads of frogs that filled the ditches at Hamaam Meskatine. At Timgad I explored the Roman ruins and this fired off a lifetime's interest in the remains of the Roman and Greek empires.

By this time, the large Llewellyn family had moved from Fairfield to The Court (now an old people's home) at St Fagans. My first pony, Fairy, and a little Welsh Mountain pony called Tommy came with us, but they did not get much exercise from me! I still used to go for occasional rides on the gentle Tommy and my enthusiasm might well have been rekindled had I not also ridden Rhys' pony, Ginny, who bolted with me for a couple of miles. For sometime after that I hated the sight of a pony or horse and would hardly go near one.

I might never have ridden again had my father not come to the rescue in 1923 and bought me a beautiful dock-tailed 13.2 hands pony called Black Pearl. She was a brilliant hunter but a quiet, affectionate little mare who never pulled and we became attached to each other. I had done a little hunting before losing my nerve and, after the arrival of Black Pearl, it became great fun again.

I received support, encouragement and expert tuition from Tom Cooper, our stud groom, and it is to him that I owe most of my interest in horses. He later told me that his greatest moment was when the Mackintosh of Mackintosh complimented him on my light hands and firm seat.

He was an active little man about five feet five, who walked around with very short strides, hissing and blowing incessantly through his lips. This he did even louder when he was 'doing' a horse. You could hear him 'wisping' from our house which was fifty yards away from the stables, where a series of thuds and hisses indicated that the horses were having their circulation brought to the surface. It was a tribute to his years of hard work that every horse looked beautiful. He was a skilful feeder and the routine he maintained (which started at six o'clock each morning) ensured that the tack and the stables were kept in immaculate order. He was also impeccably turned out himself.

In addition to being our stud groom, Tom Cooper was my confidant and friend. We enjoyed ourselves tremendously out hunting and

I remember on one occasion when the Glamorgan hounds were still running at dusk, I refused to go home. Eventually Cooper and I rode home for eleven miles in the dark singing for most of the way, and I returned to my distraught parents with a feeling of exultation rather than of shame for having worried them.

I was not, however, allowed to have it all my own way. Another time when we were out hunting with the Glamorgan, I was left a little behind and in order to catch up galloped through a gateway that was being held open by an elderly man. Cooper called me back and said: 'Master Harry, you haven't thanked the gentleman who held the gate open for you, so please go back and do so.' I did as I was told.

Tom Cooper had been an apprentice at Newmarket when he was thirteen and came into private service from racing, having worked for Sir Francis Price of Hensol before he came to us. During the First World War he was a trooper in the Derbyshire Yeomanry and he thrilled us all with stories of his exploits. We had no chance of checking up on them, but he undoubtedly played a great part in winning the war! He said his chief role was to be sent out by his commanding officer to gallop through the nearest village and then gallop back again. If no one shot at him, the regiment then camped for the night. Sadly, he was not rewarded and I think he felt this acutely. He was similarly disappointed later when riding a horse for us at Cardiff to finish fourth in a field of five. The next day, he bought every newspaper and, when he found no mention of himself, he complained about it being hard 'to get praise from the press'.

Our life at St Fagans was very happy. The Court was a big house, as it had to be in order to accommodate our parents, eight children, a governess, nurse and eight staff. This meant that we children had to use most of the rooms on the third floor, which our mother furnished beautifully for us. There were eight men in the garden under Mr Appleby. Cooper had two men in the hunting stables, while the stud groom George Legge (who came to us from Colonel Freddie Lort-Phillips at Lawrenny) had his brother and one or two others with him on our stud-farm at Llanmaes, where Hapsburg (runner-up in the 1914 Derby) was standing.

As head groom, Cooper earned £3 10s. a week all found and considered himself well off, but think of the wage bill for such a staff today! Our head chauffeur during my childhood was Knight, who had been with my grandfather and my father in Aberdare. When he died in the 1930s from a heart attack his place was taken by Dyer, the second chauffeur.

The grounds at The Court were beautiful. There were formal and rock gardens, ponds and tennis courts where well-known players like Betty Nuthall and Charles Kingsley played exhibition matches for charity. My father must have been needing cash very badly and, since he was away so often on business, he can only have maintained this privileged type of existence for the enjoyment of his children.

My mother was unwell for much of the time and she was ordered to bed for long periods, but she nevertheless continued to run the large establishment at St Fagans with extreme efficiency. She also remained loving and over-anxious about our health and well-being. Term by term, all through my school life and beyond it, she would write to those in charge saying, 'Harry is not as strong as he thinks he is.' It used to drive me mad!

My health, in fact, had improved greatly when, just before my twelfth birthday, I was at last allowed to participate in school sports. I had said goodbye to St Christopher's in Bath before my trip to North Africa and had been sent to King's Mead at Seaford, where it was thought I might benefit from the sea air. The South Coast undoubtedly helped the delicate little fellow to gain strength.

As a small, fairly active boy, I had felt great frustration at not being allowed to play games of any sort. Once the restraints were lifted, I therefore became extremely competitive and drove myself hard to make up for lost time. Within a year I was in the cricket, rugby football and soccer teams, having become Vice-Captain of the last-named game with a reputation for being a rather rough centre-forward. Though still on the light side, I certainly went as hard as anybody and nothing gave me greater pleasure in rugby than achieving a really crunching tackle. I recall being reprimanded once with a reminder that 'sport should be fun, not war'.

During those years my academic career had also suffered through my ill-health. I recall that a Mr Bunbury, who was regarded as rather a 'brain snob', said I would not have the ability to pass the Common Entrance Examination into a public school and it was then considered that I might be sent to somewhere in Switzerland, like Zuoz. However, my father wanted me to go to Oundle where he thought I might be able to develop what he believed was a mechanical 'bent'. This became a further challenge and I worked really hard during my last two terms. Oundle at that time demanded a high academic standard and set a special entrance paper. It gave me

19

tremendous confidence when I passed and learnt that I would be going into a scholarship form.

Unfortunately, whereas I had enjoyed King's Mead, I did not enjoy life at Oundle. After the initial boost to morale it seemed a dull place. There were hardly any 'horsey' people who enjoyed foxhunting, for most of the boys came from industrial areas and few were real countrymen. An exception was Peter Scott, my senior at School House, who passed on to my brother Rhys his great interest in birds. Initially, Peter established himself as a superb wildfowl artist and he was helped in this by his friend, James Fisher, the son of our splendid Headmaster. In most respects, however, Oundle was such a contradiction to the rest of my life, with the pleasures of hunting and holidays abroad, that the memory of the change from a cheerful environment to such a dreary one still sends shivers down my spine.

I longed for the end of each term all the more fiercely after my father had bought me a 14.2 chestnut mare called Golden Bell, who came into my life when I was fifteen. Golden Bell had a charming temperament, was very fast and jumped with facility over the timber, brush fences and wide reens of the Tredegar country. She had a good mouth, but was onward bound, with her ears always pricked looking for the next excitement. The mare made me really competitive in the hunting-field for together we could hold our own in any adult company in South Wales – though, in fact, no one had much of a 'go' in those days while we tried to jump everything in sight.

I particularly enjoyed the rough-and-tumble of the Pentyrch Hunt of which Lady Bute was Master. It seems that I must have become something of a nuisance because friends often used to telephone my father after a day's hunting to complain about my outrageous behaviour – not because I was interfering with the hounds but because I used to take a delight in flashing past them whenever I could.

On one occasion I rode Golden Bell in a pony race for teenagers at Hensol Castle. It was won by Cen Traherne, now Sir Cenydd, who beat me by about ten lengths. I was thrilled by this race and my spirits were not unduly dampened when my mother drew me aside and said, 'Harry, you were the only boy finishing with his tie flying out!'

I was reminded of this incident many years later when Nat Kindersley on Maguire won the National Championship at the White City in 1946, with Ted Williams second, third, fourth and fifth. The

Duchess of Beaufort turned to me and whispered, 'Serves Mr Williams right – his tie was flying out.'

Golden Bell also gave me my first taste of point-to-pointing, in a pony race at the Pentyrch meeting. So many small horses under fifteen hands went hunting in those days that there was a race for them at the end of the day, designed to give the young a chance. In this race, I fear, I showed little judgement. My racing diary reads: 'After a faller at the first fence, seven refused at the second leaving Wavelet and myself out in front for two miles when Golden Bell got leg-weary. She was so tired that she only just scrambled over the second last fence so I dismounted, led her to the last fence only to discover that it had been set on fire. It was unjumpable, so I re-mounted just before the winning-post to be placed fourth.'

My school life at Oundle was interspersed not only with my riding activities, but also with delightful family holidays, usually with members of the Berry family as our companions. We twice spent Christmas together in Madeira, where diving and swimming became our chief sports and where I formed a little society which had the object of robbing the rich hotel tables in order to feed the scraggy children in the streets. The waiters were soon in league with us and all went well until Mr Gandolfo, the Portuguese manager of the hotel, noticed a huge crowd of children assembled at our secret exchange place and realized that they were eating up the hotel's profits. Our parents were told what was happening and so this 'Robin Hood' adventure had to stop.

Mr Gandolfo, who had the Portuguese tendency to pronounce 's' as 'sh', was also memorable for the day he jumped onto a chair at one of our farewell celebrations and announced that we would all sing 'God shave the King'.

We spent several holidays in France, including one in Normandy which I will never forget. Whereas I have never been interested in betting my father was a compulsive gambler, and during our stay in France he took us all to the races at Deauville where he had a large bet on a horse called Finglas. Having cheered the horse home he realized that he had lost the ticket, so the Llewellyns and Berrys spent the rest of the afternoon searching for it. My father said he had to find this ticket, the presentation of which would pay for the whole of the family holiday in France. It was a desperate situation and we all shared my father's misery until he put in a claim to an official who checked that a winning ticket, sold at a Tote window which my father identified, had not been claimed; a month later he was paid in full.

Back at Oundle, there were a few enjoyable activities as I moved up the school. We spent a fortnight each term in workshops, where I learned how to shoe horses and ponies of every conceivable shape and size. I also learned to operate a large range of machines, from shapers, planers, millers and borers to centre-lathes and drills. This came in useful when I went into engineering later in life. All I have to show for my earlier efforts is a pair of not very finely matched brass candlesticks!

I learned to play the violin under Stephen Champ and achieved some success, finally playing first fiddle with my instructor in the *Messiah*, which was conducted by Adrian Boult and broadcast by the BBC. I also sang every 'voice' in the School Choir – treble, alto, tenor and baritone. I have always enjoyed part-singing and my father and I often lifted our voices in harmony on car journeys. It only takes two Welshmen to make a choir!

My sporting interests centred on rugby football, which was my great love, and on hurdling. I was the third-best high hurdler at Oundle, but only the best two went to the Public Schools' Sports at Stamford Bridge where the winner was our number one hurdler, Joe Simpson, later head of the Metropolitan Police.

I was also captain of tennis at Oundle and often had to play distinguished visitors to the school. One such was the Bishop of London, who proved an expert at driving his opponent to the back of the court with high lobs and then sending sneaky little drop-shots over the net. He was much amused when the headmaster asked me to comment on the Bishop's game and I said, 'He plays a dirtier game of tennis than any cleric I have ever met.'

During school holidays, I often played doubles with Rosalie Cory, the Welsh Junior Champion, at her house Coryton, which has now been swallowed up by the new road-system north of Cardiff. She had a service like a man's and could easily have beaten me. Instead she carried me through to win the Welsh Junior Mixed Doubles Championships at Penarth and got me through one round of Junior Wimbledon. I was never a good singles player, as I tried to make every shot a winner, but I was reasonably good as a doubles player.

In 1928, my scholastic career was again interrupted by illness and I missed a term and a half whilst recuperating at La Colline, a clinic near Montreux in Switzerland. I was able to ski there, but I never really took to it for I had a tendency to dislocate my joints. However,

I soon became a reasonably proficient skater and particularly liked racing round the small rink at Glion, where I must have been a nuisance to everyone.

I also took up bobsleighing and became a member of Les Collinards, the crew from the clinic. Mario Cantoni, from Egypt, was our driver and we became an extremely able crew. The World Championship had been held at Caux that year but, as a crew had been killed, another Championship was organized to provide funds for the dependants. In practice, Les Collinards returned the best time and we started favourites. Mario was an expert while the rest of us provided enthusiasm and weight; we did splendidly until we got to the Grand 'S' and went straight over the top at the first bend. This was probably fortunate, for those who had been killed in the World Cup had come off at the second bend and had landed in the trees. We turned a few somersaults but landed in the snow, and not one of us was hurt.

Another opportunity that came my way in Switzerland was to learn dressage from a part-time Instructor in the Swiss Army. My previous knowledge extended to little beyond hunting and there was no one in Britain from whom one could learn the rudiments of dressage. At that time training of this kind was much better developed on the Continent; later it was to prove invaluable to me.

Towards the spring we sailed a little six-metre boat, again under the guidance of Mario who was commandant of an Egyptian Yacht Club. Of course, membership of the crew was mixed and I formed an affection for Loteli, a charming little French girl of sixteen. In a moment of boldness I invited her to the cinema. I was more interested in her than in the film and, plucking up tremendous courage, I gave her a smacking kiss on the cheek. She rounded on me furiously saying, 'Call that a kees?'

I am afraid that was the end of our romance and, incidentally, of our sailing career together. This was just as well because, towards the end of my stay, we twice got marooned in the middle of Lac Leman and were there for several hours before poor Mario was able to take advantage of a sudden sharp breeze.

I returned home to my horses, my three dogs and the country pursuits of South Wales. In addition to hunting, we went fishing on the River Usk and shooting in the grounds of our own home and in Lord Plymouth's shoot round St Fagans Castle. My father organized shooting-parties to entertain his friends and, as a result, I think we were all quite good shots. Once we shot 1800 pheasants in the first two days 'over', which was not bad in the provinces; but before long I lost my taste for organized slaughter, which I felt was hardly sport. My later experiences of stalking game with a rifle, shotgun or camera demanded far more skill and offered a real challenge.

A hunter mare called Silver Step, bought for me by my father, was already installed in our stables by the time I returned home from Switzerland. She was a 15.3 chestnut, by Golden Bell's sire Jingling Geordie and out of a Welsh Cob mare. She was to become my first passport into racing and show jumping.

I was allowed to do some point-to-pointing in the spring of 1929 after my return, so I entered Silver Step in the Members' Heavy-weight Race at Pentyrch, carrying fourteen stone over three and a half miles. The mare never touched the brush fences or the post-and-rails that were part of this course and, after a slow start, I was able to stoke up a little a mile from home and just beat one of the leaders to finish in third place.

My father, who rode well himself, did everything he could to promote my riding in races and I was to become much spoiled in this direction. My one regret was that his heavy gambling often meant that far too much money rested on the outcome. He backed every horse I rode and, since I was never interested in betting, for me this took some of the fun out of racing.

However, the shared love of racing still bound us together very closely, so that Rhys was understandably hurt by the favouritism which my father displayed towards me. It might have been different had my elder brother continued riding, but he was run away with by my father's lightweight cob called Cherry Pie when he was still in his early teens, an event that kept him out of the saddle for ten years. His achievements were destined to be in a different field from my own.

My brother Rhys owned some Dexter cattle and also, as the result of his experiments in breeding, he had flocks of Brecon Buff Geese and Rumpless Bantams. He once won the first six prizes in the International Show at Antwerp with his Brecon Buff Geese – his were the only ones there! His experiments later earned him praise from Professor Hutt of Columbia University, who described him as 'the greatest expert on practical genetics in this country'. Their subsequent exchange of letters proved invaluable to them both. Professor Hutt wrote extensively on poultry breeding whilst Rhys wrote many articles and published a book, *Breeding to Race*.

Rhys also became an expert on the Przewalski horse and, when he went to the Serengeti, spent all his time counting the stripes on zebra. He became the first President of the British Spotted Horse Society, and later in life, we had our only serious disagreement when I had a pony stallion we called Yellow Peril gelded. 'Do you realize,' he said, 'that you have gelded the only marmalade dun in existence?' It was a crime for which he never forgave me.

My brother David and I probably had more in common with each other in our early days. He loved racing, although like my father he was a betting man. He was keen on hunting too and in the mid-thirties, he whipped-in to Bernard van Cutsem, then Master of the Cambridge Drag. Later, he married Jo Williams whose father, Bob, was Master of the Glamorgan Hounds for thirty-three years.

Sadly, we now see little of each other. David writes freely and entertainingly, but two prime ministers have told me how sad they were that he gave up his career in politics. Both Anthony Eden (later Lord Avon) and Ted Heath asked me to persuade him to bring back the 'quality in debate' in the House of Commons. He turned Cardiff North from a 2000 minority into a 10,000 majority for the Tories, then became the Minister for Welsh Affairs and was knighted in 1967. He has since become disenchanted with politics and has under-exploited his great talents as a racing gossip-columnist. He walks alone, but when the family meet he is as much fun as ever and a very wise and helpful friend and counsel.

I had four delightful sisters. The beautiful Elaine, who always looked so elegant riding side-saddle, is now the widow of Donald Anderson who was chairman of P & O. The resolute and wise Betty, the cornerstone of our family, is now Mrs David Prichard; Joyce, who died in 1976, was married to Frank Byers and lived in Northern Ireland, while Claire married Hume Stuart-Moore, chairman of Gallaher. With the exception of Betty, who became Master of the Talybont Hounds, they all complained that I put them off riding by putting them on unsuitable horses.

I saw little of my youngest brother, Rhidian, until the 1930s, except when we went hunting together. He was a good, natural horseman and he once rode a great double at the Llangibby point-to-point. Shortly before the war, he joined the Welsh Guards and he was awarded the Military Cross after Dunkirk.

During the holidays at home, my three dogs were my constant companions and I trained them to do a variety of tricks. Fury, the Keeshond bitch, would obey the usual commands to 'sit', 'lie down', 'go' where I pointed, 'stop' and 'roll over'. She would also bark to command and walk on her hind legs. Billy, a little lemon-and-white terrier from the Pentyrch hunt-kennels, achieved more or less the same standard.

The star, however, was Lancer. He looked like a blue Merle spaniel with a pink nose, but was born of Welsh Springer parents and the other five members of the litter bore the appearance of pure-bred Welsh Springer spaniels. The Corys, who bred him, swore that his mother's kennel was netted in and that no other dog had got at the bitch. So it was difficult to explain how Lancer had acquired his colouring.

At one time there was a theory of telegony which held that, due to some complicated mental process, a mammal could throw back to a previous mating and Lancer's dam had previously had an illicit love-affair with a sheepdog. I do not believe that this theory is accepted nowadays, although I have often heard it said that a mare once mated to a heavy horse could later produce by a thoroughbred foals with quite abnormal amounts of hair on their legs.

Lancer could have performed on the stage. He would twine himself through my legs when walking; upon word of command he would stop, stand up, and bow at a distance of a hundred yards. In later years he also learned a trick which Ann Bridgeman, later the first Lady Cowdray, had taught her Shetland sheepdogs. This involved his leaping into a chair on the word of command and entertaining the audience by striking various comical attitudes. Emma Hamilton is said to have produced the human equivalent of this performance at the Beaufort Hotel in Monmouth after Nelson had made his after-dinner speech to the assembled company.

I was once invited to give a display with my dogs at a show at Peterson-Super-Ely. This proved surprisingly successful and even drew some applause from my father, who, in a grey homburg hat and plus-fours, was sitting on a wagon in the middle of the arena. He always thought that I spent too much time with my dogs.

He also disapproved of me on this occasion because, for the first time, I had entered the Open Jumping on Silver Step, who in fact finished third. In those days the sport had just emerged from what was originally 'show-yard' jumping, where professionals were able to sell their horses to clients. It was not an accepted sport for hunting people, although the horsed cavalry of every nation competed against each other in show jumping, dressage and 'Le Complet' or 'Militaire', which is now called eventing or horse-trials. Originally, the latter was a test of a good military animal's ability to cross country and become an efficient military weapon.

My father would have been happier about my competing had a similar amount of enthusiasm been directed towards my work at school. My scholastic career had not only been interrupted by illness; it was also hampered by my belief that a job would eventually be found for me in one of my father's concerns, so that I felt I had no great need to work particularly hard. My mother was always anxious that I should not strain myself either mentally or physically, while my father disapproved very much of my lack of effort.

I had gone to Oundle to learn engineering but was never in an engineering form. First of all they tried me out in classics, later in history and finally in zoology and botany. The only scholastic highlight I achieved was a credit in Greek history, which I enjoyed because of my interest in old ruins. Otherwise my results were uninspiring but, at the end of my time at Oundle, I did succeed in qualifying for Trinity College, Cambridge, where I was to find more freedom to follow my natural inclinations.

Like the rest of my family, I always took an analytical interest in the things I did and wanted to shine at the activities I most enjoyed. John Miller (later the Queen's Equerry), who served alongside my three brothers in the Welsh Guards, once said: 'The trouble with you Llewellyns is that you always have to be expert on something or other!'

2   Cambridge and Canada

I went up to Trinity College, Cambridge, in September 1929, I fear thinking much more of playing rugby football and riding in races than of anything else. The opportunities for doing both seemed endless.

It was decided that it would be good for me to read economics – which, rather unwillingly, I did. I had wanted to read zoology, botany and possibly agriculture. Not only was my subject unappealing; so was my supervisor, Maurice Dobb, a famous lecturer and broadcaster who had been a card-holding member of the British Communist Party since it had been established in 1920. As the son of a capitalist, I automatically became an enemy although I was at an age when I was quite happy to listen to political views from anyone.

My father was a Liberal. He played much of his bridge at the Reform and National Liberal clubs and my uncle Bill had stood as Liberal candidate for Aberdare, having been narrowly beaten by Mr Standing who, with Lord Hall, eventually made Aberdare a safe Labour seat. We were then a Liberal family.

Mr Dobb, who usually wore a red tie, was soon at war with me, so that I began to argue just for the fun of it – and because he got so cross so quickly. My family had particularly good relations with their work-force, but he refused invitations from me to come and see that mutual respect could exist between employers and employees. Andrew Boyle's book *The Climate of Treason* describes Maurice Dobb as 'a Marxist intriguer and academic economist of subtlety and virtuosity'. He was thrown fully dressed into the River Cam more than once – but I claim no responsibility!

Burgess, MacLean and Philby, who figured rather more prominently in *The Climate of Treason*, were among my contemporaries at Cambridge. They used to frequent Gil Philips' café-cum-bar, which I sometimes visited, but no one then suspected they would prove such an embarrassment to this country by their treacherous affection for the communist cause in Russia. Kim Philby was the brightest of them all, but who could have suspected that he would infiltrate our counter-espionage and be in a position to give away the names of British agents throughout the world?

I regret to say that I was not interested in the academic side of Cambridge life. I hardly ever went to a lecture, cut several of my appointments with Mr Dobb and had a fine old time instead. I gave up lawn tennis, mainly because there were too many good international players already at Cambridge and I didn't like being beaten. After one or two attempts at hurdling at Fenners sportsground, I soon appreciated that I was out of my class, so I concentrated on rugby and was awarded my 'cuppers' as a 'fresher' during my first term.

During my first Christmas vacation from Cambridge, I hunted seventeen out of a possible eighteen days and went to an average of four hunt balls a week. This was to be the general pattern of all my Christmas holidays. I was a teetotaller and did not smoke; providing I slept for four hours I could keep going very well.

By this time I had become more interested in my father's farms. He had owned a champion herd of Herefords and bred St Fagan Paxolute, the overall breed champion at the Royal Show. This bull was then sold at a record price to the Argentine. The story went round that he was going there 'for heifer and heifer', but unfortunately he dropped dead as he was about to serve his first Argentinian love. Thus, apart from his great win at the Royal, he left behind only his photograph that always appeared on Thornybears' bags of meal.

My father similarly had success with his Clun Forest sheep; indeed I remember his cattle and sheep winning at shows everywhere. However, they proved unprofitable and at about the time I went to Cambridge, the Hereford herd was sold. It included a cow called St Fagans Pussylute which the great breeder, Dick de Quincey, later told me was the best cow he had ever acquired; she was responsible for the best blood in the Vern Curly and Oyster strains. I once heard my father talking about breeding with Dick de Quincey and they agreed that putting the best to the best was the wisest way to breed quality. They did not believe that you should breed from one moderate animal and another with a special compensating quality, in the hope that a particular fault would be eliminated by such a mating. My father was an amazing judge of animals – horse, dog, cow, or sheep – but he never tried growing orchids at which Dick de Quincey also became so expert.

Back at Cambridge for the start of my second term, Micky Stuart-Potts and I decided to join the Officers Training Corps. Micky had been with me at Oundle, where he was one of the few people with horsey inclinations; he also had a tremendous sense of humour and had helped to make school life bearable.

Those of us in the OTC used to ride horses hired out by local livery stables. We all received excellent instruction from Sergeant Brodie, who retained his cheerful attitude despite the way Micky and I played the fool. We both enjoyed pretending that we had hardly ever ridden before; when told to jump without stirrups or reins down a line of small obstacles, our cries of terror must have chilled the blood. This angered Peter Paget, the officer in charge of our ride, and he suggested that Micky and I might retire from military affairs.

Before doing so, we went to camp in the park at Arundel in Sussex, where I was appointed 'galloper'. This meant that I spent my time galloping around flat out trying to keep the various units in touch. I had three horrible horses, two of whom did their best to run away while the other reared over backwards on me. Surprisingly, I got a good chit for my energetic galloping and, when I retired from the OTC, kind Sergeant Brodie put in a good report for me. This little pseudo-military experience became of value when, at the beginning of the war, I was commissioned into the Warwickshire Yeomanry.

My interest in racing was kept very much alive during my time at Cambridge, and was a chief cause for my neglect of lectures. Since Newmarket was within easy reach, I went there for all the good races, such as the Guineas, Cambridgeshire and Cesarewitch. I was usually on the course early and I learned the signals given by tic-tac men. Although unattracted by betting, I formed the impression that to have been a 'penciller' to a good bookmaker on the course at Newmarket would have been a splendid qualification for any job.

I also furthered my experience as an amateur jockey and, on one memorable occasion, played truant in order to ride in my first race under National Hunt rules. My mount was Theorem, a horse I had schooled myself at home in Wales. I recall my father once fixing a time of 8.30 a.m. to see us in action. He was delayed, so I jumped Theorem over a couple of plain fences and our open ditch, thinking that my father would not come. Suddenly he appeared and asked me to jump the ditch again, because the horse had a habit of rapping the guard-rail. I said he had jumped it well twice and I would like

30

to leave him on a good jump, whereupon I was ordered to get off the horse. My father got up on him in his blue suit and bowler hat, then jumped the plain fences together with the open ditch quite perfectly. He was just able to stop the horse as he approached me. Then he jumped off, doffed his bowler hat to me and left without a word.

Theorem was by Bushido out of Theobald's Park and he was thirteen years old when I was given him. He was a tough, almost black sixteen-hand gelding who had won the Gunners' Gold Cup at Aldershot for Major Davey, and my father bought him for me as a hunter chaser.

He was not a beautiful horse as there was no white on him apart from a small white star. He had a long plain head and was slightly Roman-nosed, but he had all the guts in the world. Theorem was a tough guy anxious to get on with the job and he was my buddy – a change from the four gentle mares with whom my relationship had been largely based on affection. He was no sort of affectionate pet and always seemed intent on looking over my shoulder to see what was going on elsewhere, so that there was an air of rugged independence about him. He was inclined to lay on the bridle, knew how to take hold and was often difficult to pull up. He was also unbelievably bold. Set to jump a house, he would at least have reached the first floor. He was the only horse ever to run away with me. Fortunately there happened to be a haystack handy and I was able to point him directly at it. It would not have surprised me if he had tried to jump it.

Theorem came by horsebox from Wales to give me that first taste of riding under rules in the Leicestershire Foxhunters' Steeplechase at Leicester. My diary reads: 'Theorem was jumping beautifully throughout and standing a long way off his fences. On entering the straight I was immediately behind the four leaders who were in a row and until then did not move. Unfortunately, we fell at the next fence about three furlongs from home and I was slightly concussed for a few minutes. We were going well at the time. The fence I fell at had a down-hill approach and I must have been travelling too fast and uncollectedly at it. I was too near the horses in front and so probably did not give Theorem a clear view.'

I had a pretty nasty headache after the race, so I drove myself back to Cambridge and went to bed for three days in a dark room as the racecourse doctor had told me to be careful about delayed concussion.

My second race under National Hunt Rules was the Cleeve

Hunters' Steeplechase at Cheltenham, where Theorem was completely unknown. We started at 20–1 and were all surprised at the way he ran, since he finished second to Royal Arch II, a top hunter chaser ridden by Fred Thackray. Later, I was second again on Theorem at Stratford-upon-Avon, but I then had a fall at the Quorn Hunt National Hunt Races at Loughborough, where most of the course was six inches deep in water. At the first fence after the water jump, both Theorem and I slid on our sides for twenty yards in slush. This time our fall was quite painless and I enjoyed it!

1930 was also memorable for my first point-to-point win. This came in April when I rode my father's Pentyrch to win the open race at the Tredegar Hunt meeting by a short head. It was a thrilling experience and I could think of nothing else for days.

With so many pleasant distractions, I failed to pass an examination of any sort during my first year at Cambridge, and of course got into trouble as a result. Fortunately my tutor, F. J. Dykes, a rugged New Zealand academic, was keen on racing. Unbeknown to me, he had quietly been observing my progress as an amateur jockey. He was therefore less harsh on me than Maurice Dobb, whose report described me as 'indolent' and 'lazy' – indolent certainly but hardly lazy.

That happy, but academically unsuccessful, year was followed by the first of three thrilling long vacations which were interspersed with my time at Cambridge. As I was destined for the sales side of my father's colliery operations, he agreed to my starting the long vacation of 1930 by staying with Senator Lorne Webster of Montreal. At that time we had an interest in the Canadian Import Company and the plan was that I should learn about how to sell coal to foreigners. By the time I returned, months later, I had learned a good deal about many things, but very little about selling coal.

I was eighteen when I set out for Canada and I recall that my tourist third-class ticket in the *Duchess of Richmond* cost me £22 15s. My nineteenth-birthday treat was the sight of thirty-nine icebergs as we were steaming towards Belle Isle and the East Coast of Canada. On arrival, I was met by the debonair Senator Lorne Webster and his son Mac and was soon leading a life that was akin to sybarite comfort after the spartan conditions in the steerage.

Senator Webster was a brilliant businessman, who was credited with having bought and sold the Montreal Waterworks within a week. In those days he was respected an entrepreneur and empire-builder, but might now be regarded as a bloated capitalist and indiscriminate colonialist. He was very kind to me and arranged an introduction through Tom Meighen, a former prime minister, to his friend Pat Burns in the far west. I then borrowed £100 from the Senator and set off for Calgary. I went by train to Toronto, seeing in the distance the arrival of the R100 which had reached Montreal after crossing the Atlantic. Later she was scrapped after the R101 crashed with the loss of all on board. There was plenty to see in and around Toronto before I completed my journey to Calgary where Tom Farrell, the Burns' Ranch Superintendent picked me up from the Empire Hotel (two dollars a night) at seven o'clock in the morning. He was to drive me to one of Pat Burns' ranches – the '44' in Southern Alberta, where I was to earn my keep.

On the way we visited Lundbreck and I was astounded to learn later that my father, on his way to the Crow's Nest Pass, had camped in the same place. It had been given its name by Lund and Breckenridge, and he knew both men well. He remembered seeing the Blackfoot Indians pulling a dead cow out of the river there and eating it. It was odd that we should have landed up in the same place twenty-eight years apart, coming from different directions.

My grandfather had given my father £1000 to learn about American mining, and after two years he came back the owner of a small ranch and with £14,000 in his pocket. When he returned he pioneered the first electrically operated coal-cutters in Britain at his own colliery, Windber, which in twenty-eight years of his ownership never lost an hour through industrial dispute. Families who worked there have been our friends all our lives. Before he left Canada, my father had been offered a job as Chief Engineer for British Columbia. My mother, to whom he was engaged, refused to go out there; otherwise I might have been born Canadian.

Tom Farrell and I had to fight our way through a swarm of grasshoppers, which smothered our windscreen, before we reached the '44' with its spacious corrals and well-kept building. The boss was Ab Lewis and staying with him was his pretty niece, Belle Collier. The boys were mainly engaged with haying, but I was immediately given work on the basis that I would 'scrub my hutch' – in other words, work for my keep with the possibility of earning a few dollars if I was able to help with breaking horses. I was on the pay-roll at five bucks a month. I had my first job – as a cowboy.

For most of my time on the '44' Ranch I was the 'jingler', which meant I had to get up at 4 a.m., collect the horses for the cowboys and haying-crew and then help George Fenton, the head cowboy, work the cattle and horses. The other dozen men were off harvesting the hay-crop and we all worked flat out. We met at mealtimes, at a circular table around a huge cart-wheel that acted as a giant 'dumb waiter'.

The boys were all experienced horsemen who in fact usually worked as cowboys. They were high-spirited but could not have been more friendly, and they were amused by my accent. George said, 'We should be calling you Lord Chawlie, but we are going to call you Harry,' and we were all on christian name terms from then on.

George Fenton was a short, balding man of forty and as tough and hard as anyone could be. But he had a pleasant nature, was very much in love with his job, and we became close friends. He looked elegant on a horse but not on foot, and had worked cattle all his life. He had wonderful hands and was able to train a horse to neck-rein very quickly. A sympathetic instructor, he knew I was anxious to learn and he kept on giving me added responsibilities until, towards the end of my stay, we worked as a team.

I still feel the thrill of my first day when I dressed the full part in jeans, chaps and all the correct gear. That morning George started to teach me how to use a rope and a swivel bull-whip, which were essential tools of the trade. I found them comparatively easy and within a day or two could rope a calf. I also became pretty effective with the sixteen-foot bull-whip and often practised rolling a tin can with it.

When roping, the main problem was the amount of strength needed for throwing the rope, especially when galloping along at about twenty-five miles an hour with a calf in front. The rope had to be thrown with considerable force and to begin with I found that it always fell short. It was important to keep the rope supple and this was achieved by trailing it in the dust behind one's pony. A stiff, wet rope was impossible to use.

The horse that made my life on this ranch was Stockings. He was an oldish bay horse, 15.3½ hands high, with a white blaze and white socks. He was such a good pony that when I cut a calf out of a herd he followed it. I had to do nothing, since he would always follow closely on the calf's near side so that it was easy for me to rope on the off side. If I missed, he tracked the calf more slowly, still keeping him on his own while I recoiled my rope. As the calf turned he turned too, often before I was ready so that several times I nearly fell off.

34

On one occasion I was halfway down his side, holding onto the horn with both hands for dear life. Stockings then slowly came to a halt and saved me the ignominy of being a cowboy afoot.

As with all the good horses I have ridden, I immediately felt a close affinity with Stockings. I have noticed all the way through a career with horses that anybody who does well on a horse is also bound to him by a deep affection. No one could be fonder of his horses – or more solicitous for their care – than David Broome or Harvey Smith. Only the best groom is acceptable in the successful stables for show jumping, hunting, racing and eventing.

Although he had a severe bit, Stockings was immediately obedient to very delicate neck-reining and could skid to a stop from a gallop with only the gentlest pressure on his mouth. He was completely co-operative and soon we established an accord; he seemed to know what I was thinking and we were in complete sympathy with each other. He could turn very quickly with a swift acceleration; his only drawback was that his fastest gallop was rather slow so that it was difficult to rope a good-sized calf. He was about twelve years old and wonderfully sure-footed. I could even gallop him across rocks without fear of stumbling.

As soon as George was happy that I could ride, I was told we had lots of work to do and we rode out of the valley over the range into Steer Pasture where there were twelve hundred three-year-old cows and speys. Speys are heifers from which the ovaries have been removed. This operation helps to put meat on them so that they grow more quickly into prime Canadian beef. Apparently, with the worries of sex removed, they are able to concentrate on eating.

Once I got up at the disgustingly late hour of 5.45 a.m. and found that George had gone, so I went off to watch the haymaking in the adjoining hills. After being cut and made the hay was laid in lines and then great sweepers, with a horse at each side, scooped up the lines and dropped the hay at the foot of a slide. Two enormous Percherons hitched to a huge 'T' then pushed the hay up the slide from which it fell into ricks which were levelled by the stackers. This system dealt quickly with hundreds of acres of hay. Such vast quantities were necessary when snow covered the ground for months on end and there were four thousand cattle to feed.

Up at four every day, we usually went up to the canyon where George and I had a good look at the cattle before they sought shelter in the thick brush from the terrible midday heat. Once we tried to take four cows away from the boundary fence of the Bull Pasture. It was an exciting gallop over rocks, ridges and brush. Stockings was as sure-footed as a Welsh Mountain pony and I found myself galloping down precipices alongside George. Having driven back my three, I went to help George who was having trouble with a mad cow that kept attacking him. She then attacked me, so we threw our ropes round her neck and tried to pull her down the canyon to the corrals. When she threw herself into the stream bed I jumped off to help her out with my bull-whip, but she got up, dragging both horses along after me for a few yards as I scuttled for my life. After an hour we pulled her into the corrals where we left her. Two days later she provided prime beef on the dumb-waiter wheel. A rough lady like her would have taken up too much of our time on the range.

On one occasion the boys laid a great bet that I could not ride the 'sorrel', which is Canadian for chestnut. A time was fixed for my attempt but, before the appointed hour, I went to the barn and put the saddle on the sorrel. He was really just an ordinary horse with a 'cold back' so, having put the saddle on, I walked him round inside the barn but did not get on him. Then I took him into the circular corral where all the boys had come to see the fun, got on him and just trotted round gently. Everyone was amazed and I won the bet; this incident showed that kindness or, if you like, the use of a little tact, can work wonders.

Similarly, many of the horses one sees at rodeos are artificially wild. You may notice that the unbroken horses are genuine enough, but when you see a horse with a back-cinch or girth on him – look out for trouble. It is that which the horse is bucking against, rather than the man on top. Many of these horses are easily ridable, but they can get up to all sorts of tricks if they have a very tight back-cinch.

When I rode another horse called Prince using the same sympathetic approach he refused to buck with me at all. I asked about the little income I was supposed to receive from bronco-busting, and was told, 'he must have been broken before'. So I was delighted when George rode him the next day and was sent nearly twenty feet into the air! Ab Lewis then gave me ten bucks – a fortune.

In fact, Prince turned out to be a good cow-pony, thick-set but fast over a short distance. He stood about 15.3 hands and was also a good walker, which is important in a cow-pony when one has to cover long distances. I rode him a lot as he was much faster than Stockings though lacking his comforting skills and experience. The cow-ponies are trained to stand still when one leaves them; this is taught by tying the ends of the reins to a sack or log of wood and the pony is rewarded for standing still. Disaster ensues if he does not!

At this time George was breaking a Kentucky thoroughbred called 'Silly 16', who was completely uncooperative. She had a straight-forward buck but occasionally threw in a 'sunfish', which was a sort of extravagant capriole that nearly broke one's neck. The first time we took her out on the range we had to take a bunch of cattle up to the North Lake where the grass was more plentiful. When we were going up the narrow west side of the North Lake, Silly 16 decided to dig her toes in near a wire fence and would not move. So I took the cattle on.

When I returned half an hour later George was still stuck in the same place, but a little nearer the wire fence. The mare then suddenly erupted and finished up by bucking into the fence itself, which is the most dangerous thing a cow-pony can do. So, quite calmly, George jumped off, threw a rope round her two front legs and I helped him to half-hitch the rope around her two hind legs. Then we drew all her legs together in a knot. She was within a few feet of the wire. George then quietly sat on her belly, rolled himself a smoke, got out a quirt (a short whip) and gave her a whack every five minutes or so. After about an hour we untied her and rode her peacefully back to the ranch, completely subdued.

She never attempted to buck into a barbed-wire fence again, although she could be cheeky, and George often complained that he felt as if his neck was loose after just sitting her ordinary bucks. I rode her a couple of times but gave her the same kind treatment and she gave no trouble at all, by which time it could be said that she had been dominated and broken. But, had I started to rake her or quarrel with her, she would certainly have bucked.

Things certainly did not always go well for the tenderfoot. I was once on my way back from the corrals when I saw Ab Lewis and Tom Farrell, the Burns' superintendent, driving in a bunch of cattle for shipment. Instead of going back to the bunk-house, I rather stupidly went to meet them and when the leading cows saw me about one hundred yards away they charged. They were used to a man on a horse but not to people on foot and they would either run away or charge them. I got one hell of a rocket (which I quite deserved) from Ab Lewis after this incident.

Another, more startling, adventure was the one I shared with Stockings. Ab Lewis had sent me out to see that fifty-odd Hereford bulls were safely in the bull pasture, ten miles north of the ranch beyond the canyon and its two lakes. The fence had been repaired the day before and, after I had checked that it was still intact, Stockings and I made our way along the eastern shore of the lake to Jake Kearns' shack.

Jake had been one of the wild men of the area, but now had settled down and lived as a hermit many miles from anyone. No one was better at leather-work and I wanted him to put a new leather lash on the end of my swivel bull-whip. I left Stockings outside the shack, but Jake was not at home. So I helped myself to some coffee – as tradition permits – and as I came out of the door some saucer-sized snowflakes struck me in the face.

Suddenly, from nowhere on this August day, a blizzard had swept down upon us from the Rockies. I was buffeted by it as I climbed aboard my faithful Stockings and rode to the top range aiming for home. After ten minutes of swirling snow and gale-force winds I was completely lost. For a minute or two, we turned our backs to the storm in a small coulee. Then, quite suddenly, Stockings decided it was time we were off. So, with his head down and my scarf over my face, we drove into the full fury of the blizzard as the snow swirled into us. Once or twice Stockings was nearly blown over, while I had to 'reach for leather' and hold onto the saddlehorn. I had no idea where we were but, as Stockings obviously knew the way, I made no attempt to guide him. Both of us were blinded but he knew by instinct where to go.

After very nearly an hour we came to a fence, touching it before we saw it. I had no idea which way to turn but Stockings was confident; he turned left and within a hundred yards we came to an opening in the fence which I recognized. I knew that I was within half a mile of the ranch buildings and, as we approached them, cheers and catcalls went up from the boys who had organized themselves into a posse to come and look for the tenderfoot who was suddenly emerging from the icy armageddon. About an hour later this freak blizzard swept away, leaving the whole prairie a foot deep in snow with the wheat to the east of us completely flattened.

Another incident that stands out was the driving of our cattle for shipment at Claresholm. We had to collect them, corral them, treat them for sores, and then set off for Claresholm twenty-two miles away. We took off across country and soon a cow took the lead, as always proves to be the case. We established a small leading group of about fifty well-behaved animals who gave us no trouble; behind this bunch, some fifty yards distance, the rest of the two-hundred-

and-fifty-strong herd followed, looked after by two cowboys. My job was to keep the two bunches apart.

When we came to the wheat-lands all our worries seemed to be over as there were fences on either side. We were aiming for the station corrals but, as we got to the first house, a minute terrier appeared from behind a shack. None of our cattle had seen such an extraordinary beast before. The leading cows stopped while the second bunch moved up into them. There was nothing my bull-whip and I could do to stop the two bunches merging and I found myself in the middle of them. Stockings extricated me from this perilous situation, in which the cattle could have trodden me into strawberry jam. Many cowboys have been killed in just such a way – but I had been saved again by the resolute, sure-footed Stockings.

All three hundred cattle now started milling. They went round in a huge circle – round and round – ever faster. We tried to chase the terrier off but he always appeared somewhere else and started yapping. The cowboys were shouting, the cattle were bellowing and the situation got out of control. Suddenly, the leading cow came out of this mêlée and set off straight for the nearest wheat-field as fast as she could go. The others followed and, as they went through the wire fences, I remember hearing the wire play a pizzicato tune, like some skilled violinist, as each strand broke. The cattle did a lot of damage to the crops and an inquiry followed. Burns' Corporation had to pay for the damage, but apparently this was a pretty usual occurrence and they were insured against it. Nobody was blamed for the incident.

My last night made me· feel sad. I went for a walk, took a long look at the Rockies thrown into relief by the orange-red sky to the west and went to bed with my rope and bull-whips before being lulled to sleep by the coyotes.

On my way back to Calgary, I called in at the 'EP', the Prince of Wales' ranch, and spent half a day there. It was encircled by Pat Burns' Bar 'U' ranch which held 10,000 head of cattle.

In Canada the Prince of Wales was looked upon as rather a naughty boy. He often used to climb out in order to go to parties and as a result was very popular amongst the Canadians. But it was his general friendliness which won him so much admiration.

I did not think that Bar 'U' was anything like our '44'. It had a few visitors and looked like turning into a 'dude' ranch. As we were a cattle-ranch we also felt rather disdainful about the 'EP' ranch. However, it was about this time that the phrase was coined, 'a dood ranch pays but a cattle ranch don't' – and dude ranches were soon to proliferate all over America.

It was early September when I left Claresholm by train from which I had my last view of the foothills where I had spent such a thrilling time. The Rockies were away in the distance, while to the east there was an endless, vari-coloured plain from which the grain harvest was being gathered by huge combines. After a change of trains I was heading for Banff, and soon we were twisting round the foothills of the Rockies and winding up through the fir forests. This train stopped for anyone who waved at it from the side of the track.

I got fixed up at Banff's Homestead Hotel and awoke in the morning to a breathtaking view. The Rockies seemed quite different from any other mountains I had ever seen. They are said to be the result of volcanic disturbance and there were huge lumps of ground distributed at the oddest and most irregular angles. Mount Rundle, which overshadows Banff, had had one side levered up to a height of nearly 10,000 feet.

The stables in Banff were run by Miss MacLaren, who was the only woman guide in the Rockies, and as tough as any cowboy. I went there and chose Buckskin, a rich dun with a brown stripe down the middle of its back. Later, I escorted Miss MacLaren to the local cinema. It was hardly flattering that she was soon asleep and snoring loudly! Nevertheless, she promised to take me to the Game Warden the next day as he wanted help riding herd on his buffalo. They disappear, as any sensible animal would, into the thick scrub in the heat of the day, but this means that the passengers in passing trains cannot see them.

The Game Warden took me on and I found myself, adorned by a Deputy Warden's badge, driving these uncooperative, shaggy brutes out of thick cover down to the railway a mile or two away. It was interesting and dangerous, for if one got too near the beasts they promptly charged. Owing to its queer shape, a buffalo can turn round almost on a sixpence. Its heavy front acts as a pivot for its much lighter back end and it can soon set off at top speed in the direction from which it has come.

During the previous week the Warden had been chased for a half a mile by an infuriated bull, and I established a vendetta with two young bulls who took it in turns to defy me. I never thought that I would see their great-great-grandchildren half a century later, by which time the buffalo were in smaller paddocks and people were not allowed to get out of their cars.

One evening I rode off in the direction of the garbage heaps behind the Banff Springs Hotel where, I had been told, bears frequently came to scavenge for titbits and I hoped that I might see some. By this time it was completely dark, and I was quite alone. It was an exhilarating experience riding along on a beautiful pony with the fir trees high on either side, and I was probably over-relaxed when, suddenly, Buckskin whipped round at incredible speed. I found myself being bolted with back down the road we had come. Had I not been riding in a western saddle and caught hold of the horn I would most certainly have fallen off, which could have been most unpleasant for I had just caught sight of a black shadow by the side of the road about ten yards away. It was certainly a black bear that had made Buckskin react so violently. I have since wondered what would have happened had I been deposited ten yards from the bear; I have a pretty shrewd idea that we would have bolted in opposite directions as fast as we could!

This was literally the last impression I had of Banff. Buckskin, once he was headed for home, did not relax until we reached the streets of the town itself. The next day I was at the station in good time to catch the *Mountaineer*. It was equipped with a solarium, smoking-lounges, buffet services, an observation-car, a large library and a valet service. During its long journey to Chicago, many of us indulged in welcome shower-baths during the day at fifty cents a time.

From Chicago I travelled to New York City, where the heat and the noise contrived to give me miserably sleepless nights. I still remember the all-night clamour from police sirens and the peep-peep of the cars. Happier memories are associated with the day I spent at Belmont Racecourse, which was beautifully laid out with lawns and flower-beds in the middle. The first race I saw was a steeplechase for three-year-olds and upwards. Pete Bostwick, well-known in England, fell at the first fence – his accident being eloquently reported in the paper as 'horse lost rider'!

I had been taken there by Mr Horgan (of the Horgan Fuel Corporation), who introduced me as one of Britain's leading trainers – which must have seemed remarkable considering that I was still only nineteen. As a result of his introduction I was allowed to have a good look at the fences and was surprised to find that they were made of box-privet which could be hit a couple of feet from the ground without making any difference to the horse.

The final stage of this memorable long vacation came when I

boarded MV *Britannic* and sailed for home, travelling cabin-class in tremendous comfort. As we steamed up the Irish Channel and saw Britain again, I realized what a wonderful country it was. Most remarkable was the vivid green colouring of the fields. I was soon brought back to reality by under-cooked whiting, tasteless mashed potatoes and repulsive coffee (made with multi-boiled hot milk) on the train that took us to London.

It seems to me that setting out on my own at the age of eighteen, having left school only a year before, had the effect of making me a very independent character. I knew I could get by on my own and having to work on a tight budget gave me a real sense of the value of money. The final entry in my diary of the trip reads: 'Of all the places that I visited, Banff in the Canadian Rockies must take first place. I hope to go back there some day.' Half a century later, I was to do so.

3   Winner Under Rules

There were many ways in which I wasted my time at Cambridge. For example, I should probably have given up water-pistol activities years earlier but, skilfully used, I still found them great fun. On one occasion, I aimed my pistol out of a window and bought a shower of water down on the head of my brother Rhys, then had to hide in my tailor's shop to escape his anger. Climbing was another popular activity but I did not have a head for heights and I nearly fell when climbing into Pembroke down the front of the building, whereupon I gave this sport up. It was due to David Haigh Thomas's guts and resolve that he succeeded in climbing to the top of King's College Chapel, and tied an umbrella to one of its spires.

During my time at Trinity I first 'kept' at 29 Thompson's Lane where a fellow-traveller was Maurice Edelmann, later the Labour member for Coventry and a distinguished author. Later I 'kept' at Whewells Court, 'H' Court in Trinity itself, then at 11 Green Street where we had a very accommodating landlady called Mrs Cairns. She always charged quite a lot extra for broken crockery at the end of each term, which was in fact a kind of hush-money because she never reported anybody absent if they did not come back for a day or two.

There were frequent jaunts to London and, owing to the cooperative indulgence of Mrs Cairns, we were able to go to quite a few deb dances and even stay away for them. Of course the early summer months were always great fun. May Week, which traditionally took place in the first fortnight in June, usually led to all-night dancing and punting, with breakfast at Huntingdon or some nearby place.

Although I had come from an unfashionable public school I was soon made a member of the Pitt Club, no doubt because of my horsey activities. After a year, I also became a member of the Cambridge Athenaeum which had its premises facing the main entrance of Trinity. These Clubs provided me with much congenial horsey company.

I was rarely idle at Cambridge – except in the academic sense. My chief interests remained rugby football and steeplechasing, and, during 1931, I achieved one great goal in the latter sphere. I won my first race under National Hunt rules.

Theorem had been brought down at Stratford in my first race that year but everything went right for us in the Basset Hunters' Steeplechase at the Glamorgan Hunt meeting at Cowbridge. The course contained the only fence in Great Britain which was jumped from both directions in the same race. This fence was just in front of the stands and it caused many thrills, particularly if someone had been tailed-off or had remounted.

The race was by no means a pushover for Theorem because two and a half miles was not far enough for him; he could gallop for ever in spite of his fourteen years. But we succeeded in beating Meyerling, ridden by David Thomas, the brother of our farm bailiff Thomas Thomas. David had been one of the top amateurs and had won the Welsh Grand National on one of my father's horses, 'Miss Balscadden'.

Those two rides were my only races that year. My father would not allow me to ride in any more until I started doing some real work at Cambridge. When Theorem finished third in the 1931 Liverpool Foxhunters' he was ridden by Evan Bowen.

In spite of my many frivolous activities, like other undergraduates I occasionally had time for more serious thoughts about politics and religion. By the time I left Cambridge I knew that I was a Christian – but without a belief in the hereafter – and nothing has happened since then to change my views.

When young I had enjoyed going to church and was impressed by the devout faith of my parents, but I hated the compulsory church services at my public school. Recently the US Supreme Court decision to ban compulsory prayer in public schools encouraged the American Civil Liberties Union to press for a legal ban on Christmas carols, but surely this is carrying things too far! My family have always rejoiced with Christmas carols and sing them rather well. My sons Dai and Roddy organized the carol-singing at our local church at Llanfair Kilgeddin for many years and nothing, to us, is more fun than joining in with the carol-singers and welcoming local parties who make Christmas very special by bell-ringing or bringing the 'Marie Llwyd', a broomstick white horse, into the house. Carol-singing brings people together and if it does so in a religious sense, so much the better.

I have given much thought throughout my life to questions relating to religious beliefs. Man alone can think and make deductions. But the interrelationship between conscious deduction and the soul is not a clear one; when does a man's mind become his soul? Shakespeare said, 'Tell me, where is Fancy bred, or in the heart or in the head?'

Some philosophers maintain that one's mind is merely an instrument of the social structure but how does a man's soul relate to that situation? Some believers hold that man's superconscious takes over on death, but philosophers differ in their definition of the superconscious, the subconscious and the unconscious. Others believe that when one dies there must be some residue left, even if only a molecule of nitrogen; but does the soul transfer itself to a component of a killing-gas, or become a dewdrop on an orchid or a dandelion? I hold that one can in fact be a good practising Christian without having to believe in an afterlife, and that there must be God who created heaven and earth and who is responsible for our being here.

In this connection, I have wrestled with the conundrums posed by physicists and biochemists. For some time Dr Moorpath of Oxford University dated as the oldest known sediments on earth the brown-black rocks in Northern Greenland, estimated as being 3.85 billion years old. Maryland's Laboratory of Chemical Evolution recently claimed to have found extraterrestrial amino-acids in two meteorites preserved in pristine condition by the deep-freeze conditions of Antarctica. These meteorites are believed to have come from the asteroid belt between Mars and Jupiter and are 4.6 billion years old, which dates them back to the beginning of the solar system when the Earth and other planets were formed out of gas and dust. Of whatever age, they were part of God's creation. He made us and when our course is fully run we will return to dust and gas and be available for recycling to extend the Universe which God created at the beginning of time.

So if I have to be classified as anything perhaps I am a deist. The Holy Gospel according to John relates that after the death of Martha's brother Lazarus, Jesus said to her, 'Whosoever lives and believes in me will never die, do you believe this?' And Martha replied, 'Yes, Lord, I believe that you are Christ the son of God, the one who was to come into this World.' Perhaps, if she had said '*one of those* who were to come into this World', she would have got it right. In a way the Islamic faith is more ecumenical than the others. It lays down that God had four prophets, Noah, Moses (for the Jews), Jesus (for the Christians) and, the last to arrive, Mohammed (for themselves).

However God is worshipped, a standard of behaviour is laid down to govern the conduct of the lives of human beings; these codes of behaviour are vitally important – it is easier to relax standards than to maintain them. I accept the Christian code regarding the manner in which we should conduct our lives. I do not wish to take faith from others – nor would I seek to hurt or offend those whose religious views differ from mine. Above all we need tolerance of the beliefs of others. It is only recently that the World Council of Churches posthumously absolved Galileo, who was denounced nearly four hundred years ago for saying the world was not flat. Bully for the World Council of Churches.

My own standpoint can be summed up briefly – live and let live, believe and let believe.

As I was still being aimed at the sales side of the coal business, my father decided that I should spend the summer of 1931 in Spain in order to learn Spanish. We sold millions of tons of coal to Spain, bought iron ore from the North, had bunkering businesses in some of the ports, including Gibraltar, and were developing a new bunkering facility at Ceuta, on the African coast. It seemed a fine idea to me but our local Master of Hounds, on hearing of my proposed visit, confided to his wife, 'I always knew Harry was mad – he's missing the Puppy Show again.' The Vale of Glamorgan in those days was a very close-knit community. It had the coalfields to the north, the sea to the south, and only England to the east. My friends there thought it unbelievable that somebody with the advantages of living in Glamorgan should ever want to escape from it for the three months of the summer vacation. But apart from the Merthyr Mawr Tennis Tournament there was very little local junketing, at least little that came my way.

So I set off happily by train en route for our office in Madrid where I was to meet Jack Gridley and Moreno Luque, both of whom were extremely kind to me. They put me up with a well-matched pair of Spanish beauties, who were instructed to speak only Spanish with me.

Nearly opposite lived a young lady called Pilar Gondalez Conde de Bourbon of whom I was to see a good deal. When first I asked her out to tea, she came alone and we had a fine time. I then asked her out to lunch and her mother came too. I was rash enough to ask her out for a third time. On this occasion it was to dinner and not only her mother but two portly, frigid aunts came as well! Apparently, to ask a lady out so often over a period of a fortnight indicated that I was pretty serious about marrying her. So I had a quiet word with Moreno Luque and asked him to explain that in England things were a little different. If I asked her out again, would it be possible for her to bring only one chaperone and not three? A deal was done so that Pily, her mother, and I had some really splendid evenings. We were particularly good at the tango and often danced at Los Perdices outside Madrid, while her mother gradually went to sleep over a bottle or two of red wine – a splendid chaperone at the price of some pretty nasty Spanish plonk! Pily could not speak English and therefore I learned Spanish quite quickly.

I visited many places in the area including Toledo, where the magnificent Alcazar building was still standing. King Carlos had abdicated in April of that year and there had been riots as the Republic had been declared. Written all over the Prado and other main buildings were notices stating '*Publico Esto Edificio es Tuo*' – 'This building is yours'. This was in an attempt to avoid unnecessary damage. I was involved in one very unpleasant incident in the Puerto del Sol when a tremendous crush killed two people. I managed to climb up on to a grille protecting a window. Nothing would have happened had the police not got panicky and fired a shot or two over the people's heads.

The University district was a tricky one at this time and the students were continuously making trouble. I once stopped a young man who was running down the street and asked him where he was off to. He said he was going to the demonstration. I then asked him what it was in aid of, to which he replied, 'I don't know but I will be told when I get there.' This seemed to reflect the aim of many of the students who were really just out for a bit of fun; it did not seem surprising that, five years later, the whole nation was embroiled in the fierce civil war which was to burn up so much of their surplus energy.

Whilst in Madrid I used to have three lessons a week from Mr Morquende, who was then Librarian at the *Biblioteca Nacional*. He was also the bullfighting correspondent for the *ABC* – the Spanish equivalent of *Paris Match* or *Life*. Through him I learned to understand a much misunderstood sport.

Until then I had only seen one bullfight. That was in San Sebastian during our family holiday of 1926, at a time when they did not use padding (*petos*) on the horses. We were all completely disgusted and left after we had seen a horse badly gored; its entrails were falling out, only to be stuffed back in again with straw in the hope that the animal would be able to stand up to the buffeting of the next bull.

The introduction of *petos* altered my attitude altogether, for this meant that the horse would sometimes go through a whole season without sustaining a serious injury. Moreover, as is the case with other sports, when you fully understand its intricacies, when you know what calls for skill, and what represents clumsiness or lack of guts, it is possible to appreciate bullfighting a great deal more. Somehow the mind then transcends the sight of the bull's blood.

At the beginning of a fight, the measurements of the bull's horns are given and then compared with the size of the *torero*. Obviously a short bullfighter with short arms has less chance if he draws a bull with very wide horns. One learns to notice the initial cloak-play of the supporting *matador*'s team, as this is meant to test the reactions of the bull – whether he looks at the man or not, or whether he hooks to the left or to the right. The *banderilleros* place their *banderillos* expertly while running across the bull's front, and this requires a high degree of skill. After this comes the action of the *picadors*. One could never like these heavily armed men on horses; they have thick lances with which they gore the bull in the area of the withers. The energy used by the bull in challenging the horses, and the damage done to the muscles of his neck by the *picadors*, reduces him to the state in which he can be killed and this does not seem fair or acceptable. Then comes the action of the final play by the *matador* with his carmine-coloured cloak, the *muleta*. The manner in which he stands into his bull without moving his feet, and the various difficult passes, can be better appreciated when one knows them and understands how difficult some of them are to execute. The final killing of the bull with one thrust calls for great skill and bravery.

Even so, I find it difficult to analyse my own attitude. Having been brought up with animals, I have truly loved many horses and dogs to the extent that their slightest scratch has worried me. Yet I can watch a bullfight, if it is a good one, with a feeling almost of exultation. Others too have found this contradiction hard to explain. How can a man who jumps off his horse if it has only a slight over-reach wave handkerchiefs at a bullfight so that the *matador* may be rewarded with two ears for his skill? One person, it seems, can be many people. I am not proud of the fact that I like bullfights, and make no excuses for myself, except to say that I do understand what happens, and appreciate the skill that is required.

I became so keen on bullfighting that I decided to fly off to Barcelona for a couple of days to the Fiesta, to see a bullfight one Sunday. I flew for the first time in my life in a three-engined Junkers aeroplane. We flew very low over the Spanish mountains and I was so sick that I had to go to bed for nearly a day when we reached Barcelona. However, I managed to get to the bullfight. I clearly remember Alcareno Segundo, who was a very small man, being very neatly caught by his bull on one horn, tossed into the air, caught on the other horn and killed instantly.

We looked on this sight in amazement. I can only suppose that in all of us there remains an element of the crowds that used to turn out at Newgate to see a hanging; or, further back, of the enthusiastic mobs who went to the Colosseum in Rome to see the lions killing Christians or gladiators chopping each other up. Even now, crowds cannot be kept back from major accidents such as a pile-up on a motorway or an aeroplane crash, and often impede doctors and ambulances on their way to help the injured. Such a reaction must, like my own to bullfighting, reflect some deep-seated barbaric instinct in one who tries to live as civilized a life as possible.

Some people, like my wife Teeny, will not go to bullfights. Once in the mid-sixties we took her to a mock fight which my daughter Anna wanted to see. Even then, Teeny had to go out when Anna kept on asking, 'Daddy, where's the blood, where's the blood?' On another occasion I took my elder son Dai to a bullfight at Nîmes in France. It was an extremely hot day, which may have caused him to faint; on the other hand, as far as I know he has never fainted at any other time.

Whether one reacts with elation or with horror, bullfighting is bound to be an emotive subject. In the United Kingdom especially, most people loathe everything associated with it. Yet perhaps this can be a little discounted as being part of our national tendency to criticize other countries about subjects of which we know little.

The most extreme example of my own attitude came towards the end of my stay in Madrid. I used to go to the office for about two hours a day, and learned how to handle Spanish correspondence. By this time I could speak the language quite well. I was then sent off to Gibraltar, where our business associates were Gueret Imossi. Lionel Imossi gave me a wonderful time, but best of all I remember visiting the bullring in Tarifa. There was no *contrabarrera* and no passageway between the ring itself and the front lower seats. So, horror that I was, pulled the *banderillos* out of the bull as he passed underneath me in the small Tarifa ring. To my undying shame, I then took the weapons back to Cambridge and had them crossed over my doorway, bloody points and all.

Since that long summer in Spain in 1931, I have loved the Spaniards as a race. To this day I speak fluent 'kitchen' Spanish, and find it very useful. When I got back to Cambridge I discovered that I could take a Spanish exam at the beginning of the term, so this I promptly did and passed, second class – not bad for a three-month holiday. If you want to learn Spanish, get a 'Hugo' book, live in a house with two pretty Spanish ladies, make friends with the bullfighting correspondent of the *ABC*, and travel about a bit. It then becomes an easy language to learn!

After my Spanish holiday it was decided that I should take a Commercial pass degree. Having passed my examinations in economics and Spanish, I then took a pass degree in law after two terms work. This nearly ended in disaster as I was still failing to attend most of my lectures, and my extramural activities continued to handicap academic progress.

Fortunately, there were some splendid books. One was called *Torts in a Nutshell* and another *Contracts in a Nutshell*. I shut myself in my room for three days and read them through time and time again – and in the end I passed quite easily. Consequently, my father's anger over my lack of diligence had somewhat subsided by 1932 so, to my great delight, I was allowed to take up steeplechasing once again.

I had two marvellous days at the Cambridge University Steeplechases at Cottenham (which is now a popular point-to-point course) where Theorem was the first to carry me to the winner's enclosure. He had won the Stewards' Cup over four miles despite facing the wrong way at the start. Then he was carried out by a loose horse at the water-jump so that I had to turn him round and he then jumped the fence out of a trot. A fence behind the leaders, I could waste no time. I caught Magistrate, ridden by Ken Urquhart, after about a mile, which left Greenhorn in front ridden by Simon Digby. Theorem won in a canter by four lengths. This was a great performance as he was carrying thirteen stone and giving pounds away all round – an amazing performance for a fifteen-year-old horse.

On the next day I won the University Challenge Whip Steeplechase on a horse called Silver Grail, who had come into my life just before my vacation in Spain. He was a beautiful chestnut gelding by Prince

Galahad out of Silver Patch, and had been trained by Bay Powell at Aldbourne. Among our opponents in that race at Cottenham was a good horse called Steady Johnny, ridden by Ken Urquhart.

He went off at a fast gallop but fell, leaving me alone in front. Silver Grail was always sticky without company, so I waited until Steady Johnny was remounted and he had rejoined me before I had gone another half-mile. With Steady Johnny alongside again the race was never in doubt. This was the most sought-after race at Cottenham but on this occasion it turned into a six-furlong sprint. There had been great rivalry between these two horses and it was sad that we had not had a straightforward encounter.

I next rode Theorem in the Foxhunters' at Cheltenham and Liverpool. In the first I hit the second fence hard which lost me a dozen lengths, but made up ground in the last two miles to finish a fairly close sixth. In the Liverpool Foxhunters' I was brought down at the first open ditch.

Later, Theorem was second at Wincanton, going under by fifteen lengths, to Bobby Petre's Hero Lass, ridden by Fulke Walwyn. This was the only time that Theorem ever jumped badly, no doubt as a result of his Liverpool fall. Normally he would have beaten Hero Lass who was, as I wrote 'at her best, a very moderate mare'. But, of course, she had a superb jockey.

In April 1932, towards the end of a hard season, Theorem was last in the Hunter Chase at Monmouth. This meeting I remember not so much for the racing as for our mission when the last race of the day was over. It was then that all the jockeys trooped out to look for Eric Foster's teeth, which had been lost in the water at the bottom of the open ditch. It took us half an hour, then Billy Stott offered them back to him on the condition that he would not wear them again in a race.

Later, I recorded Theorem's performance when finishing last. 'He jumped beautifully. Theorem, I am afraid, is getting very slow, which is not surprising at the age of fifteen.' The old horse did, however, succeed in winning a point-to-point the following week.

Silver Grail's main objective that month was the Holman Cup at Cheltenham's April meeting. Unfortunately, I made my effort too soon and, having hit the front at the bottom of the hill three fences from home, we were beaten into fourth place. I wrote: 'I feel sure that with a lazy horse there is definitely a psychological factor involved and he would have run much better if kept with the field and only asked to pass them once. A lazy horse often loses interest if there is nothing alongside to race with him and he will not make two efforts.' As it transpired Silver Grail was to make two glorious efforts in one race the following year, but a great deal was to happen to me before then.

4 Safari and Silver Grail

I came of age as we crossed the equator. With Lionel Devitt, one of my friends at Trinity College, I was travelling to Rhodesia on board the *Edinburgh Castle* with her two high thin funnels. We had been invited by Donald Low, who had been up at Trinity with us, to join him in Rhodesia for his twenty-first birthday party which was to be followed by a hunting-trip. This holiday was to be the last of my memorable long-vacation journeys.

My own birthday was celebrated after ten days at sea, and I was thoroughly spoiled by everyone on the ship. I was given a huge six-foot-high silver key (to manhood) and a bouquet of vegetables made to look like flowers by the skilful chef. Twenty-one of us sat at a special table and I still treasure the menu. After Consommé Llewellyn we had Salmis of Game Tally Ho, followed by Roast Leg of Lamb Rhodesia, Cardiff Green Peas, Salad Plain Harry and Trinity Pudding.

At the end of seventeen thoroughly enjoyable days we were soon through the Cape Town customs, leaving our guns and trunks to be sent in bond to Bulawayo. If they had been opened in the Union we would have had to pay customs on them. In order to afford £17 second-class return tickets to Bulawayo we had to obtain a refund on our return journey on the *Windsor Castle* by agreeing to go steerage. I later noticed my ticket had been made out for Mr Levy Ellen — which to my surprise proved to be valid.

Lionel and I shared a small scruffy coupé. The scenery was flat and boring but I saw lots of springbok from the train before arriving at Kimberley, where most of our passengers left us to catch the train to Johannesburg. We passed through Mafeking and from the train it looked a most unattractive place. Said Lionel, 'Why was it ever relieved?'

Halfway through the night we were aroused by Immigration officers and later we were met at Bulawayo station by Donald Low and his father, a prominent lawyer, and by Colonel Sonny Webb. The two of them together ran the firm of Webb & Low, Solicitors.

One evening we went to dinner with Colonel Webb and found him in the middle of his hall wrapped up in sleeping-blankets, surrounded by guns, rifles, revolvers, boomerangs and ammunition of all sorts. This was to impress upon us that a trial run was necessary before the hunting-trip proper began.

At that time Rhodesia was Great Britain's youngest colony and had its own responsible government after a referendum taken in 1923. Before that it had been controlled under Charter by the British South Africa Company which still owned vast properties in both Northern and Southern Rhodesia.

My diary reads: 'Such restriction must eventually cause violent reaction, but is probably unavoidable when people who consider themselves educated are in control of those they consider uneducated.' I recall sympathizing with the comparatively well-educated blacks. Their situation was a fundamental cause of why the world now looks upon 'colonialism' as a dirty word. Yet the colonists eventually developed such countries as Rhodesia to the ultimate advantage of all concerned. I wonder what the reader would have felt in those days.

We had a day or two at the races where bells kept ringing for no apparent reason. The horses walked to the start and waited ten minutes or so for the starter, while one or two bolted round the track for something to do. Most of the jockeys were black and lay down in the paddock before the races while the horses were being walked round although half the horses did not come into the paddock at all. Auction sales were held between the races. A man bid 5 shillings for one horse and I bid him up to 7s. 6d. and was nearly landed with the animal. I gathered that the whole object of the operation was to do dirty tricks to other people. The better you did it, the higher standing you achieved – rather in the manner of snooker.

Don's twenty-first birthday party was a marvellous occasion and, when it was over, we concentrated on our preparations for the hunting-trip. I put in some practice with a .303 VII rifle, with mark VI ammunition which caused the rifle to shoot 16 inches higher in a hundred yards; but it was a very good high-velocity weapon. I practised off both shoulders, as I had taught myself to do this in the OTC at Cambridge, where I had been classified as 'First-class' shot.

The day arrived when we laid out our kit including several pairs of thick socks and two pairs of *Veldtschoen* boots. My armoury consisted of a .303 VII Medford rifle with 70 rounds of soft-nosed ammunition and 10 rounds of hard-nosed ammunition; a 12-bore Greener shot gun with 50 No. 4 shot cartridges, 25 AAA shot cartridges and 25 SSSG shot cartridges, plus a .32 Browning automatic with 100 rounds of ammunition. All of us were equally well-equipped. I had a small 120 Ensign camera and a 9-mm Pathé cine-motor camera with six charges. Sadly these cine-films were destroyed when my office in Merthyr House was burned to the ground at the end of the war.

The hunting-party consisted, amongst others, of Colonel Sonny Webb, his brothers Mac and Chap, and Don Low and Lionel Devitt. We set off in three cars – an open touring Naish 8, a Buick lorry and a Willys. On occasions we stopped for a walk-about to shoot something 'for the pot'.

My first opportunity to take a shot came on the second day, when we saw in the distance a large herd of black animals that I thought were wildebeest. After a long stalk I saw a bull which was about a hundred and sixty yards from me. I shot him off my right shoulder, steadying my arms on the knees of my crossed legs. When I fired, I knew from the thud–smack that I had hit him, but he disappeared from sight. We soon found his blood-spoor and after a quarter of a mile found him dead. He had been shot through the heart but had managed to go this distance before dropping.

It was now getting late, so we cleaned him out, put him in a tree, and covered him with a lot of thorn-bushes to stop the hyenas getting at him. Ten miles further on we made camp in Reit Spruit near Oliphant's Pit. We selected two huge leafy trees and dug up the ground beneath them to make it softer for our beds before setting up camp and building two fires. The night was silent except for the lowing of cattle and the beating of tom-toms, probably announcing our arrival.

Early the next morning we sent oxen and a sleigh to get my buck which in fact turned out to be a tsessebe. The boys who brought the bull in said that lions must have pulled the branches away as they had disembowelled it. Fortunately, they had left its horns and head-skin intact. On arrival at camp, Colonel Webb said that it was the best Tsessebe horn he had seen in Southern Rhodesia and advised me to take it home. A couple of months later, when I was back at Cambridge, my mother telephoned to say that an evil-smelling tea-chest had arrived from Beira. I asked her to send it to Rowland Ward to have the contents mounted. A week later I had a letter which read: 'Dear Sir, I have the pleasure to inform you that you have shot the world's record Tsessebe'. The horns measured 17½ inches and were entered in the Rowland Ward 1935 book as the world record Tsessebe. Later, Frank Wallace was to put them on show at the Field Sports Exhibition and, later still, they went to Berlin to Goering's International Hunting Exhibition, where they won first prize and a gold medal.

This was fantastic beginner's luck: my first shot at a wild animal in Africa, of a breed which I had never previously seen, turning out to be a world record. It remained one for several years, until Botswana was opened up. Now there are a few ahead of my Tsessebe bull, which has been relegated to a place on the cellar steps and is usually referred to as 'the cow'.

It has, however, had its other moments of glory. It was in the Museum of Wales during the war, and was later given the place of honour above the throne in my loo at Gobion. We had a very Welsh maid called Ethel at that time who held this head in great awe. One day she came in to tidy up and must have slammed the door rather hard, whereupon she complained, 'The cow did jump out of the wall and attack me!' When Ethel had recovered from her faint she declared, 'It is the cow or me'; and I am afraid I chose the cow. So poor Ethel packed her bags and was seen no more. The mark of the horn is still imprinted on the lavatory seat at Gobion.

My time in the African *bundu* was bliss and I immediately fell in love with that life, promising myself that after a year or two I would set up as a white hunter. Being of an independent nature, I was usually allowed to take out two boys, Ndala and Mashaba or Sixpence. We shot plenty of kudu, impala, zebra, and tsessebe, while there was a lot of elephant and lion spoor about. There were a few sable and roan antelope, and many warthogs, the comedians of the veldt who trot away with their tails straight up.

Each day we used to walk about ten miles in the morning, come back for a rest and then go out for about another five miles in the evening. There were a few ostriches about. During the time we were there we shot stenbok and impala for the pot and I was lucky enough to shoot an impala which is still just in the record book as 23 inches. This is good for Southern Rhodesia as there it is a slightly different breed to those in Kenya where the horns are longer.

After shooting the animals we brought them in on sleighs drawn by oxen and this attracted both lions and hyenas into the camp area. On occasions they made a tremendous noise at night. The Webbs had shotguns by their sides loaded with SSSG and AAA buckshot, as these heavy shots are the best defence at close quarters against lions and leopards, of which there were several in the nearby *kopjes*.

One day Trooper Hunt of the British South African Police suddenly arrived, claiming to have been thrown from his horse near the camp. He knew the area well and said he had had a donkey killed at our camp-site by a lion only a few weeks beforehand. On his way in he had seen some giraffe spoor and a lot of wildebeest near our camp. As our stories got taller and taller he capped them all by telling us that he once arrested General Smuts, who had crossed the Limpopo into Rhodesia and was shooting without a licence! Hunt firmly believed that cannibalism was occasionally practised in the area. He had, he said, found human remains stripped to the bone near villages. On his way up he had been presented with two goats by a native woman, because she thought that a son rather than a daughter had been born to her as a result of his having given her De Vetts kidney pills.

During the trip I learned that the main skill with game is to hunt into the wind and approach as quietly as possible without making any noise. Elephants in particular have an acute sense of smell; it is said that they can smell a man at a mile up wind and a woman at two miles – possibly because 'Arpège' or 'Je Reviens' is out of place in the bush!

When shooting on your own you have to learn to clean out the animal quickly, which is not difficult as long as you have a sharp knife and a right 'go' at it, getting your arms into the belly cavity as far as your elbows. But I found skinning rather more difficult, particularly when it came to the head-skin.

I soon learned that it is important when walking to keep one's feet in good order. I often bathed mine in lukewarm water with white alum, and always wore thick socks well soaked with vaseline on the inside. The boys' feet, however, got so hard that they could walk on a sharp thorn without feeling it.

In the evenings we would walk round our *kopjes* looking for the leopards. All we saw were lots of dassies, rock rabbits. Often I would go out without having a shot at all and still enjoy every minute.

We had not yet seen a lion, but we came across plenty of spoor and plenty of lions' kills – mostly sables. Only once did we run into a big bull-elephant and his younger satellite bull. We knew we were coming up with them because their droppings were wet, warm and steaming. These two elephants did not like us at all but after a bit of trumpeting and shaking of heads they moved away. We were nowhere near a game reserve, and no doubt they had been shot at by natives keeping them away from their gardens.

Both roan and sable have been known to attack their tormentors as they make a big low sweep with their long, curved horns. One day I was lucky enough to shoot two sable bulls, one of which had a horn 40 inches long and 13 inches between the points. This also was in Rowland Ward's record book for some years.

Although I have not shot for a trophy in Africa since that safari, I will play my part in shooting for the pot or culling. I will not shoot, though, unless I am nearly 100 per cent sure of hitting the animal in the shoulder or heart. There have been many times when I have refused to shoot because I was not sure, and this refusal has not always been understood.

I do not feel so squeamish about shooting predators because they 'live by the sword and should be prepared to die by the sword'. Colonel Webb took me out early one morning to try for a lion which we had heard fairly near the camp the previous night. With Ndala in front of Colonel Webb, Mashaba in front of me, and Sixpence behind me, we approached the area up-wind with great stealth and soon were following some spoor. We tried to keep in sight of each other but while I was crossing a *donga* I heard a shot on my left – and then silence. So the three of us dived to the ground and kept absolutely still. Complete silence ensued and then the finest flow of language I had ever heard in Africa – which at least meant that Colonel Sonny was all right! So we carefully threaded our way through the fairly thick bush in his direction, and found him still giving forth and using a lot of new words I had never heard before. He was looking at a dead, tawny-coloured cow. The colour was right but the species was wrong.

About a mile up Reitspruit we found the spoor from a great many animals, including kudu, eland and giraffe which had been watering at one large pool. So one evening Donald, Lionel, Chap and I went up to it well before sunset and hid ourselves round it in different places.

I tucked myself down behind a small bush on the down-wind side and we waited patiently without anything happening for half an hour. Then a noisy herd of about thirty zebra came down and watered, splashed about and suddenly trotted away. Again there was silence and it became dark. Nightfall is very quick near the equator, but soon we could see quite clearly a magnificent sable bull coming down to drink. He stopped halfway then suddenly he made the sort of noise with his mouth that most animals make from their other end and sped off. Obviously he had been alarmed.

As it was getting dark we started to make a move, whereupon a tawny shape seemed to spring out of what had appeared to be open ground, leapt the stream near Chap Webb, took five more strides and jumped straight over me. I had already begun to feel cold but had been told that if any predators appeared to keep absolutely still and not reach for Sonny Webb's shotgun, which was lying at my side loaded with heavy SSSG shot. I lay as still as I could but, by this time, the cold and the fright of this animal leaping over me caused me not merely to shiver but to shake like a leaf. It must have been a combination of excitement and sheer terror. After a few minutes Chap said, 'Up, everybody – and home.' We told everyone of our adventure and Chap said that he thought this animal was a hyena, but when we returned the next day the spoor told us it was quite definitely a full-grown lion. When coming straight for me it was difficult to identify, because my head was down. People who have been charged in earnest by lions and leopards stress the smallness of the target and the fantastic speed at which they travel. Fortunately I do not think this one had seen me but was merely jumping the bush behind which I was hiding.

When we returned to Bulawayo we boiled the head part of the game we had shot to kill all the maggots, and picked out the sable, tsessebe and zebra head-skins to dry them in the sun. We rubbed them with a mixture of three-quarters Fullers Earth and one-third salt on the non-hairy side.

Later Anthony Howie (also up at Trinity) joined Don, Lionel and myself when we took a train up to the Victoria Falls. There we found an impressive scene with strong green tropical vegetation against a deep blue sky, and the 'smoke that thunders' rising from the Falls. With the hand of man nowhere in evidence this setting was made even more inspiring.

By this time I was a dangerously over-confident hunter and was quite determined to shoot a lion. I was told that there were lions down near Viljoen's farm at Matetse, and an article which I wrote shortly afterwards on our days at the Victoria Falls included an account of my pursuit of them.

I will proceed to relate the chief episodes of the inglorious hunt after these lions which one of my friends, a keen cinematographer and I, an equally keen 'shot', undertook. Immediately after lunch on the next day we set off in a car we had hired from Livingstone, fully equipped with cameras, rifles and provisions, and arrived at Farmer Viljoen's house near Matetsi, after nothing worse than three punctures, fortunately all on the same tyre, en route. Viljoen told us that one lion had been killed, and another wounded, on the road half-way to his brother's farm sixteen miles away near Gazouma Pan. He advised us to avoid these lions at all costs, as their mates would almost certainly charge at sight. He also told us that his brother would show us a troop of thirteen lions as they were in the habit of passing the same spot early each morning on their return from water. He provided us with a hunter 'boy' and we set off for his brother's farm with night practically upon us. Let it suffice to say that after one puncture and a burst tyre, we eventually had to pull the car across the road, and prepared ourselves for the worst.

Our first difficulty was to collect sufficient firewood to make fires on both sides of the car. This we had to do by ourselves as the terrified 'boy', after much chattering, dived under the car and stayed there for the rest of the night. We decided to take the night in two-hour watches, and all went well until two o'clock when the silence was broken by a series of roars from a lion, or lions, which to us seemed very close at hand. Our feeling of insecurity increased when switching on the headlights of our car half an hour later, we saw a great yellow shape bound into some long grass about two hundred yards away. Although nothing else happened in the remaining hours of darkness, the suspense was dreadful, and we welcomed the dawn as never before.

Our adventures for the rest of the day consisted mainly of mending punctures, and pushing our car out of sand-drifts and dongas. We travelled for the most part on flat tyres across the open veldt, as this offered a smoother passage than the road. We took the 'boy' back to Viljoen, who informed us, from our description, that we had camped for the night within a few hundred yards of the place where the lions had been wounded.

At length we had to desert our car, with two flat tyres, an empty radiator and a cracked carburettor, and set out on foot for the remaining twelve miles to the Falls. Fortunately, we were picked up a little later by a truck and returned to our Hotel. Within a very short while, with the gentle murmur of the 'Smoke that Thunders' in our ears, we were deep in the arms of Morpheus, forgetful of all Africa – and her lions.

We returned to Bulawayo where Lionel and I were soon making sad farewells to our wonderful, hospitable Rhodesian friends. I had a lump in my throat as the train pulled away from our last glorious Rhodesian sunset.

After visiting Johannesburg, Lionel and I were broke. At Cape Town half the crew of the ship that was to take us back to England turned out to laugh at us as we lugged our heavy bags aboard, refusing the aid of numerous down-and-outs as we could not afford even the 3d. 'ticky' as the South Africans call it. Table Mountain, with its tablecloth of clouds, looked beautiful as we saw it disappear into the far distance. A few weeks later, it was home, sweet home, at last – to Silver Step, Theorem and Silver Grail – and, of course, to my beloved parents and family.

I had passed the necessary Cambridge examinations for my degree. I was then left with two terms in which to find something congenial (and not too arduous) to study.

I therefore perused the curriculum carefully and found that Portuguese was one of the subjects for which one could obtain a Certificate of Diligent Study. I further confirmed that there was no one at Cambridge qualified to teach Portuguese and immediately decided to take this subject. This delighted Mr Barker, my Spanish tutor, who came to tea with me a few times in 'H' Court, gave me some Portuguese books to read and helped me to acquire a Certificate of Diligent Study in Portuguese.

My good friend and tutor, Mr Dykes, was aware of the fact that I had been racing all over the country and had not attended a lecture during the past term. He suggested that I chose a subject for which at least three appearances a week were required. Between us we examined the curriculum again and found that Fresh Water Fish and Fishing would provide a field of interest for my future studies. I duly turned up three days a week at the Law Schools to listen to lectures on crustacea, fishes and fishing, which proved extremely interesting and at the end of the term earned my Certificate of Diligent Study. In such a manner did I become a Bachelor of Arts.

During those last two terms, I was even more anxious to get a Blue for rugby football. Each year I had been troubled by my fibula bones on both legs; my bones did not break but my joints were apt to become dislocated, which had been one of the reasons I could not ski.

I had kept Charles Taylor out of the Trinity team and was told I was going to have a trial early in the Lent term and asked to keep fit during the holidays. So I still had great hopes when I played for the Aberdare Rugby Club at the Ynys and scored three tries, before being asked to play for a Cardiff 'A' team against the Glamorgan Wanderers on the Three Elms Ground at Whitchurch.

During the first half of that match, I was completely starved of the ball and touched it only once. So, with a view to being given a game with the main Cardiff team should I prove my worth, I was asked to play inside three-quarter. Making my first run, I managed to elude one or two people before being tackled by the back and another three-quarter. It was really more of a collision than a tackle. My opponents were groggy while I finished up with a badly dislocated elbow, which was a good four inches out of its joint and required an immediate hospital operation to put it back. My father was with me and I remember him taking me to Harry Banks at Aberdare, the son of the doctor who had delivered me and who had advised my parents to get me my first pony.

Harry Banks put my elbow back and I was shown an X-ray of the two bones in my forearm which, I am told, is still exhibited. It shows that young bones can bend instead of break, though this is usually only the case with much younger children. Although I later dislocated my collarbone several times, in twenty-one seasons' steeplechasing I only cracked the tip of a transverse process (false rib) and never actually broke a bone. I was similarly unscathed during twenty-five years show jumping and it was only when a horse turned over on top of me when I was out hunting at the age of fifty-five that some of my bones capitulated and I cracked three ribs.

However, my dislocated elbow meant that I had played my last game of rugby football so that any dreams I had of playing for Cardiff and later getting a Blue had gone.

I was not deterred from continuing to ride racing. In March, six weeks after dislocating my elbow on the rugby field, Silver Grail gave me my first ride in the Amateur's Handicap at Newbury. Since the elbow was strapped up and I was riding with only one hand, I was pleased to get round – although I referred in my diary to Silver Grail as 'very lazy on this occasion'. However, a few days later he won a Hunter Chase at Wye, after which I recorded that Bay Powell (Silver Grail's former trainer) told me that I was riding with too short a rein. I resolved to avoid doing so in the future and thereafter tried to model myself on Danny Morgan, one of the great jockeys of that time.

My most memorable ride on Silver Grail was also in 1933, in the Pershore Hunters' Steeplechase. This Beau Brummel of a horse took on a good-class field that included Colonel Morgan-Lindsay's Ego, ridden by one of the top amateurs, Perry Harding, who had won the National Hunt Steeplechase at Cheltenham on him. My racing-diary recalls:

'Silver Grail jumped perfectly and I passed quite a few on the inside going to what I thought was the last turn. I came away from them as I liked and passed the winning-post ten lengths in front of everybody. I thought I had won and pulled him up very nearly to a trot. People were shouting at me, however, telling me to go on and I realized I had finished a circuit too soon! By this time a few horses had passed me and Ego was making the running. I was desperate and managed to pass Ego on the inside. We drove hard at the last four fences and Ego came again but he could not quite catch us and we beat him a neck. Not many horses have won the same race twice in the one day!'

That year Silver Grail was considered too good to go to Cottenham for the Cambridge University meeting so I rode Yellow Oriel, a horse I had often hunted, to win the Red Coat Race; I also had two wins on Happison, by Hapsburg out of Cymar, whom we had bred ourselves.

Happison was lucky to start in the first of his two Cottenham races, which was over hurdles, for my right stirrup-leather broke on the way to the post. I was grateful for the sportsmanship of the other riders who waited for me to change saddles. After we had won the race, George Loraine-Smith (who was second on Shiny Knight) received a rocket from his owner for being so kind.

We pulled Happison out again on the second day when he won just as easily, this time over fences. I recorded: 'I had never jumped a fence on him before that but he jumped perfectly throughout. One of twins, he had been partially blinded at birth by straw in one eye and his full brother had not survived. Although I was not aware of it, Richard Blunt was coming up on the side of his blind eye, but Happison heard him and pulled away to win by ten lengths'.

One of the regular riders at Cottenham was Anthony Mildmay, who was up at Cambridge with me and whose first efforts as a jockey inspired more amusement than admiration. On one occasion at Cottenham he had just jumped the fence in front of the stands when his horse decided it was time to return to the paddock; so the animal whipped round and poor Anthony was deposited on the ground in front of all his friends. Later, no one showed more determination and consistent courage to become an extremely efficient top amateur rider – winning 197 races – and a Steward of the National Hunt Committee, affectionately known as 'Lordie'.

After his two wins at Cottenham, Happison won the Open Race at the Glamorgan point-to-point. During a busy season, he also scored by fifteen lengths in a Hunters' Chase at Newton Abbot and went on to give Gate Book (ridden by 'Minnow' Prior-Palmer, uncle of Lucinda) a five-length beating in a Hunters' Chase at Colwall. We then knew he was a useful horse; later, at Cardiff, we discovered that he did not like hard ground. He hit almost every fence, including the last, and was both shin-sore and foot-sore for days afterwards. My diary noted that 'it was obviously unwise to run such a thin-soled horse on the hard ground'.

I was allowed to ride Silver Grail in that year's Inter-University Race in the Warwickshire meeting at Somerton for which he was favourite. Alas, I risked running a good-class steeplechase horse to beat point-to-pointers all for nothing, for I was far too confident and was many lengths behind two fences from home. In the end I failed by a length to catch the leading horse. More important, Oxford beat Cambridge by one point and I knew it was all my fault.

Later, I rode Silver Grail in the Welsh Grand National where I carried second top weight. The ground was hard which did not suit him and I finished fourth. Lord Glanely won this race with Pebble Ridge, trained by Ivor Anthony and ridden by Dudley Williams. It caused quite a sensation at the time because the horse had finished last in all his previous races, yet he had been backed down to 6 to 4 against. One can only assume that Pebble Ridge must have gone much better at home!

I then first rode my father's Breconian, who was trained by Colonel Morgan-Lindsay. He was a fine dark-golden chestnut gelding, by Lorenzo out of Fortura, who stood 16.1½ hands and was the most beautiful jumper. In that first race at Cardiff I was beaten half a length at level weights by Mrs Mundy's Dove's Pride, ridden by the famous Billy Speck. Later we were third at Monmouth (again one place behind Dove's Pride to whom I was trying to give thirteen pounds) in a race won by Billy Parvin on More Magic.

Sadly, on my last night I was caught by the 'progs'. Otherwise known as proctors they were a kind of University police. There were three sets of them that night and they quite definitely admitted that they had disposed themselves so as to catch me. I had sworn not to wear a cap or gown during my last term at Cambridge but was run to ground in Gil Phillips' bar. As the progs came to the door, everybody rushed to find me a gown and I quickly acquired a smart velvety one.

Unfortunately, I could not find a 'square' – otherwise known as a cap. The progs took my name with a broad smile. I was summoned to see Mr Portway, the Senior Proctor, who also took charge of anything connected with motorcars and was known as 'the motor prog'. As I entered his room he said, 'Mr Llewellyn, you have been fined three guineas.'

I said that I was a first offender and that the fine for the first offence was traditionally only 6s. 8d. Whereupon he rose to his feet, stood in the window of his room with his back to the light and in the solemnest of tones said, 'Mr Llewellyn, you have got your degree – God knows how – and if I were you I would pay up and say nothing.'

He knew as well as anybody that I had in fact been the leader of what was in effect the Prog-Baiting Society in which we set out to irritate the progs, run away from their assistants known as bulldogs – 'bullers' – and escape. Until now I had succeeded in doing this over the whole of my time at Cambridge. All my friends had been caught at various times and had therefore given it up as a sport, because if you were caught three times by the progs you could be sent down.

I had many secret hiding-places, but I think that the best one was a six-foot-high wooden crate that I hired from Eaden and Lilley's store, when I 'kept' at 11 Green Street. I had this crate left outside my 'digs' with an open side against the wall. If I was far enough ahead of the progs I could quickly pull away the case, stand inside it, pull it back against the wall and completely disappear from view. This is the first time that I have revealed the secret of my many escapes!

Sometimes, when I was in my packing-case hiding from progs and bullers, a policeman would pass by and knock on the door at 11 Green Street. This was frightening for me until I discovered that he was paying court to Dolly Cairns, whom he subsequently married.

I made many friends at Cambridge, among them the Masters of the Trinity Foot Beagles – Peter Paget, who was killed in the desert during the war, and Bob Hoare, who was to become a well-known Master of the Cottesmore and later the South Notts Foxhounds, before dying so unexpectedly from a heart attack in 1977. John Nelson, who 'kept' with me in Green Street during my last year, was Master of the Cambridge University Drag Hounds and later, as General Sir John, commanded the British troops in Berlin. Another friend, John Russell, managed to remain Master of a pack of foxhounds in Kent even when he was *en poste* as British Ambassador in

Addis Ababa, Rio de Janeiro and finally Madrid. His father, Russell Pasha, taught his camel to jump and I have a photograph of him taking part in a hurdle race near Cairo.

When I visit Cambridge nowadays, I often feel sorry for the students, mainly because they have to work so hard. Before the war, there was more time for the wide-ranging discussions that often took place in the Pitt Club, or over late-night scrambled eggs in the 'Scotch Hoose' or while mixing with the clientele of Gil Phillips' café. It is surely much better that young people should discuss their opposing points of view in the period before they are projected or launched into their careers.

It seems that now it is necessary to be academically highly qualified in order to get to Cambridge, but I have discovered through a multidimensional life that acceptability is as important as ability. Certainly the way in which scruffiness seems to be encouraged and far-out tactics employed by some undergraduates will prove of doubtful value to them later. This is of course an older man's pronouncement on the young, and I accept the charge that I am out-of-date – thank Heavens I am!

5 Trade, Travel and Show Jumping

My new role as a trainee shipping agent did not at first seem likely to be a congenial one. When I came down from Cambridge my first job was in the offices of Gueret, Llewellyn, & Merrett in the main street of Port Talbot. Here I started my working life by licking stamps, dealing with the letters and correspondence, and gradually becoming responsible for the bills of lading which I found an endless and rather boring task.

Fortunately my boss, Nelson Merrett, was not a hard task-master and he tried to teach me all sides of a shipping agent's job. My father, on the way down to see his collieries, would visit me and have lunch with me at the Italian café opposite, where the back room was put at our disposal by the expansive Mr Franchi, who had the largest hands of any man I ever met.

Amongst my tasks was that of Inspector of Coal in the waggons before shipment, a particularly tricky job on a night shift. When inspecting coal to see that it was free from what we called 'mam-glo' (mother-of-coal) and iron pyrites, one had to jump from waggon to waggon – rather alarming when a train of these waggons was unexpectedly shunted.

These night shifts, however, were made much more enjoyable by systematic rat-hunting in company with Ernie Hayes, the flower of local communism. He could not read but I supplied him with comics, which he enjoyed, and we became real buddies. Furthermore, he had a splendid terrier which, together with my Billy, disposed of hundreds of rats.

Ernie's politics did not affect our friendship. I have always said that sport should keep bridges open and believe this is even more important today. It has never been possible for me to hate politicians who hold different views from mine. I have never had that particular fire in my belly and possibly this is why, later in life, I was able to

act reasonably successfully as a liaison officer, peacemaker and nego-
tiator. Perhaps Ernie started me down that path.

Later I was to go into lodgings with Mr Giles, the saddler at the
top of Sketty Hill, Swansea, and spent many enjoyable months under
the direction of Philip Holden and Gwyn Powell, a great hunting
man, inspecting the screens (through which coal is sized) throughout
the Amalgamated Anthracite Group. The classification and sale of
coal became my speciality and I wrote many articles for the *Western
Mail* on the subject.

By this time Mr Giles had retired, but he taught me how to stitch
saddles and about leatherwork generally. His instruction supple-
mented the knowledge that I had acquired from Mr Howes, the
saddler in whose shop I had spent many hours when I was deprived
of horsey friends at Oundle.

Opportunities for riding were greatly curtailed during my initiation
into the coal business. I did, however, find time for some show
jumping. Silver Step won a class at Dunraven in 1933. For the rest
of the season, we competed against the professional travelling show
jumpers of those days such as Tommy Glencross, Doug Dobson and
the Woodhalls from Cheshire, Adcock from Leicester and Skidmore
from West Bromwich.

They were too good for Silver Step and myself at such shows as
Monmouth, Abergavenny and Devynock. Locally, Hubert Taylor
with Tuskar was usually too good for me, but not on every occasion.
At Usk Show Silver Step excelled herself and was acclaimed by
everyone as the winner until the results were announced. For the
only time in my life I disputed the decision and asked to see the
judge's marks in front of the stewards. As he did not produce them,
I wrote to the British Show Jumping Association and reported the
judge, but the BSJA in those days was rather a sleepy affair.

We started off the 1934 season rather better, being second in the
Open class at the Cardiff May Day Show, with the great Tommy
Glencross third, fourth and fifth behind us. Later, I took the mare
over to the indoor school at the Horse Gunners' Barracks at Newport,
where she jumped freely and well; I therefore decided to enter her
for the civilian classes at Olympia.

The big London show was to be a memorable occasion. I stayed
at Chartwell with Winston Churchill and his family at the invitation
of his daughter, Sarah. My father knew Winston and admired him,

having stayed at Chartwell when his advice was sought on stopping the 1926 General Strike.

Winston was charming to me and I advised him on what type of stoker to put into the swimming-pool which he was at that time building himself. I have never been a political person but I sat spellbound listening to the great man discussing every national issue then at stake. He took great pains to bring me into the conversation when he could, particularly in relation to South Wales and the coal business.

By this time, Silver Step had become about the best show jumper in South Wales, but Olympia proved to be a disaster for both the mare and myself. The crowds round the ring, the vast flower arrangements and the general hustle and bustle of this huge indoor show unnerved her; the country cousin was not happy. At the end of the week I had to my credit ten refusals and only one fence jumped.

During the week, Reg Whitehead arranged with Bertram Mills for me to jump indoors at the Duke of York's school. I conceived the idea of opening the end doors and taking Silver Step through them at a grand gallop in the belief that, when presented at the first fence which was plain brush, she would think it was a steeplechase fence and jump it.

I was wrong. She put the brakes on going into this fence and smashed it to smithereens. Without actually falling, we finished up in a tremendous jumble and I saw Reg Whitehead had collapsed with laughter. Apparently what he had found so funny was the expression of complete fury on Bertram Mills's face at his prize fence being demolished by this 'wild man from Wales'. I offered financial recompense which he refused, complaining that my offer was adding insult to injury but, before the week was over, he had accepted my apology.

Each night I had to return to Chartwell where I was quizzed by Winston and had to report my dismal failure. His counsel was simple: 'Pershevere, and you will succeed.'

Sarah Churchill had been a great friend from my Cambridge days and she often hunted Silver Step with the Glamorgan hounds. When she was a deb I loved her dearly. She was a marvellous dancer and I was often called upon to see her learn to dance for the stage at the Da Voss School for Dancing; later she appeared in one of C. B. Cochrane's musicals as a wounded pheasant. This was the start of her theatrical career, which took her out of my range. Within a couple

69

of years, she had changed her affections to Mr Vic Oliver and had taken off for America.

I had no opportunity to return to Olympia with Silver Step for she started to fade away the following spring and would not eat. She did not have redworm and we never discovered what really killed her but, when she was opened up after she died, her liver was found to be badly infected by some bacteria which was not identified.

As she weakened, we spent much of our time trying to persuade her to eat any delicacy that we could find and she would occasionally play with a sweet mash with molasses in it. It was sad to see her fade away. To keep her warm, Cooper covered her whole back with cow muck. This gave her, as it were, a permanent blanket whilst leaving the lower part of her body free and unencumbered.

Eventually, she could not get to her feet and Cooper and I were with her when she died. It was late at night and we both had hurricane-lamps. While trying to give her some sugar, she gently nickered, laid down her head and stopped breathing.

She was the last of the four sweet mares who had ensured that horses would play an important part in my life. After the motherly Fairy, the rompworthy Black Pearl and the enthusiastic tomboy, Golden Bell, there had come the talented Silver Step, who had started me show jumping and steeplechasing, and now was gone. I never cease to wonder why animals do so much for us for so little reward.

After my inglorious efforts at Olympia in 1933, I set off to 'do' Rome with Geoffrey Wilson, who was a great friend from my Cambridge days – indeed I had met Sarah Churchill while staying at his home in the New Forest. We did not, however, set about our sightseeing in quite the same spirit as an American mother I once heard say to her child, 'You "do" the Pantheon while your father and I "do" St Paul's.'

We had taken the trouble to read up our Roman history beforehand and were able to relive it vividly in the place where it all happened. It had long been my ambition to merge myself with the distant past and I look back upon this as an exhilarating experience. We came back through Venice where the Piazza San Marco stands out in my memory for I had the thrilling experience of hearing Gigli sing there. A less satisfactory experience was observing Mussolini strutting up and down the bridge of his yacht *Eleana*.

We then took off for Innsbruck and Munich before returning home and I believe it was this trip with Geoffrey that made me determined to see as much of Europe as I could, which resulted in my going there every year until the war. I never suspected that many of the places that I then visited could not be comfortably seen again by most of the young. With the exception of Lisbon I went to every European capital.

Later in the year the Valentine's Steeplechase at Liverpool became my objective, assuming that Silver Grail remained fit. This race was run over 2¾ miles of the Grand National course and was confined to amateurs. I wrote afterwards: 'The little horse obviously did not like jumping these big, green fences. He had never jumped them before and appeared frightened of them. I jumped Becher's on the left and Silver Grail also jumped to his left. This, combined with the fact that Becher's is also at an angle, meant that we landed practically in the ditch. Silver Grail came right on his head and floundered about for quite a while before he finally recovered. From that point on he jumped the Aintree fences beautifully. I saw I could not catch the leaders and eventually finished eighth.'

That winter, for the second year running, I qualified my father's Breconian as a hunter with the Glamorgan hounds. He had been blistered earlier in the year after his suspensory ligament had given way, but he was fully sound for the hunting-season and for some racing the following spring during which he won the Malvern Hunter Chase at Colwall and was second in two other races. Breconian was a meticulous jumper and, though he was not bold enough to give a lead to the 'first flight' when out hunting he never made a mistake with me on a racecourse.

The 1934 Grand National, won by Golden Miller, was the only one I missed during the pre-war decade. By that time, I was employed by Powell Duffryn and, using their laboratories at Mountain Ash as my base, I learned a good deal about the analysis of coal. I also carried out the inspection of every single Powell Duffryn pit with detailed drawings of their screens and methods of classifying coal. It proved a fascinating aspect of the business.

During my time at Mountain Ash, Lloyd George visited Nixon's Navigation Collieries and I was detailed to show him round the pit-head and the newly installed miners' baths. At that time I believe he was seventy-three but he scuttled round the place and it was difficult to keep up with him. I had heard that he was apt to do this but I was astonished by his energy and rapid-fire questions, all of them very much to the point. He also made a stirring address at the Three Valleys Festival at Mountain Ash when I was there. A friend described him as 'starting off like a visiting clergyman and ending up like a town crier.' Lloyd George told the story of how someone in Caernarvon had asked him if it was true that his father had driven a donkey-cart around the streets of that town. He replied that it was perfectly true; he had often seen the cart but this was the first time he had heard the donkey bray!

I succeeded in getting enough time off from my work at Mountain Ash to win two races during the spring of 1935 on Colonel Morgan-Lindsay's great horse Ego – of whom much more later. I was also given a week's leave after dislocating a collarbone while schooling one of our horses. During this time I was asked to help Randolph Churchill fight the Wavertree by-election. It sounded fun and Diana (later Bailey), Sarah, Randolph and I all put up at the Adelphi Hotel.

Randolph was standing as an Independent Conservative against Mr Platt. During this time Winston came and spoke for his son and they succeeded in creating 10,000 votes in ten days. Conservatives looked upon this as disgraceful because as a result Randolph split the Conservative vote, letting the Labour Councillor Cleary in with a good majority, and eventually making Wavertree a safe Labour seat.

Both Randolph and his father were unpopular with the Conservative Party. But despite this I thoroughly enjoyed my role as a canvasser, going from door to door and meeting with different kinds of reception. Most of these interviews ended in a good-natured way but, once or twice, I was told to 'FO' – and on one occasion a rather drunken lady threw some milk over me. At the end of the campaign I was appointed Randolph's scrutineer in the Cotton Exchange at Liverpool when the votes were counted.

In spite of my injury I was able to drive with one arm and spent much of my time transporting Randolph round to his various meetings. He was never a close friend of mine but I admired his guts and his ability to speak knowledgeably 'off the cuff', although he had a habit of shuffling forward on the stage with his toes slightly off the edge of the platform. Instead of listening to him, his audience was more interested in waiting to see whether he was going to fall off or not! On one occasion his rivals had encouraged some young men to make 'raspberry' noises through a door at the back of the stage.

Randolph responded quickly by asking if there was a doctor in the house as there were evidently gentlemen in severe distress behind the stage!

A month or so later, during the summer of 1935, my brother David and I set off to visit Europe. We were ostensibly going on a fact-finding tour of the coalfields of Germany, Russia, Poland and Turkey, and we were armed with many stamped documents, including official recognition by the Mining Association of Great Britain. We flew from Croydon to Brussels on the *Syrinx*, owned by Imperial Airways, which was a bi-plane with four engines between the wings. Just a week later, this plane crashed at Brussels Aerodrome.

There were many diversions to be found, including a miniature train which went round the Brussels Exhibition much too fast, and a fun-fair which included a hundred-foot tower from which people could simulate a parachute-drop. Having watched a few, I thought it would be rather fun. The principle was that you had a free drop until about halfway, then the parachute opened and the slack was taken in by a strong steel wire going back to a centrifugal brake. This left the jumper suspended about five feet above the ground. In order to encourage the sale of tickets, one or two people had been paid to jump and I was fooled into going up in the lift. When I got to the top I was terrified. I noted that nine out of ten people who got up there decided to tear up their tickets and take the lift back down again.

I did not have the nerve to do the same, so I was launched into mid-air. The free fall convinced me that the equipment had broken down but, gradually, I felt the pressure on my harness increase and I was duly deposited on the ground in one piece. Looking back, I cannot imagine why I was so foolish. It did not give me one bit of a thrill; my only sensation was one of terror.

Armed with our official introduction from the Mining Association of Great Britain, David and I took the train to Essen where we moved into a hotel in the middle of the town, next door to the GAU Headquarters of the *Sturm Abteilung*. Military bands played continuously in the square and the whole of Essen was turned upside down because Hitler himself was due to appear.

The Mining Association provided us with an SA guard called Jupp Frohn and a car driven by an SS driver. We were taken through the Krupps Works, where we were not allowed the freedom to go where

73

we liked, obviously because they were actively engaged in manufacturing arms which they did not wish their visitors to see.

Many mass meetings were taking place, and we persuaded Jupp Frohn to take us to the Essen Aerodrome where there was a gathering of 100,000 SA to greet their *Führer*, who made one of his ranting, raving speeches, all of which fortunately was lost upon us. Sometimes, remembering all the Swastika banners that we saw, I wonder how it ever came about that we were driven as representatives of the Mining Association to this grisly Nazi festival. I know that both David and I realized then the tremendous power that was behind the Nazi movement. Nothing that happened in subsequent years surprised us, as Hitler gained power and eventually took on the world in a war which he felt confident he would win and which he believed would enable him to impose himself and his philosophies on a world-wide basis.

Whilst in Essen we were impressed with the Matthias Stinnes pits with their railway-tunnel-like drivages underground and the efficient manner in which they used their coal-cutters, brought their coal to the surface and classified it. In this respect they were probably, on average, technically ten years ahead of British mining methods. Nor could we fail to be impressed by the accommodation provided for the workers at the Zollverein XII Pits. This encompassed miners' apartments, gardens and a specialist school for the mineworkers' children.

But the shattering exuberance and ominous threat of the SA, the SS, the Hitler Youth, and the BDM, with Hitler and Goebbels prancing around triumphantly in front of their admiring millions, remain my most indelible memories of Essen.

We took the night train to Berlin and spent two days there in the Adlon Hotel. I still have my collection of photographs of all the main buildings, including the *Reichstag* in its full magnificence as a piece of architecture rather than, as when I last saw it, a monument to Hitler's failure. At that time too, the balcony, later to become so famous, was being built outside the *Reichskanzlerpalais*. From it Hitler was to address his mobs in years to come. As we toured the city the Germany army, re-formed in March of that year, was marching up and down the *Unter der Linden* to the sound of bands playing.

David took me flat-racing at Hoppegarten and to the trotting at Ruhleben where he made several successful investments. He has always been a shrewd gambler on the course; I was always rather more interested in the horses, their equipment and the technical aspects of racing.

From Berlin we travelled across Poland, stopping off in various places before boarding the train for the Russian city of Kiev, where the most outstanding building is the Perchersk Monastery. Its bell-tower looks like a three-tiered wedding-cake and the building is quite unique, each level boasting a different architectural style from Doric through Ionic to Corinthian.

David led me to more trotting-races in Russia, where he punted away successfully while I made myself rather sick on sticky red caviare which one could buy in huge tins – half a kilo for about thirty shillings! The Nazi flags of Germany were here matched by massed red flags on most buildings as various anniversaries and jubilees were being celebrated.

Whereas the Mining Association had some influence remaining in Germany, it had little or none in the Soviet Union. However the Horgan Coal Corporation of New York had arranged introductions for us to the mining and port authorities, and Ugleexport gave us a special guide called Peter Sidorin who took us to the Don Basin. At that time American trade was important to the Russians as they were selling a huge tonnage of coal to America. The Russian coal had to be mixed with British coal which we supplied to the United States; of the two, our fuel had a much lower ignition-point, and therefore the Russian coal could be more easily fired when they were blended together.

We were first taken down to the port of Mariupol on the Sea of Azov, from which was exported most of the coal from the Don Basin. Although it was officially *niet*, I managed to take photographs of the port installations, basically for our own interest, but also in order to furnish a report to the Horgan Corporation concerning the Russian ability to supply the coal they needed. I had taken a good Zeiss Ikonta camera with me.

Later, when the war started, military intelligence learned that I had been to the Don Basin and I supplied them with a lengthy report, illustrated by photographs, which was gratefully received. British ships had occasionally gone into Mariupol but always everyone had to stay on board, so I had enjoyed a facility which no other Britisher had been given. As we never fought Russia, I could not then see why this information should have been valuable, except possibly in enabling us to gauge the potential of the German thrust down the Caucasus later in the war.

After seeing Mariupol we came back to the Don Basin to visit washeries near Stalino and a coal-mine. Here the washeries were huge contraptions with a small and rather inefficient output, while the collieries had the reputation of being unsafe in which to work. At one pit they asked me to go underground but, as all the surface buildings and the shaft itself shook violently whenever the elevator car went up or down, I found an excuse to stay on the surface.

Some sophisticated machinery had been acquired for classifying the coal. The large coal was passed onto conveyor belts from which impurities such as iron pyrites would be extracted. The flow was controlled by thickset ladies who perched themselves above the belts, allowing the coal to go down under their skirts and between their legs while they regulated the flow with their hands – another example of the contrast between modern industrial methods and the old-fashioned use of human hands.

At Stalino we were entertained to dinner by the engineers in their mess. No doubt they were looking forward to a good party and had got themselves well-oiled before we arrived, only to discover that we were both teetotallers. This did not discourage them and every single engineer had passed out before midnight, which enabled us to creep away unnoticed to our hotel.

The food we were given was excellent, with lashings of caviare, *foie gras* and assorted cold meats. There was also a kind of goulash-cum-Irish-stew-cum-Scotch-broth, thickened up with chunks of different varieties of meat with plenty of salt and pepper added. Something must have gone wrong with the salad, however, as David and I were sick the next day when we went by train to Odessa, where we both spent a day in bed.

After two days we caught a Russian boat of the *Sovtorgflot*, the SS *Frantzmerinj*, and set off across the Black Sea in rough weather. We arrived in Istanbul and, since David was severely ill from dysentery, I had him removed immediately to the American Hospital where he was put on a diet of apples. He was found to be suffering from the 'Shaiga' dysentery, about which not much was known in Europe apart from its initial discovery when isolated in some Paris hospital.

My parents contacted St Thomas's and we were advised to leave David in the American Hospital to recover his strength; he ended up staying there for a month. Tolstoy's niece, Marina, was a nurse in the hospital and she also acted as my guide round the town and surrounding area during that time. I spent many days swimming off the superb beach at Florya, eating my daily omelette at the small beach-bar before returning on the rickety, ever-whistling puff-puff to Istanbul in the evening. I was able to keep fit; the bathing must have been some of the best in the world. For half a mile out one walked through clear calm clean water, which never came above one's shoulders. It did not take long for Florya to become the principal resort in Turkey and I gather it now looks like Benidorm, with its shore crowded down to the water's edge.

While in Istanbul, I took the opportunity of going to the Turkish Army Riding School where I was given instruction by an extremely efficient sergeant on a grey horse called Tom. He had no real mouth but, if I ever wanted to adjust his stride, I dropped his head on the approach to a fence when he would shorten and meet it right. I later adopted the same method on my show jumper Monty.

After three weeks I could see that David was getting weaker, so I made preparations to take him home. His dysentery was not cured and he was getting dangerously thin with a hollow, parchment look about his face. I booked him back on the Simplon Express and it was interesting to note that, as soon as the train started moving, his dysentery improved. I have since been told by doctors that the constant movement and shaking that takes place in a train can cut down bowel activity.

The train journey itself was uneventful apart from the measures taken at each frontier, where guard-dogs inspected the train. When we arrived at Trieste we found crowds of Italians who had been mobilized to go to Abyssinia. We journeyed through the Simplon Tunnel into France, then sped to Boulogne where we were met by Dyer, my father's chauffeur, with a carry-chair in which two brawny, very able seamen were able to carry David to our car. This took him straight to St Thomas's Hospital, the only place at that time which we felt was capable of effecting a cure. It took him many months to get over this illness and I do not think that he would welcome another evening in a Russian engineers' mess!

6　　　　Ego

Ego, an aptly named son of the stallion Pomponious and the mare Eggs, had come over from Ireland in 1933. He was then a raw five-year-old chestnut gelding with a biggish head. His new owner was Colonel Morgan-Lindsay, who had ridden a hundred winners on the flat in South Africa during the Boer War and later trained about a dozen horses at Ystrad Mynach, with gallops and schools on wonderful going on the mountains and hillsides nearby. I was then riding early morning work at Ystrad Mynach, just as Fulke Walwyn and Evan Williams had done before me.

I had given Ego his first school over fences on the Llanharan mountain. He loved the job and skipped over the schooling-fences as if they were nothing, which they probably were in comparison with those he had met in his native Ireland where it was assumed he had been hunted since he was two years old. Never has there been a bolder horse.

I was not then asked to ride Ego on the racecourse – partly, I believe, because I could not have done the weight in the National Hunt Steeplechase in 1933 when he won it as a five-year-old carrying 11 stone 5 pounds. Furthermore, although I was already being offered rides in amateur races and point-to-points, at that time my father wished me to work harder and not ride other people's horses.

So it was a great thrill when Colonel Morgan-Lindsay first asked me to ride his great horse in a steeplechase and my father made an exception to his normal rule. I won two races on Ego during the spring of 1935. In the first, at Newton Abbot, he carried top weight and won easily; all I had to do was to sit there and stop him over-exerting himself.

Our next joint venture was at Buckfastleigh, where he jumped the first fence very much to the left and allowed Peter Cazelet to come up on my inside. My diary records: 'I allowed him to come there to make sure that Ego did not run out on this National Hunt course which has no rails and only a few flags at turning-points. Coming to the straight he was well in front. He dropped the bit but on seeing the last fence he took hold again and galloped up the straight like a lion. I discovered the reason for his easing up like this was probably because the gate through which he had entered the course was only a little distance away to his left. He had often been known to hang like this on the way to his box before.' He was never a nappy horse but he certainly had ideas of his own.

Ego was kept going through the summer while David and I were in Eastern Europe. I next rode him at Colwall in October, where he again won a three-mile chase, but he had some difficulty giving 22 pounds to Comedian ridden by 'Ginger' Dennistoun (father of Lady Oaksey). A week later, in a two-horse race at Cardiff, he beat Fred Rimell on Brave Cry by two lengths – but it could have been more. My father then bought a half-share in Ego. Our objective had been the Becher Steeplechase at Liverpool, but dear old Colonel Morgan-Lindsay died reading *The Racing Calendar* a few days before this race so we ran Ego in his name and carried his colours.

Ego obviously enjoyed jumping these big Liverpool fences. Normally, on a standard National Hunt course, he would rather slop over the obstacles. He was too bold, did not respect the fences and often hit them quite hard. He never pricked his ears and looked at them, and I am quite sure that he did not regard them as serious obstacles to his progress. But when he got to Liverpool he soon realized that these very strongly built fences required much cleaner jumping so he looked at them, backed off a little and tried hard. Interfered with in the approach, he hit that nasty fence between Bechers and the Canal Turn, came right down on his head and cut his lip. I do not believe he ever forgot that lesson.

I was nearly put into the wing by Inversible who ran across the fence, but Ego, obviously enjoying Aintree, galloped on stoutly to finish third. The two and a half miles was too short a journey for him but he had proved that he was a Liverpool horse and much easier to ride there than round provincial and park courses.

A week later I rode him at Cheltenham in a three-mile race and found myself in front at the last fence and going very easily; but without company he 'scotched' a little and I blamed myself for not keeping him about his business. Meanwhile, Fred Rimell on Brave Cry had passed us at great speed. Having lost his momentum at the last fence it was difficult for Ego to get going again, just as it would be to try to start a heavy car in top gear on a hill. I just failed to catch Brave Cry which beat me a length. I threw this race away.

Had Ego not come into my life at that particular time, I would probably have given up steeplechasing, although I loved every minute of it. My weight was becoming an impossible problem. Even using the 1½ pound saddle made for me specially by Boyce & Rogers of Newmarket, it had been a struggle for me to carry only 13 stone when I rode Breconian in March 1934. Incidentally, Pete Bostwick (the great American rider) had an exact copy of my saddle, which had a special tree with a double-rolled steel arch in the front to give it strength. There were benefits in riding in this beautiful saddle which meant that I was always close to my horse and, even when I had to put up extra weight, I still rode in it or in the second one I had made as an exact copy.

Now that Ego had proved that he was a good Liverpool horse, I had before me the glittering prospect of riding in the 1936 Grand National and every sacrifice became very much worthwhile as far as training was concerned.

When I had been at Cambridge my fit weight for rugby football was 12 stone 7 pounds; in 1934, when I had ridden racing very little, I had gone up to 14 stone. As I knew that Ego would be given somewhere in the region of 10 stone 7 pounds in the following March, I went into rigorous training over the winter of 1935–36, having lost half a stone swimming daily at Florya on the Marmora Sea in the summer. I had been able to ride Ego at Liverpool in November at 11 stone 9 pounds which meant that I had already reduced my weight to about 11 stone 4 pounds stripped. It was the removal of this final stone which was to prove so hard to achieve. I was forced to become a recluse and attended no social functions at all. I had my meals by myself at the end of a small table in the kitchen and never ate with my family.

Fortunately, my father could see the sense in this routine. I then came under the devoted care of our cook, Mrs Stinchcombe, who had been a kitchen maid at Badminton, and quite rightly, a devotee of the horse-loving Beaufort family. She weighed everything I had to eat. This consisted mainly of small quantities of meat, vegetables and oranges, with a rationed input of liquid. My breakfasts consisted of two raw eggs in a glass of vinegar and I had no fat or starch of any sort. Once I was on this routine, retaining it became comparatively easy except when I had to travel to race-meetings and saw the lovely food being eaten by my friends!

When I went hunting I had two layers of wool next to my skin and then a mackintosh shirt and shorts, so that in a day's hunting I was able to sweat off several pounds without much pain. On almost every night for months on end I would go off for a run round our cricket-pitch. Ten times round this was the equivalent of three miles. I put on several pairs of woollens and then zipped myself up in an airman's suit so that only my face was exposed in order to breathe.

Occasionally I used to take laxatives when I was desperate to do the weight, and on one occasion I recall taking off nine pounds in a single night in order to ride in a race the next day. I was careful not to overdo the restriction of such liquid that I took – mostly tea, water or orange-juice – as I was told that my kidneys would suffer if I did. Even when I was down to about ten and a half stone I was extraordinarily fit and used to exhaust the two chauffeurs, Knight and Dyer, plus Cooper and the two lads, when I shadow-boxed them several times a week.

When I hear about people slimming these days I wonder how many of them reduce their weight from 14 stone to 10 stone 3 pounds as I did before I finally rode in the Grand National of 1936. I looked so thin that one racing journalist, Quentin Gilbey, wrote that he could not believe that anyone who had lost so much weight would be strong enough to survive the National course. This upset me, so I wrote him a letter challenging him to a race immediately after the National – twice round the paddock or parade-ring for £100. He did not accept the challenge but later wrote me a charming letter of apology.

Ego's first outing in 1936 was in the Crawley Steeplechase at Gatwick over stiff, upright fences. I record that this was a disappointing display, although the distances behind the winner (Davy Jones) and the runner-up (Remus) were only three lengths and six lengths. I dead-heated for third place with Knuckleduster, ridden by Gerry Wilson, because I had dropped my hands near the post and Gerry had come 'with a wet sail'.

We were third again at Kempton in a three-mile chase behind Deminkoff, ridden by Fulke Walwyn. Ego then won a three-mile chase at Hawthorn Hill when he was giving a lot of weight to many others, beating Applaud, ridden by Gersham Wood, by a head in a rousing finish. One of the professionals, Billy Parvin, paid me the compliment of having 'ridden it like a pro', and the *Sporting Chronicle* awarded me the 'Best Performance of the Week'.

Honours for the Best Performance of the Week go to

MR H. LLEWELLYN

who rode a brilliant race on Ego to beat Applaud at
Hawthorn Hill on Monday, winning in the last stride
after being four lengths behind at the last fence!

In races at Cheltenham, Hurst Park and Kempton, my horse was
off the bridle the whole time but I was delighted with the way he
jumped, for I knew he did not really have the speed for a park track.

Ego was 100–1 in the ante-post betting for the Grand National,
but he was considered to be an outsider who would probably jump
the course and his odds were eventually halved. He had been given
10 stone 6 pounds in the handicap and I was able to do 10 stone 8
pounds on the great day, which meant that I weighed only 10 stone
3 pounds without my saddle.

My father and I spent the night before the National at the Gros-
venor Hotel at Chester. Having ridden the course a few times before,
I decided not to walk round as I knew the fences well and they were
(as they are now) still in the same places. I am glad I did not look
at them again as walking round Aintree is a frightening experience.
One wonders how a horse just over sixteen hands can survive over
a long series of solid fences which are mostly five feet high, with the
open ditch – the famous 'Chair' in front of the stands – at five feet
two inches.

Any feelings that I had were not of fear. I had absolute confidence
in Ego's ability to jump the course and my only worry was that he
might not be fast enough to go with them in the first part of the race.
One hears stories of jockeys taking alcohol before the National but
I never saw anyone take to the bottle.

The routine of the changing-room under the eyes of the valets was
the same as anywhere else. My valet was Arthur Lord, who had
looked after me so well and cheerfully since my first ride at Leicester
six years previously. Changing, weighing out, saddling-up, were the
same as always. One simply did not have time to sit down and worry
about the immediate future. It is a wonderful feeling of elation to
have a ride in the Grand National at all and, if I felt anything, it was
exhilaration. I am not trying to show off when I say that steeplechasing never frightened me; it was simply that my mind was occupied with other considerations, mainly – would I win? I had a
tremendous ambition to *win*. I would prefer to have one winner rather

than fifty seconds. Later, Mike Ansell had the same philosophy in regard to show jumping, and there was seldom an occasion when his guiding genius and great leadership restrained him from sending a telegram which usually read – 'Bloody well win!'

Another reason for my lack of fear was that, having ridden only one or two bad jumpers, I knew what a really good jumper was and should be. As a result I had few falls. I was able to choose my rides and, being heavy, only rode in hunter chases or on highly handicapped horses which therefore must have been good. Most professionals did not have this choice – they had to ride everything they were offered. Another fact was that I never really hurt myself. My bones must have been made of pretty hard material because I never broke one during a steeplechasing career that spanned more than twenty-one years, although I dislocated rather more easily. Actually my face suffered most and I had teeth knocked out on seven separate occasions.

Up to this National, however, I can really say that I had never been hurt and this helped me not to be frightened in any way. When riding one could soon detect when some of the older jockeys had seen the 'red light', and they quickly withdrew from the game. The professional jockeys were wonderful people but I saw many of them have a raw deal. I never envied the professional trainers, either. Many of them led a precarious existence and were badly treated by their owners. I was quite determined never to take up a professional career with horses and suffer from the actions of a mainly fickle owning fraternity who, to be as kind as one can about them, were at best a pretty mixed lot.

Returning to the Grand National of 1936, my diary records: 'Ego was considered to have an outside chance and started at 50–1. I had much to win and nothing to lose. The scene in the changing-room was the same as in any other and it was hard to realize that I was about to ride in the Grand National.

'In the parade, however, I became conscious of the vast stands packed with punters and the persistent murmur of the crowd. As we lined up, I chose a place towards the outside. All of a sudden we were off. We raced towards the first fence as if in a five-furlong sprint. All the horses seemed unbalanced and they floundered as they crossed the tan on the Melling Road, but we were off again and charged that first fence like tanks going into action.

'Ego had not the speed of the others and we were nearly last going into this fence. My most vivid recollection of the race was the crashing and breaking of thick sticks as five horses fell in front of me. I became conscious of the crowd shouting and screaming at the side. Ego sailed into the first fence and jumped it beautifully. Over the first four fences we kept our position on the outside and hardly noticed the drop at Becher's. There is the danger on the inside of being crowded into the corner and jumping into the brook on the far side. Becher's, like most of the Liverpool fences, is at an angle. We all converged to jump the next fence. At the Canal Turn a horse fell on my left but Ego jumped to the right and then turned left on landing. Horses get to know the Canal Turn and I knew one must be careful not to become unseated when they turn sharply to the left.

'At Valentine's, Blue Prince fell in front of us and I still wonder how Ego kept his feet. We were brought to a standstill and must have been a hundred yards behind the leaders. However, Ego still jumped beautifully and was only twenty lengths behind the leaders coming on to the racecourse. We caught them going into the country for the last time but only just succeeded in avoiding Avenger, who had started favourite and fell and broke his neck at the next fence.

'At Becher's second time round I was eight lengths behind the leaders. I had been off the bit all the time but, knowing that Ego was a true stayer, I realized that my only hope was to keep in touch. I kept this position until the Canal Turn when Reynoldstown and Davy Jones raced ahead. At this fence I was badly stopped by Keen Blade who cut in front of me. I was passing Keen Blade when he fell at the third-last fence. Davy Jones ran out going into the last fence and this enabled me to finish second instead of third, officially beaten twelve lengths, having eased him in the run-in, with Bachelor Prince six lengths behind.'

The buckle joining Davy Jones' reins had broken and poor Anthony Mildmay had been unable to steer the horse to the last fence – which was terrible luck. My diary continues: 'Whereas Davy Jones lost his Grand National in full view of everyone, Ego probably lost his when he was badly interfered with by Blue Prince. I still feel that I was on a horse that was quite good enough to have won, but soon rejoiced, realizing that I was the second-luckiest man in the world.'

After the National there was traditionally a party at the Adelphi Hotel with the names of the first three horses being placed above a long high table and the owners, trainers and riders invited.

Naturally, we were delighted to have been second. I could not help feeling that I might have won had Davy Jones and Reynoldstown fallen when they collided landing over the fence after Valentine's last time round. The BBC film shows them both on the ground. However, they recovered, and had not the rein on Davy Jones' bridle broken I would have been third instead of second. It was to Anthony Mildmay that everybody's sympathy, including mine, went. Opinions vary, but most thought that Davy Jones was going the better of the two leaders at the time. Reynoldstown had carried the huge weight of 12 stone 2 pounds for four and a half miles.

Among the telegrams I received after the race was one which read: 'Warmest congratulations. Winston and I both backed you. Clementine Churchill.' Another, from Mary Churchill, simply said: 'Whoopee and love.'

Evasio Mon had fallen at the first fence in the Grand National and Thurstan Holland-Martin had hurt himself, although the horse was quite all right. He asked me to ride this champion point-to-pointer in the Liverpool Foxhunters' Steeplechase on the following day, for which he was much fancied. This beautifully schooled horse was a marvellous jumper. Nothing ever took the Chair and water-fence better than he did.

His splendid jumping took us into the lead and I wrote: 'Going out into the country he was pulling far harder than anything else and I felt certain that he would win. I pulled him back as much as I could and was soon joined by "Minnow" Prior-Palmer on Tullamaine who was eventually fourth.' We were having a wonderful time on two superb animals jumping perfectly. He shouted across at me, '*C'est la crème de la crème!*' and I replied, '*D'accord, d'accord,*' and then promptly fell at the next fence!

For some extraordinary reason, Evasio Mon had put in a short one at the second fence into the country and had turned a complete somersault. He then got loose and tried to jump some spiked railings which cut his chest about terribly and this injury put him out of racing for the rest of the season.

I rode many other horses that spring, all under National Hunt Rules. Silver Grail had been regenerated and I had ridden him at Birmingham where he was third; in the Melton Hunt Steeplechase he was second, dividing the Bissill brothers on Royal Ascot and Lurid. After this race, Olive Partridge schooled round the course on a hunter without permission, possibly as an early expression of women's lib, but the stewards reported her to the National Hunt Committee for having done so.

Silver Grail then returned triumphantly to Wye, beating Leconfield II (ridden by Anthony Mildmay), and then to Colwall Park where he beat Cheerful Marcus by twenty lengths and was in front of Pucka Belle when she fell at the last fence. Pucka Belle had been Filmer Sankey's champion point-to-point mare before being bought by Eric Bailey, who had only learned to ride four years beforehand and won many races on her – a tremendous achievement.

My father had relaxed his rule after the National and I was therefore allowed to ride other people's horses. I went to Stratford-on-Avon where Paulerspury's jockey had not turned up, so I had a chance ride on this good point-to-pointer who proceeded to win the Warwickshire Hunters' Chase, running away by fifteen lengths from many good established hunter chasers. I again rode this horse in the Cleeve Hunters' Steeplechase at Cheltenham which he won equally easily. I was grateful to Cliff Beechener for giving me the ride and to Perry Harding for persuading me to take it.

For the first time I rode China Sea, who was jointly owned by Carmen Cory and Ben Roberts. He was bold, but a clumsy jumper and he hit many of his fences without ever looking like falling. He was unplaced at Worcester before winning at Cowbridge. Other rides included Richard Blunt's Peritate and Mrs Nellie Roberts's Henry VIII who gave me a crashing fall in a hurdle race at Windsor having taken off ten yards from a hurdle which he dived through.

I also had a couple of rides on my sister Betty's Bunfight and these proved a mistake. I fell at both Ludlow and Cardiff with him and, on the last occasion, was hit by another horse's foot above my right eye. For many weeks I could not see out of the top of the injured eye, and foolishly told no one about it. I have never enjoyed receiving sympathy, which is possibly a reaction to the over-anxious care bestowed upon me by my mother, my Aunt Maud and various school matrons when I was young.

I felt that the best way for injuries to repair themselves was to keep going and to keep *fit*. As it turned out, the damage incurred in that fall with Bunfight has affected my eyesight for the rest of my life. Apparently the grey shade at the top of my eye was probably blood in the bottom of the eyeball and, when it finally disappeared, it left me astigmatized in my right eye.

Apart from our horses I continued to take a keen interest in the home farm and stud and learned much from Thomas Thomas, Sam Haydon and old Joe, who looked after three Guernsey cows which were hard at work supplying our large family. I was particularly interested in my father's cattle and sheep and, for a while, found myself helping to run the farm as well as the stud.

Jim Edgel came into my life as the purchaser of thousands of pit-horses for the collieries and he became a great friend of mine. When Ego looked like becoming a good National horse, I persuaded my father to send Edgel to Ireland to buy his sire, Pomponious, instead of having a big bet on my Grand National mount. Unfortunately, on his first trip, Edgel got in with some over-hospitable Irish hosts and spent most of the money he had with him on forty donkeys. The next day, feeling penitent, he telephoned me and confessed what he had done. He said he could not resist them as he had bought one charming mare for 7s. 6d. and what was he to do with them all? I told him to send them home and they duly arrived at St Fagans station, making a tremendous noise so that their arrival could hardly have been kept a secret. I made arrangements for them to be put in a field at St George's and I paid the full purchase price. Despite the donkeys, Pomponious did eventually join Hapsburg and Chin Chin, the other two stallions standing at our stud at Llanmaes.

Unfortunately, Jim Edgel, his son and I were discovered by my father driving the donkeys up the road past our front gates, but he had little time in which to chastise us as he was late for a meeting. By the time my father returned that evening he had seen the funny side of it and I was allowed to retain the donkeys providing they were not kept upon his property. I kept the ten best and sold the remaining thirty for much more than Edgel had paid for the lot. I had also paid for their journey over but at the end of the transaction, I still had a little money in my pocket and ten beautiful donkeys, which soon proved pleasant to ride and formed the nucleus of the 'donkey polo' which we often played at St Fagans.

The system in our unique brand of polo was to have goal-posts about one hundred and fifty yards apart and two people, both with walking-sticks, allotted to each donkey. We played with a regulation football, and whilst the rider tried to strike the ball with his walking-stick his partner belaboured the poor donkey from behind to position the rider so that he or she could hit the ball. When a rider became tired, he changed places with his partner.

We often played this wonderful game when we had house-parties for the young, and it was particularly useful when a meet of the hounds was cancelled owing to frost after one Glamorgan Hunt Ball.

From time to time the donkeys took it into their heads to withdraw from the game and bolt with their riders, and one of the funniest sights I ever saw was that of Anne Bridgeman being bolted with by a donkey. Later, I presented her with a foal which she retained for many years and called 'Eeyore', and which must have reminded her of our donkey polo.

There were several other young families in Glamorgan who shared our various activities. In the twenties I recall often going to Coryton, where Rosalie Cory, my partner in tennis mixed doubles, was the calf-love of my life. Carmen was the one who shared my interest in horses and I occasionally rode her Pastime show jumping. Their parents, Sir Herbert and Lady Cory, were wonderfully kind and they shared with my father a mania for bridge, so when we went to dinner at Coryton we young ones were left to do as we liked.

Lady Cory had a habit of making everyone get up and make a speech, recite a poem or sing a song, which was usually embarrassing for the young, but later the ability to stand up and make a speech proved an advantage. Proceedings were always opened by Sir Herbert – known as 'Sherbert', because he pronounced his 's's' as do the Portuguese – singing the song, 'Pretty Jemima, don't say "No" ', and then we all had to take our turn.

Edmund Hann's family were also great friends. He was Chairman of Powell Duffryn when it took over my father's group, Welsh Associated Collieries. Joan Hann was the nearest to my age and I often used to go to Lanelay Hall to play squash. She was also a beautiful dancer and I was sad when she got married shortly before the war. A compulsive rug-maker, she was making a black rug at that time and allowed me to put two scarlet loops in it to record my bleeding heart!

In the thirties, we saw a great deal of the Boothby family; indeed Hugo and Serena are still close friends. Their mother always insisted that whenever I went anywhere I must go back and tell her about my travels – which was not all that easy as she had become very deaf and relied on the use of an ear-trumpet. In spite of being the fifth son, Hugo's father had inherited the Boothby title, which is the senior Welsh baronetcy. The previous baronet had been a Trappist monk near Stettin in Eastern Germany. Few people knew he lived there or that he had died, and Sir Seymour did not even know that he had succeeded to the title until more than a year later.

We saw much of the daughters of Bob Williams who lived at Bonvilston and was Master of the Glamorgan Hounds for thirty-three seasons. They were our constant companions and shared our love of hunting and racing. Sue went like a bomb side-saddle, while Jo did not ride but was one of those foot-followers, like Daphne Moore, who were always there before the mounted field. Jo is now married to my brother, David; while Sue has continued her interest in racing, with such good horses as Tree Tangle, Successor and others, and has become the first female steward at Chepstow racecourse.

The Boothby, Llewellyn and Williams families formed the Bonfonagan Hounds, which met every Sunday. It could be described as a very mixed trencher-fed pack as all our dogs, sometimes numbering a dozen, were accustomed to hunting rabbits or hares. We seldom killed anything but had exhilarating hunts over the land at Bonvilston, Fonmon Castle and our land at St Fagan's, hence the name Bon-Fon-Agan. It was not unknown for us to net a rabbit, put a little aniseed on him, and take him from one property to another so that he would not find his own burrow for our homes were eight to ten miles apart. Lancer and the Boothbys' dachshunds had the best noses, but the Williams' Scotties, Hugo Boothby's Kerry Blue and various terriers all played their part. My Keeshond, Fury, was a courageous 'tufter' and she would hurl herself through any bush at anything moving.

I had spent over a year working at Mountain Ash when I managed to organize myself, rather skilfully I thought, to move to London in the spring of 1936. I went to work in the mileage depot of Bradbury Son & Co., coal distributors, and came under a splendid gentleman called Mr Gadd, who buzzed around like a bee and was probably the finest coal salesman in the world.

I was instructed in the full art of the 'knocker' trade – that is knocking on strange people's doors and trying to sell them coal. My other duties were to call on every laundry in Acton and try to sell them anthracite grains for their boilers. This was less exciting but rather more fruitful, and Mr Gadd commended me for increasing the sales. My method was to try to get people interested in racing and give them a series of tips! If successful, they were honour bound to buy their coal from me. Perhaps this was an unusual approach to the job – but it worked.

Of course, one of my principal objects in getting a job in London from May to July was that it meant that I was in London for the Season. I seemed to be on quite a lot of 'lists' and therefore was asked out to dinner before going on to a deb dance every day of the week. My only expenses were the bus-ride to the Mileage depot and 1s. 9d. for a multi-tiered sandwich in Whiteleys' store nearby, plus the cost of producing a stiff shirt and two collars for each night's activities. It was all 'white tie' in those days. I was only one of the dozens of young men 'freeloading' in this way; but, after all, few girls would have had partners had we not been available.

Interspersed with these dances were many enjoyable weekend parties, and we were able to return the hospitality we had received in London by asking people home where they always seemed to enjoy themselves. Apart from organized festivities we could always swim in the Freeman-Thomas's natural pool – many hundreds of feet deep – at Maindy, play donkey polo, or enjoy a day with the Bonfonagan Hounds for which there was no 'close season'.

I was an energetic dancer and specialized in the Viennese waltz, on occasions reverse-turning at speed throughout the whole dance. Vincent Paravicini was one of my chief rivals in this; another was George Townshend, of whom I still see a good deal. He is Chairman of Anglia Television, while his wife breeds some splendid Arabian horses.

Whatever one says about the London Season, those privileged to take part in it made lifelong friends.

I eagerly accepted another invitation that summer, which was to go to Hungary and ride a horse called Tammuz, which was their top hurdler. He was set in the handicap to give 40 kilos (6 stone 4 pounds) to the bottom weight and 13½ kilos (nearly 30 pounds) to the next top weight. He had proved himself the best hurdler in Central Europe but was too wilful and strong for the average small Hungarian jockey. Someone from Hungary had seen me ride in the National and thought I looked big enough and strong enough to ride this horse and get him to start. I was to discover that Tammuz's reputation as a rogue was entirely justified.

'He was also the biggest "dog" in Central Europe', I wrote in my diary. 'On this course he had often been known to refuse to start altogether. He stopped several times with me during the parade which, incidentally, was in front of Admiral Horthy, the Regent of Hungary. I noticed the other jockeys were riding shorter than the

British jump jockeys. We were then allowed to jump a preliminary hurdle in front of the stands. Tammuz approached this both sideways and backwards and I only had him straight enough just in time to jump it beautifully. He then objected to going down to the start and napped every few strides. Eventually at the start he jumped off towards the stables instead of towards the contest and nearly had me out of the saddle by so doing. The starter fortunately called them back but, even at the second attempt, Tammuz refused to jump off properly and merely cantered into the first hurdle. After getting round the bottom turn however, he suddenly shot off like a streak of lightning when he realized it was the quickest way home. He sped down the course and jumped perfectly. I finished fifth amongst cheers and whistles, but everybody seemed pleased that I had got him round.'

I was then offered more rides and would have been able to take them had I been able to do the weight, but I was out at grass for the summer and was more than two stone heavier than when I had ridden in the National.

I thoroughly enjoyed life in Hungary, where we danced until early morning on Margareten Island before riding the first lot of horses at Alag at about 4 a.m. and the second lot at 6 a.m. followed by breakfast at 8. Then we slept until going racing in the afternoon. I was offered two rides in the Pardubice Steeplechase but was unable to take them as I had other plans.

My main objective was now Berlin, where the Olympic Games were about to be staged. I went up the Danube by boat to Vienna, spent a day at the Spanish Riding School, and then went to Prague, where I had a surprise meeting with my brother David.

I had known that David was likely to be in the area, so I went round one or two hotels before visiting the Sroubec. Quite suddenly I saw him with Nick Elliott and Mr Routh, his 'beak' at Eton, walking down some hotel stairs. David and Nick were astonished as they had no idea I was in Europe and indeed thought I was at home. David was so shocked he did not recognize me for some time. He had just written a letter to me in England.

I spent the next day with them before catching the night train for Berlin. I had tried a new technique when travelling by night between Budapest and Prague; it involved putting out all the lights in my compartment, drawing the curtains, eating some oranges and leaving the peel on the seat, then snoring loudly whenever anybody passed. This ensured that nobody wished to share my compartment with me and so I had most of the night to myself. I tried the same trick on the way to Berlin and this cut the occupants down to two; but the rest of the train was crowded. At full stretch I spent a good night. Looking back, I am a little ashamed of my tactics – but a lone traveller has to survive.

When I reached Berlin, I made a point of reporting to the German authorities, because no Customs people had seen me when I entered the country. No doubt they had been deterred by my orange peel, but I did not want a problem when I left. I begrudged the three hours that I spent in the *Devisenstelle* before being able to obtain a form which showed how much money I had brought in. I then set off by underground for the Olympic Stadium; this meant an hour's hot clanking run during which time I had to stand amongst a plethora of Nazi flags, and those of some other countries.

I spent most of my first day at the stadium watching the *Grande Épreuve de Dressage* – in German the *Grosse Dressurprufung*. I was particularly interested to note that the *Piaffe*, when all four legs simulate the trotting action without the horse moving forward, was not as clear or as distinct in the hind legs as when carried out by the Spanish Riding School. The Germans, who won both team and individual gold medals, had a much more rigid way of performing than did the riders of other countries. Every movement had to be straight and correct, if rather stiff. The French and the Swiss had a distinct *élan* about their performances, which were fluent, much freer and more pleasant to watch.

The following day I went to see the dressage for the *Concours Complet d'Équitation*, which is now called horse trials or three-day-event. The standard was a good deal lower than on the previous day and, although I enjoy dressage, I found it rather boring. So I went to the *Deutchsland Halle* which, thirty-five years later, I was to visit with the British Show Jumping Team. Here there were some splendid boxing events. In the Bantamweights a lightning-quick black American knocked out a Filipino. As in the case of Jesse Owens in the track events, it was interesting to note the hostile reception by the crowd of a coloured winner. These were the Games when Jesse Owens won three events and Hitler was so incensed that he left the stadium in a fury and would not congratulate him.

In those days I was not much interested in horse trials but I went to the cross-country day and I recall standing next to a fence where all the German competitors seemed to jump well into a water-splash and then emerged successfully. It was subsequently discovered that there was one hard area where horses could land safely and this seemed to be known to the German riders but not to the others, most of whom floundered or fell. Whether the gold-medal-winning Germans knew about this beforehand is questionable, but certainly the other riders should have walked the course more efficiently than they did. Nowadays, gumboots are the order of the day to walk in the water and find out the good spots for landing.

I was unable to wait for the show jumping *Grand Prix des Nations*, also won by Germany, and I was soon on the train for Amsterdam. Here, I went on my usual *rundfahrt*.

The Duke of Kent had opened an English art exhibition and I spent half a day looking at beautiful paintings. If I had been allowed to take home one irrespective of value, I would have chosen Ford Madox-Brown's *Last of England*, which shows a man with his wife and child looking back pathetically as the boat on which they are emigrating leaves the British shore.

The exhibition was a visual feast of fine paintings and I found myself exhausted. I felt like a cat that had had all the cream. It was almost a surfeit of good things. But I felt equally that I had learned much and was particularly proud of our British artists.

I sailed home from the Hook of Holland to Harwich and, for the first time in many years, arrived feeling really seasick. I was then – and for the only time in my life – given a thorough going-over by the Customs. I cannot think why I should have appeared to be such a suspicious character apart from the fact that I had bought a Czechoslovakian mackintosh because my own coat had been stolen!

7   Aintree Days

Back home in England, my thoughts turned to steeplechasing and to the prospect of another ride on Ego in the 1937 Grand National. But first I rode China Sea, who had been kept in training for most of the summer and was fit enough to win the Hereford Amateur Riders' Steeplechase at Colwall in September. A month later he won the three-mile Town Handicap Steeplechase at Tenby where we made all the running to beat the odds-on favourite, Vive L'Amour.

This was the last meeting at Tenby, where David Harrison had been the outstanding trainer in recent years. The Tenby area was responsible for the production of the Anthony brothers – Ivor, Owen and Jack; the last-named won the Grand National three times. Bilbie and Fred Rees had also come from this area, but another claim to fame by Tenby was related to the great coup that had been engineered for Oyster Maid.

There are many versions as to what happened but the one I believe was that hundreds of telegrams were handed in a couple of minutes before the 'off' so that it was impossible for the bookmakers to know how much money had been laid on this mare in time to shorten the odds. The result was that Oyster Maid, previously regarded as a moderate mare, won at a starting-price of something like 10–1, beating horses that had much better form.

China Sea recorded his fourth successive win with me when he trotted up at Cardiff in the Llanrumney Handicap Steeplechase. The official verdict was six lengths because I had eased up after I had looked round. I wrote: 'Although Know-Alls in the stands might resent a jockey looking round it is far better to win by a smaller margin in view of future handicapping – and why exert the horse unnecessarily?' Handicappers are not always easy to fool merely by elbow-wobbling while holding a horse tightly by the head. On the other hand, looking round can unbalance a tired horse and going for your whip can have the same effect.

At the same time we were naturally making plans to see if Ego could go one better in the next Grand National. He had been sent to Frank Hartigan who approached his training programme rather differently, often giving him only a sprint of three to four furlongs a few days a week. He gave him no middle-distance gallops as he wanted to get Ego faster and fresher – jumping out of his skin or 'cherry-ripe' as he put it.

The horse's first outing since the previous National was again to be at Liverpool, this time in the Valentine's Steeplechase of two miles seven and a half furlongs. I spent a few mornings at the great trainer's establishment at Weyhill and learned much from him. He spent the first part of the morning in bed in those days, looking out of the window at his horses doing their work and at the same time doing his paper-work. He was surrounded by copies of the *Racing Calendar* and form books.

At Liverpool where Frank Hartigan insisted I should jump off quickly with Ego, we made a good start and jumped the first two fences in the middle, lying about the centre of a field of thirteen. My diary reminds me: 'There was a "schemozzle" at the Chair and Ego was confronted, when only a stride away, with one horse in the ditch and one on the fence. We did a quick swerve to the left and jumped the fence without losing any ground. People standing at the fence thought it was a miraculous escape. We were fourth over the water-jump into which all the remaining competitors jumped in turn, probably blinded by the strong sun which shone straight down the course at this November meeting.

'Capt. R. E. Sassoon on Airgead Sios, the champion 'flyaway' of his day, made the running with Drim about five lengths in front of Drinmore Lad and myself but the two leaders fell at Valentine's. The absence of noisy crowds was noticeable, in contrast to the Grand National, and it seemed odd to be out there jumping those big, solid green fences by oneself in peace and quiet.

'Drinmore Lad was always going better than Ego and he won by six lengths. This was excellent form for Ego's first run of the season, taking on Drinmore Lad at level weights and being beaten only six lengths.' Drinmore Lad was ridden by Evan Williams and owned by Paul Mellon with whom I had stayed at Combe a few years beforehand. Paul had been keen to ride in a race. I had walked him round the Chiddingfold Farmers' point-to-point course, given him a few tips, tied his cap up, practically dressed him, and was then delighted to see him get round.

At the end of December at Cheltenham, Ego was unable to give weight away all round having been given a higher weight after his performance against Drinmore Lad. Frank Hartigan knew that he was not fit and he was timing his preparation for the Grand National. Ego had been physicked by Frank, who had given him a complete rest and laid him off. He had done no work over a longer distance than one and a half miles at half-speed. In this race he tired before he came into the straight but chugged on to be fourth.

A week later he was made the hot favourite to win the Stayers' Handicap Steeplechase at Manchester over three and a half miles. Frank Hartigan had suggested that I kicked Ego hard for the last three strides before every fence. As a result he hit the third-last fence. This lost me valuable ground and I was fairly easily beaten six lengths by Lazy Boots. I told Frank that indiscriminate kicking of this horse would not work. He and I had been accustomed to measuring our fences from a long way off and I knew him so well that I was able to help him to help himself. The trainer agreed with me for he was aware that I had schooled the horse from the time he came over from Ireland as a four-year-old and knew the best way of riding him.

In his last run before the National I rode Ego at Hurst Park, where we were second favourite and finished fifth. He jumped beautifully but did not have the pace to go with such high-class horses over a park track.

Although Ego's preparation for Aintree had dominated the winter, Silver Grail, revived after a season's hunting, now came back into the picture. We brought him out in the two-and-a-half-mile Sandown Hunters' Chase in mid-February. I always found that in these amateur races it was better to get quickly to the 'inner', as so many of those who did not ride very much tended to bump round the middle and there was often more room on the inside. I was tucked in nicely and thought I had plenty of room at the 'pond' fence; but perhaps I had not for he hit it very hard, giving me the worst fall I ever had on him. Horses galloped all over us; they rolled me along as I was kicked by several of them. Apart from a bad bruise on the inside of my right shin which hardened off into a lump I was unhurt.

We then went to the Hunters' Chase at Newbury. There was a terrific mix-up at the water-fence – 'so many horses falling that as I jumped I was confronted with a sheet of spray', I wrote. 'Silver Grail landed with all four feet in the water and slipped along the ground for nearly twenty yards before scrambling to his feet. We set off in pursuit, but three-quarters of a mile from home we were nearly put over the rails by Winter Knight who seemed out of control. I managed to get to the last fence upsides with Duan Mor and Winter Knight. The last-named was on the outside but swerved across Peter Herbert on Duan Mor and me on Silver Grail, making us pull right back. Peter Herbert objected to Winter Knight after the race and I had to appear before the stewards to give evidence. As a result Duan Mor was placed first and Silver Grail was placed second.'

This was by far the best performance Silver Grail had put up for years but he must have ricked his shoulder at the water-fence and, as he was not sound for six weeks, we gave him up for the remainder of the season.

My racing had to be fitted in with my working-life which was made much easier for me when, on 1 January 1937, I acquired (in partnership with Norman Merrett) the Rhigos Colliery and C. L. Clay & Co., the coal exporter in Cardiff Docks. We each put up £15,000 but had to rely on a £70,000 debenture to acquire a £100,000 colliery which had lost £109,000 in the last three years.

The early months of 1937 saw me battling once more to reduce my weight (drastically). During the previous summer I had been up to 12 stone and, as Ego had been given 10 stone 10 pounds in the Grand National, it meant I had to get down to 10 stone 4 pounds. I trained largely on steaks, fruit and vegetables and took haemoglobin supplied by my doctor; I also ran several miles every day. Once again, I lived the life of a hermit, spending much time in my room reading or writing, or sitting at the end of a small table in our kitchen being fed by Mrs Stinchcombe. Again I hardly saw anything of my family – in fact, I avoided any social life at all. As a result of these strictures, I succeeded in doing the weight.

I spent the night before the National in a small hotel at Southport and, as I was returning from a three-mile run dressed up in my zipped-up airman's suit with many layers of wool below, I was pursued by a policeman. I could not explain exactly what I was doing, as I was completely out of breath, and so was very nearly arrested! But suddenly he took in the situation, when I said between gasps, 'Llewellyn – Ego – Grand National' – He patted me on the back, which nearly sent me flying, and said, 'Best of luck – you certainly deserve it if this is what you have to go through!'

Ego was the overnight favourite and I felt confident that he would win. He was wonderfully well and very fresh, as Frank Hartigan did not believe in giving steeplechase horses long-distance work. He was much sharper than the previous year and had become better able to lie up with the leaders early in a fast-run race.

I again started from near the outside and had a good start. Ego jumped like a stag and I had an unhampered ride as far as Becher's. At the next fence a horse kicked us as he fell – which lost us some ground. Drim set a fast pace with Ego just behind the first bunch until the open ditch after Valentine's. Here I could see trouble brewing, and although I was on the inside I managed to pull in behind Golden Miller as he started to hang to the left. Though he had won the Grand National in 1934, Golden Miller never liked Liverpool or its fences; he half-jumped and chested the fence shooting poor Gerry Wilson off on the landing side. No rider, even if he had been glued to the saddle, could have stayed on.

Drim fell at the next fence and then no one wanted to make the running; we led for a few strides before Pucka Belle, who nearly went the wrong way going on to the racecourse, went ahead. At the Chair she was well ahead accompanied by two loose horses. Out into the country again Drim and Royal Mail moved up just ahead of us, but Ego was still on the bit and jumping beautifully as we flew Becher's for the second time.

Going to the last open ditch, Ego was alongside Royal Mail and I had a 'double handful'. I thought to myself, 'Winning the Grand National cannot be as easy as this.' I could not believe that I should be sitting there on this beautiful jumper who showed no sign of fatigue; he was literally pulling my arms out as he always did when he knew he was on his way home at Liverpool.

Royal Mail and Ego had been dogged by loose horses during the second circuit of the course and this race was afterwards known as 'the year of the loose horses'. The riderless Drim was in front of us approaching that last open ditch. He had been jumping to the left, so I pulled out more to the centre of the course; but this proved to be a foolish move. Suddenly Drim saw my bright-primrose colours as I was almost upsides with him on the right, and instead of jumping to the left he jumped to the right immediately in front of me as I was taking off. Ego stumbled over the take-off rail and plunged through the middle of the fence. He lost his hind legs, slid on the ground and my first thought was to pull him up. How he stood up I shall never know; but we came to a standstill and, as he started to trot, I spent the next few seconds divesting myself of the spruce which (without exaggeration) cluttered the whole of the area between poor Ego's head and mine.

As the horses kept passing us he suddenly took hold again, but coming on to the racecourse we were very nearly last of the ten left standing and some thirty lengths behind the leader, Royal Mail. But Ego was now bounding forward again. He passed horse after horse and in fact jumped the last fence third, just behind Cooleen. After a hundred yards of the long run-in suddenly Ego had shot his bolt; and so, although I could hear something behind me, I did not go for my whip but rode him home with my hands to keep him as balanced as possible. For the first time Ego was very tired. He had jumped beautifully throughout but the effort of catching up had been too great. Perhaps it was my concern for the horse that allowed Pucka Belle – that great point-to-point mare ridden by my friend Eric Bailey – to come and beat me for third place. Royal Mail, under his big weight of 11 stone 13 pounds was also tiring and won by only three lengths. He was giving Ego one and a half stone and, wonderful horse though he was, I don't believe he would have stayed with us over the last half-mile had we not been hampered. However, his rider, Evan Williams, still disagrees. Jack Fawcus, who was second on Cooleen, asked, 'What happened to you – you were trotting up!' To his dying day he believed that I should have won that race. In the previous year he had been third on Bachelor Prince and we had two splendid years riding round together, just ahead of Ronnie Strutt (now Lord Belper) who was fourth on Crown Prince in 1936 and fifth in 1937. When he was Master of the Quorn, Ronnie sometimes told me to 'go on with the huntsman', saying that he had long ago got used to the sight of my backside!

One cannot talk about bad luck in the Grand National because so many wonderful horses have suffered misfortunes and other riders have thought they were winning when disaster struck. Think of Dick Francis and Devon Loch when they were coasting home twenty lengths in front and then belly-flopped on the ground only ten lengths away from the winning post! What a wonderful example Queen Elizabeth the Queen Mother showed us by her calm and sporting acceptance of this calamity – and the same can be said of poor Dick Francis.

Then again, think of Foinavon, a reject from Anne, Duchess of

Westminster's stables, who was a rear marker when the rest of the field either fell, was baulked or brought down at the fence between Becher's and the Canal Turn in 1967. You ride in the Grand National knowing that luck is going to play a great part and I accept the fact that I was the fourth-luckiest man in the world on that day.

I had again practically killed myself in training to do 10 stone 10 pounds on Ego so my mother took pity on me and sent David and me down to Nice to spend ten days at the Hôtel de Paris. This was wonderful relaxation. During my preparation I had limited the amount of liquid and, when I went to Nice, I found myself compulsively drinking any liquid in sight – fortunately in those days I was a teetotaller. The increase had the effect of making me get cramp whenever I exerted myself as I did when I played tennis. I did not appear to be particularly hungry; I ate little more than normal and kept away from fattening foods. However, this great increase in liquid consumption put my weight up by a stone and a half within those ten days, proving what an important part liquid plays in weight-control.

On my return from Nice I was offered many rides but soon learned it would be wise to choose them carefully. I rode H. Dyke-Dennis's Ty-Coch in the Bryn-y-Pys Steeplechase at Bangor-on-Dee where I was only just able to do 11 stone 7 pounds. I nearly fell at the last fence, but David Harrison had specially wanted me to ride the horse as he thought I would stop him putting in short ones, or 'fiddling' as it is now known. I only partly succeeded and decided not to ride this bad jumper again, which did not please his trainer who had previously paid me the compliment of saying that all horses seemed to jump well for me.

I had a couple of rides again on Paulerspury, who started favourite in the Hunter Chase at Worcester. We were second to Winter Knight, now ridden by Eric Bailey, but were easily beaten. In this race Peter Herbert had a nasty fall with Kitty Fisher and was galloped over by a lot of horses. He nearly died from a perforated lung.

I was then due to ride Paulerspury again, this time at Market Rasen. I was not quite sure where Market Rasen was but had been asked by Lady Bradford, Anne Bridgeman's mother, to stay with them at Weston, near Shifnal to the north of Wolverhampton, as she thought the racecourse was near. Just before going to bed, I discovered that she had thought I meant Market Drayton and not Market

Rasen, which was two hundred miles away on the other side of England! This meant getting up at four o'clock in the morning to motor there in time to walk round. I did not think we would beat Herod Bridge, the champion hunter chaser of that time; in fact we were only able to finish third.

Paulerspury, back on his home track at Huntingdon, was favourite but here could do no better than fourth; 12 stone 12 pound was too much for him. Two great characters won the race with Lovely Rheims. They were Tom Masson, the owner who was formerly a successful show jumper, and the mare's rider, 'Washy' Hibbert, subsequently a successful Clerk of the Course. A loose horse prevented us doing our best. This came right across me at the open ditch, jumped over the wing and landed on top of a car in the car park in which a family was having a peaceful cup of tea! Fortunately nobody was hurt but poor Paulerspury had broken down and this was the last time I rode him.

Later in 1937 my sister Joyce and I decided to set off for a Northern Capitals cruise on a French ship with many amusing young French men and women on board. The pre-war Baltic scene proved fascinating: we visited Oslo, Stockholm and Helsinki, and spent a day in Leningrad, looking at the beautiful pictures in the Hermitage. We flew to Moscow where we saw a mass drop of parachutists, and then returning through Leningrad, visited Riga and Danzig before passing through the Kiel Canal on our way back to Le Havre.

Fully refreshed after steaming round the Baltic, my next objective was to have yet another crack at the Grand National. Frank Hartigan wanted Ego to have two outings before going to Liverpool for the Valentine Chase and I rode him at Chepstow (carrying 12 stone 4 pounds, which made me eleven pounds overweight!), and at Hawthorn Hill – both times unplaced. Ego was not fit; nor was I.

Carrying 12 stone 11 pounds he duly ran in the Valentine Chase in mid-November. Afterwards I wrote: 'I was surprised at the ease with which he seemed to clear those big fences, never seeming to get far off the ground. I certainly felt no drop at Becher's, which I jumped towards the outside, nor at any of the other drops on the Aintree Course.'

His jumping brought him very close up behind the leaders. He was trying to give a stone to Brendan's Cottage, who subsequently won the Cheltenham Gold Cup, and to Royal Danieli. We finished half a length behind Mount Hermon, who was third, beaten four lengths and a neck. Thus Ego had run five times at Liverpool, completing seventeen and a half miles over this course without once having made a mistake. He was referred to by some at that time as the 'Modern Manifesto' because of the performances which had proved him to be a real Liverpool horse. It was the same in the case of Red Rum who, many years later, demonstrated that he was stones better at Liverpool than on any other course.

At the end of November, I rode Ego in the Whitelaw Challenge Cup Handicap Steeplechase at Fontwell Park for which he was favourite. Sea Trout was in front when he refused across me at the last open ditch and I was forced into the left-hand wing. Ego was so bold that he jumped straight into Sea Trout and between them they razed the fence to the ground. I was up before the horse but it turned out that I had suffered a 'sub-luxation of the acromio-clavicular joint'; in other words a dislocation of my right collar-bone. I refused to be treated by a bossy, meddlesome doctor who wanted to pull my arm about, and Eric Bailey kindly took me back in the thickest of fogs to Cheltenham, where I was X-rayed, skilfully strapped and given a suitable sling to support the arm.

This meant, of course, that I was unable to ride for several weeks and so I took the opportunity to go off to St Moritz, where I had ambitions to go down the Cresta Run. I could not ski or skate as my right arm was strapped into my side, but I saw no reason why I should not bobsleigh or luge. The Cresta, unfortunately, had not had enough snow, so I spent part of my time tobogganing down roads and ski-slopes.

I returned home exultantly looking forward to Gatwick where Ego, now one of the favourites for the 1938 National, had been entered for the Stewards' Handicap Steeplechase over four miles. I quote from my diary: 'I was soon well in front and led the field for over two miles. Ego took a strong hold and I attributed this to the fact that we ran him in a rubber bit for the first time. He faltered before jumping the last open ditch where Blue Shirt, the winner, passed Ego who did not seem to gallop nearly so well over the last mile. I was surprised as he usually put in his best work at the end. The reason was soon apparent, however, for on dismounting in the paddock the poor old horse dropped and died before I could get the saddle off him.

'He went out in a blaze of glory and I believe I shall never ride such a horse again. I had schooled him since he first came over from

Ireland as a four-year-old, had ridden winners on him for Colonel Morgan-Lindsay and my father. No horse has ever jumped Aintree more faultlessly or in better style. The post-mortem showed that he had burst his heart which was nine times the normal size.'

I was naturally upset at losing such a close friend but my fellow jockeys were wonderfully kind and sympathetic. They may appear to be the toughest lot of people but they are also the kindest. No one could have had better friends and not one of the professionals ever did me a dirty trick the whole time I was riding.

Gerry Wilson was particularly helpful to young amateurs and his persistent, dogged courage won all our admiration. But there were many others such as Billy Parvin, Eric Brown, Jack Moloney, Danny Morgan and Tommy Elder, who were always most helpful. I particularly admired the riding of Danny Morgan and Jack Moloney. There were a couple of dozen supreme horsemen riding under National Hunt Rules in my time; also among them were Fred Thackray, Fulke Walwyn, Evan Williams, Jack Fawcus and, in my early days, Billy Stott and Billy Speck, otherwise known as 'Stotty' and 'Specky'. Another of the great jockeys was Bruce Hobbs, who went on to win the 1938 Grand National on Battleship.

The rest of the 1938 racing season had much less meaning for me after Ego's death, although I was to ride several good horses.

Possibly the best novice in Great Britain was a five-year-old called Talybont which my father had bought. This horse was trained by Peter Thrale, who said that he would be as good or better than his champion horse of the time – Macaulay, with whom he did his work.

Going down the hill at Warwick I was coasting along behind Jim Pointer and the leaders. When I aimed my 'torpedo' between the two leaders – who were jumping away from each other at each fence – I ran out a surprisingly easy winner by four lengths.

Two days later I rode my father's Tapinette at Derby. Hugh Lloyd Thomas made the running on Periwinkle II but he was going round the middle of the course and I found myself on his inside with Tapinette, who pulled like a fiend and jumped all her fences quickly and cleverly without a mistake. She carried her head low and I soon realized I was on a safe jumper. I quote from my diary: 'I had intended to ride a waiting race, not being sure of the mare's ability to stay three miles. I found myself six lengths in front without having moved. I then dropped my hands and was surprised to find her producing more speed. The going was firm and up to that point her time was the fastest ever returned for a three-mile steeplechase at Derby.'

I completed a treble a week later by winning again on China Sea at Nottingham in a selling steeplechase. He won easily by two lengths, but my luck turned the next day when I rode Talybont in the New Century Steeplechase – possibly the most important novice steeple-chase in the country at that time. I quote: 'Peter Thrale had told me not to ask him too much in the early part of the race as he is a long-striding horse. I moved up behind the leaders as we went towards the straight where he was going splendidly. Savon crossed him jump-ing the last fence before coming into the straight and he hit it so hard that he slid along on his belly on the other side before recovering himself. At the time he was going a lot better than Victor Norman, the winner. When he fell he severed the tendons of his near foreleg and his fetlock-joint dropped to the ground. His leg was put in plaster of Paris but he never raced again. He certainly was the most brilliant novice steeplechase horse I had ever ridden.'

Tapinette returned to Derby on 22 February for the Harrington Hunters' Steeplechase, after which I recorded: 'Tapinette was going nicely and lay just behind the leaders. She jumped perfectly and very cleverly, putting in a wonderfully quick and clever jump at the second open ditch. Periwinkle II soon went into the lead but jumped mod-erately. I lay second, but a mile from home Renown II passed me. Entering the straight Periwinkle II led from Renown II with Tapi-nette and a few others just behind. I was carrying a big weight and was waiting to come from behind. I started to move on her between the last two fences. She passed Renown II and came up alongside Periwinkle II going into the last fence. Hugh Lloyd Thomas had thought that he was winning until he saw us coming and at the last moment pushed Periwinkle, who was visibly tiring, into the last fence. I pulled well to the right as I feared they would fall and, sure enough, Periwinkle II put in a short one, throwing his jockey on to his head. Tapinette went on to win with the greatest ease as she would have done in any case.'

Sad to say, Hugh Lloyd Thomas broke his neck when he fell and was dead before he was brought back in the ambulance. This distin-guished diplomat, who had been the British Minister in Paris, lived at Tredilion, forty miles from my home in Glamorgan, and had always been charming to me.

Arthur Lord, my valet, somehow got it through to Sir William

Bass that I was very upset that this accident should have happened, although my horse was nowhere near Periwinkle II at the time. As a result, the Stewards held an inquiry, and Sir William himself came to tell me that I was in no way responsible and must try not to worry about it.

Stewards like Sir William Bass make racing. When I later became a member of the National Hunt Committee in 1946, Fred Withington came up to me one day and said, 'Harry, remember one thing – we are here to look after the professionals, particularly the professional jockeys, and the good name of the sport.'

Fred Withington understood the sport from A to Z and was particularly respected by the trainers and jockeys. If he thought they were starting to cheat he would prefer to talk them out of it rather than hold damaging Stewards' Inquiries. On the other hand, if people did not take his advice he was very firm in his decisions when it came to punishment.

That season continued to be an eventful one for me. China Sea came back on the scene and on him I was second at Gatwick in a selling chase. By this time my weight was worrying me again, and I had taken a Turkish bath the night before and another on the morning of the race. I was very tired and had I been a little fitter the 'head' decision might have gone the other way.

After China Sea had won yet another race at Lingfield Park, I wrote: 'We went into the last fence level-pegging with Port Said, who jumped it well, but China Sea met it all wrong and put in a short one. As a result he galloped straight through the fence without rising an inch. He catapulted me in the air and I cannot imagine why he did not fall. I landed over his head but fortunately my feet stayed in the irons. Helped by this I gradually climbed back from between his ears and slipped back down his neck. By this time Port Said was two lengths in front of me, but as soon as I set China Sea going he stayed on wonderfully to win by two lengths.'

This particular episode won for me the *Sporting Chronicle*'s Award – publicized on their front page – for 'the performance of the week'. I only wish I had a film of it because it took me a hundred yards to get back in to the plate and feel safe again. How China Sea kept going with me sprawling all over him I shall never know!

When 'Tubby' Martyr asked me to ride his Ablington in the National Hunt Chase, Stalbridge Park, ridden by 'Babe' Moseley, was the hot favourite. Ablington behaved badly in the paddock. As I was thrown up on him, he reared, slipped down on to his haunches and slid me off over his tail. I am quite sure this had nothing to do with Tubby asking me to ride the horse but everybody seemed to be amused, especially as he kept on fooling about even when I was on him.

I asked the lad to let go and went cantering round the enclosure sending quite a lot of people scuttling. He then tried to run away going to the start and, as this was the first time I had ever seen the animal, I wondered what lay ahead. Ronnie Bennett, who trained the horse, led me round in short circles. Ablington was sweating so badly that I could not hold the reins and had to get a handkerchief to dry them before the start. I found myself last over the ridge-and-furrow before he settled down to jump. He then passed the whole field on the inside and by the time we reached the bottom of the hill behind the stands we were actually the leaders. He never stood off too far and put in short ones in the neatest possible fashion. I realized I was on a super-jumper and started to enjoy my ride. K. D. H. passed me but I soon passed this mare again; Hector Gordon, her jockey, gave my horse a whack on the behind and shouted, 'Good luck!' I jumped into the lead at the third-last fence but Ablington faded going up the hill and I finished a close-up fifth. He had run a splendid race and given me a wonderful ride.

On one horse, I came close to killing myself. This was in March whilst I was riding Mrs Charlie Jones's Adamant. I landed on my face at the fourth-last fence and nearly broke my neck. I had to ride in a neck-guard for the rest of the season; the ligaments were still sore from the middle of my back to the top of my head months later when I was doing the rounds of the horse shows.

During the summer of 1938 I decided to go on another cruise, as the Baltic one had been so exhilarating. This time I chose the Mediterranean starting at Genoa.

There were a number of high-spirited young Americans aboard the SS *Roma* and I formed a group with three Princetown undergraduates. We styled ourselves 'The Four Musketeers' and had what I suppose would nowadays be known as 'a ball'. My companions were the plump 'Blimp' Ferris, whose grandfather invented the Ferris wheel; Alan Grady, son of the producer of *Rose-Marie*; and Joe Gidding, who said he owned a couple of blocks in New York – and did!

Joe subsequently joined the American navy and was the sole sur-
vivor of a submarine; he fortunately came up in the air-bubble. Some
twenty-five years later, when he came to stay with me, he had acquired the nasty habit of smoking all night and set one of my beds
on fire. He claimed to have been at school with Prince Philip at
Cheam, and organized a party in New York for me to which he asked
every Head of State and well-known film star. I could not go, but it
seems quite a lot of rather amusing people turned up who certainly
had never heard of me and were hardly surprised when I did not
arrive.

Our cruise took us to Athens, which was *en fête*, so the Acropolis
was closed and carefully guarded. Blimp Ferris and I decided to
climb in and, with little trouble, we scaled the wall. Between us we
had the whole Acropolis to ourselves. As luck would have it, our
entry had been observed, and as Blimp climbed down the way we
had come in he was promptly arrested. Fortunately, he persuaded
the police to take him to the American Embassy, where he was able
to identify himself as the son of the president of a top bank in Dallas.
He was returned unharmed to our hotel. Meanwhile, when the coast
was clear, I climbed down by another route and was soon joining the
crowds enjoying their feast-day. I wonder how many people have
had the Parthenon all to themselves in recent years! On the next day
we all went there again and found it painfully overcrowded – full of
beastly tourists like ourselves.

Apart from our adventures in the Acropolis, SS *Roma* took us to
Libyan Tripoli, Beirut, Haifa, Jerusalem and Cairo. Near the last-
named city 'The Four Musketeers' borrowed some horses from Su-
leiman the boss dragoman at the Pyramids. We simulated a midnight
attack by bandits on the tourist camp near the Pyramids which
housed some of our fellow-passengers. All went well until one of us
collided with a pup tent, leaving an elderly, rather drunken gentleman
stranded over a long-drop loo. Later, he complained to the Captain
of the *Roma* who said that although he could marry or bury people
when at sea, he held no jurisdiction over bogus Arab bandits on
shore.

The cruise included visits to Rhodes, Constanza, Bucharest, Istanbul, Venice, Palermo and Naples. My first-class cabin, with an outside porthole, cost me £51 for four weeks – not bad for a dozen cities
and a good deal of fun.

8   Enter Maza

After another enjoyable London season, I became very attached to Teeny Saumarez, who was one of the most energetic of the ex-debs. She had previously been a girl-friend of my brother Rhys, but when she had come to stay with us at home a misunderstanding took place during a game of 'Truths'. Everyone was asked how much out of ten they liked other people. Asked how much out of ten she liked Rhys, Teeny politely said, 'Eight'. Much later in the game she was asked how much out of ten she liked me. Unfortunately, she had no head for figures and had forgotten how many marks she had given my brother. She attempted to give us both the same but, by some mistake, gave me eight and a half. So vain are men that this little bit of flattery really started off the love-affair which eventually led to our marriage after the war.

By now, Maza had been installed in our stables at St Fagans. A mare by Zarope out of Pop Off, she had been bred by Sir Alan Anderson, my sister Elaine's father-in-law, at Notgrove in the Cotswolds. He had given her to my sister Betty when she was Master of the Talybont Hounds, but she had been lent to me to train as a hack.

The ever-resourceful Cooper tackled this new challenge with the interest and enthusiasm of a schoolboy. 'We'll show them,' said he, and instructed me in the use of Professor Litchwark's method, which his former employer, Lady Price of Hensol, had used in New Zealand.

Maza had a temper, was nappy, held her head high and stuck her nose out. Initially, I tied her head down with a standing martingale to the noseband and used a fairly severe double bridle. Within three weeks she had learned to canter slowly, by which time I found that a Hanoverian Pelham bit suited her better, although she would flex only for short periods.

The Litchwark, however, bent her neck just behind the poll – not easy at ten years of age. For gradually increasing periods, Maza wore a special contraption which consisted of a crupper under her tail to a rein running through the rings of her bit or back of her noseband, and back to a roller or the 'D's of a saddle. Gradually she gave in, and we were able to tighten it up, and Cooper and I drove her in long reins in the Litchwark. I then rode her in the contraption so that she could never evade my hand because any pull that she made was immediately related by her to a strain on the crupper under her tail – and no horse likes to pull against its own tail! Looking back, it seems rather unkind, but all this was done in slow, progressive stages.

I rode this little mare daily, sometimes in the evenings, from about the time of Ego's death until the outbreak of war the following year and she added an exhilarating new dimension to my life with horses. We had started on her in March and, much to my surprise, she was called in fifth in the Open Hack class at the 1938 Royal Show. This was the first time she had ever been shown in the ring. She had given a particularly good show, having first done an eight-metre figure of eight on one leg and then on the other, the judge saying that the performance given was the best in the class. In those days points were given for conformation and manners but much depended on the hack achieving a high standard of dressage when giving its show.

During the 1938 show season, Maza was closely rivalled by Mrs Dorothy ('Pug') Whitehead's cream hack, but towards the end she always beat him and then fought off the challenge of Ted Havard's Princess the following year to become unbeaten and unbeatable.

She was a beautiful chestnut with little white about her, standing 15.1½ hands, and she seemed well up to my weight which was then around twelve stone.

Maza was probably the most comfortable animal I ever sat on and every judge liked riding her. She won many lightweight hunter classes, although she was really too small and her greatest triumph was at the Gower Show where she won the hack class, was second in the Open Jumping, won the Handy Hunter and, on her performance in the hack class, was judged the best light horse in the show.

Meanwhile I was also becoming more involved in show-jumping. There had been a two-year gap after my disastrous efforts at Olympia until, in the late summer of 1937, I had brought out a horse called Bombed which we had bred ourselves. He was by Sky Rocket out of

War Baby and was a beautiful if rather long-legged bay with a tremendous natural 'lep'. My diary records that, at Abergavenny, Dick Friedberger won the main event while Bombed went round very happily hitting everything!

The ever-cheerful Doug Dobson and the graceful Mrs 'Pug' Whitehead were then going strong and usually we were not good enough to beat them. I did the round of Lampeter, Kington, and other shows without any success. In the Monmouthshire Hunter Trials, Bombed's performance was marked the best, but the judge had to put me down owing to the fact that Bombed had been 'fired' as a young horse in his racing days. Judges were influenced by the value of the horse as well as his performance.

I believe that the experience I was gaining in show-jumping and hunter trials during 1937–38 helped me to become accurate in the approach to a fence, and I developed an 'eye' for distance which was to help me later. Anyone can pull back and then do a 'one, two, three – over' in the last strides. The real art was, and still is, to be able to adjust a horse's stride while maintaining a fair pace. No one has been better at this recently than David Broome.

They were thoroughly enjoyable competitions but Bombed would have been better suited by post-war conditions over FEI courses. He started getting minor placings but was nevertheless a beautiful horse to ride – pleasant, good-natured and cooperative. He never really folded up his long legs as well as he should have and was classified as a 'dingle-dangler' – which was no good in those days when there were slats on top of the fences.

The experience of Bombed and the taste I was acquiring for show-jumping led me to the purchase of Dick O'Rhigos, whom I renamed Overorthrough for obvious reasons. I purchased him from the Cwmgwrach Colliery which adjoined my Rhigos Colliery, as I had heard that he kept jumping out of his field when he was out at grass during his summer holiday.

We took him home and, before we competed at the Wenvoe Show in 1938, Cooper spent two days washing him to rid his coat of coal-dust when I was away having an enjoyable time in the hack classes with Maza. I returned to find that he had been transformed from a dingy dirty dun into the most beautiful golden dun with black points. I have never seen another like him. His colour was once referred to as 'burnished gold', but to me it was a vibrant yellow and was easily distinguishable hundreds of yards away. We left his black feathering on as well as his mane; and this, combined with his thickset body, made him unique. The *Western Mail* reported him as 'a heavy cart-horse type'; others would call him 'heavy cob', but in fact he was a pit-horse, having worked underground and on the surface.

He loved jumping but there was scarcely any chance of my being able to 'place' him as he usually bolted round the course, shortening as he came into his fences, and there was little that I could do about it except steer him. If I could stop him going too fast he would not hit anything, and very soon he achieved a major triumph at the Vale of Glamorgan Show at Cowbridge.

Dressed up in his pit-horse's 'straws', he was placed third in the Open Pitter Class. Without changing his hairstyle in any way I jumped him in his straws in the open jumping which he won. I then took him round many shows with Bombed, where he was often placed, but he will be best remembered for his display at the Aldershot Show in July 1939.

I had hoped to do well in the international class on Bombed, but he staked himself on the trial jump before the class, so I rode my pit-horse instead. I could not turn Overorthrough round to the right after the third fence. I pulled as hard as I could but the reins snapped and I had to jump off, fortunately without hurting myself. He stopped when I did this. I tied up my reins and set off again. He jumped all the most difficult fences with ease. Having cleared the five-foot gate with inches to spare he charged the red wall and smashed it to smithereens!

Unfortunately, there was no spare wall available and to this day I am reminded by friends of the chaos created by an army of carpenters having to build another wall on site before the competition could continue. The remainder of the round was clear except for his getting his hind legs in the water.

Although I had a dozen horses to train, I found myself becoming increasingly involved and interested in the coal business. When two lots of horses were going out in the morning I could seldom get to my office before 10.30 a.m. – but by this time I was my own boss and the owner of Rhigos Colliery at the head of the Neath Valley.

I would motor up to Rhigos two to three times a week and on many occasions went there on my return from a race meeting – sometimes going down with the men on the night or repair shift. In a way this was good because nobody ever knew when I would turn up. I knew hundreds of men by their Christian names and there was never any risk of industrial dispute except on one occasion, when the men under the screens complained that they had to buy their own mackintoshes. These had been supplied but they had 'disappeared', so I went into a shop in Cardiff Docks, bought twenty-four macs over the counter and took them up to the colliery. This ended the dispute.

I also became a director of Norths Navigation Collieries, the Meiros Colliery and Tondu Engineering & Wagon Company. Thus my absorbing interest in horses did not prevent me from establishing a firm base in industry.

I am not sure if my colleagues were overjoyed when I turned up unexpectedly. I once recall riding in a race, seeing the men go on the night shift at Rhigos, and then motoring down to St John's pit near Bridgend to see some repairs being carried out underground.

This was, for me, a fairly normal lifestyle during the National Hunt season of 1938–39. By then I had acquired Rubin Wood, who was by Duncan Gray and had been the lead horse for Precipitation and Omaha when trained by Cecil Boyd-Rochfort. His determined independence had been misinterpreted and he was described as a 'dog'; he was not even a good lead horse since he refused to gallop – hence the reason he was sent to the Newmarket sales where Cecil Boyd-Rochfort persuaded me to buy him.

After he had won a point-to-point when ridden by my brother, Rhidian, I took him to Towcester for the Hunters' Grand National Steeplechase. I wasn't expecting anything much and was not greatly surprised when he did not take hold for the first two miles. But at the bottom of the hill he suddenly realized he was on his way home and he sped past the rest of the field to win on a tight rein by six lengths. Rubin Wood thus proved that he was an out-and-out stayer.

L'Estaque, who had been schooled to jump fences at home, was beaten by half a length when I finished second on him in an amateur riders' race that season. I then brought him out on a very foggy day at Manchester at the beginning of January 1939, by which time he had shown that he was such a talented horse at home that my father backed him heavily to bring his price down to 8 to 1.

The fog was so thick that no one could see from one fence to another, but it was perfectly safe for the jockeys, so the stewards wisely decided to hold the meeting. On passing the stands the first time, I was last of the fifteen runners. L'Estaque then steadily made up ground and going into the straight I was just behind the leaders

– Soldeno, ridden by Dan Moore, and the favourite, Black Knight, ridden by Gerry Wilson. These two horses swung wide towards the stables and the only way I could go was to nip up on their inside – a step one tried to avoid when riding against the top professionals.

Dan Moore often tells the story of how Gerry shouted out, 'Stop him!'

'I can't,' Dan replied. 'He has passed me; but don't worry, he'll come back.'

'The bugger's gone!' Gerry cried, as I disappeared into the fog in front of him and arrived at the winning-post ten lengths ahead, out of Dan Moore's sight. Black Knight was a bad third – lost in the fog! No one could believe that I had not cut a corner but this was impossible at Manchester.

I often think of those conditions when stewards attempt to cancel racing when there is a little fog about. This involves tremendous financial loss for the riders, owners and trainers. Presumably, and perhaps mistakenly, the stewards feel that their main responsibility is to the spectators who cannot see the horses.

Possibly, L'Estaque's best performance was when he was second, beaten four lengths, in the Sefton Steeplechase at Newbury. His worst performance was undoubtedly at Cheltenham. There were not many good Gold Cup horses about that year; so, believing that L'Estaque stayed for ever, we thought we would chance our arm in the 1939 Gold Cup. As he often jumped the first fence stickily, I had been in the habit of going down to the start early and jumping the first fence on him. We were allowed to do so in those days. Unfortunately, when I did this at Newbury, my current lady-friend had accused me of showing off. So at Cheltenham, where she came to watch me, I fell in with her wishes and this resulted in total disaster.

There were only five runners – with Morse Code, ridden by Danny Morgan, the odds-on favourite. Nobody wanted to take the lead and there was a contest to be last at the first fence – which I lost, because I arrived in front and promptly got thrown off when L'Estaque refused! I landed on my feet on the other side of the fence holding the reins while L'Estaque laughed at me from his side. So much for taking a girl-friend's advice! George Owen swept past us and went on to win with Brendan's Cottage.

However, my father's Tapinette, who had given me a good season's hunting, won the United Hunts Steeplechase. The going was holding and I came to the last fence alongside Small Hours, ridden by Peter Herbert. Our horses had tired before they had to face that last punishing hill to the finish and, after the final fence, Peter Herbert reached for his whip. This unbalanced his horse, then a length in front of me; I decided to keep Tapinette on an even keel and I rode her home with my hands to finish two lengths in front.

When I look back, certain compliments are more valuable than others. The three Anthony brothers, who had backed me that day, came into the dressing-room after the race and glowered at me in a way which was often misunderstood. Suddenly, Owen barked out, 'Ridden like a Welshman!' Whereupon they all marched off to leave me with a compliment that I shall always treasure. I repaid the compliment when I called a pub after them on the site of the previous Cardiff open ditch when I was chairman of Rhymney Breweries in the sixties.

There is little room for vanity in steeplechasing. One day you could be riding the best animal in England on four sound legs; the next day he could have only three. One often gets polite comments from one's friends but, frankly, one sets little store by many of these. When the experts who are doing the same job as yourself go out of their way to commend you it is a very warming experience.

I was to ride several other good horses in the spring of 1939, winning on my old friend Silver Grail at Plumpton, on China Sea at Hurst Park and La Petit Savoyard at the last Cardiff meeting ever held. I also rode Black Hawk for Jimmy Jones at Warwick, where he failed by only two lengths to give 26 pounds to Peter Herbert's good mount, Post Horn. He jumped beautifully for me, although he had a reputation as a 'hit or miss' merchant and had given Eric Brown a nasty fall at Sandown.

I was offered the ride on Black Hawk in the 1939 Grand National – mainly, I believe, because I was strong enough to hold him and, by that time, had a reputation for being able to stride a horse. Jimmy Jones and John Goldsmith, the horse's trainer, said they would like me to ride in the Grand National if I could do 11 stone 3 pound, which was nine pounds above the horse's weight in the handicap. I thought carefully about this interesting proposition, but came to the conclusion that Black Hawk was the wrong type of jumper for Aintree, as he was apt to hurdle his fences and often took off early, seeming unable to 'fiddle' or shorten his strides.

Imagine my feelings from the stands as they came back on the racecourse for the last time and I saw Black Hawk upsides Workman.

Black Hawk appeared to be going the better of the two but he got too near the second-last fence and came down, leaving the race at the mercy of Tim Hyde on Workman. Poor Jack Moloney, who was the brave rider of Black Hawk that day and was convinced that he would have won but for his fall, was later killed walking across the road at Newmarket.

That spring, while Maza was proving invincible in the hack classes, Sid Woodhall asked me to ride Brimstone (formerly Old Joe). He was the first really high-class jumper I rode. We were equal first at Cardiff; and then, at the Royal Richmond Show in June, were equal first in one class and second in the championship jumping for the Coronation Challenge Cup after two jump-offs over a five-foot course.

I next rode Brimstone at Olympia the same month, but asked him to stand off too far at the 'garden gate'. He put in a short one which resulted in us crashing through this heavy obstacle, giving me a pretty hard fall. I record: 'We both rolled for yards. I remember noticing how wholly silent everybody was. I was up before the horse, which was dazed, and apparently it looked to be a bad fall.' Apart from this occasion, Brimstone was the cleverest horse I had ever ridden at getting underneath a fence and still jumping it.

By this time I was beginning to feel in need of a change of scene. Not only had I been racing, showing and show jumping; I had also become deeply involved in my business. Both Rhigos Colliery and C. L. Clay & Co. were proving successful and they took up much of my time. I was also involved in various directorships, so that I had perhaps an over-full life which seldom allowed me to spend more than six hours a night in bed. But I was fit; I did not smoke or drink and I enjoyed every second of my time.

The opportunity for a change came when I was invited to take a team of British steeplechase horses and riders to Hungary to compete at the European Amateur Riders' (Urlovas) Championships at Megeyr, near Budapest. I was able to persuade tall, thin Tom Hanbury, one of the better and more stylish 'bumpers' under rules in those days, to make the trip. Mark Pilkington, who had ridden in a few point-to-points, also accepted; he was already due to visit that part of the world through his involvement in something called the 'Ruthenian White Count', which I never quite understood. I also managed to get Susie Bligh to ride in the ladies' races. After the war she was better known on show-hacks as Mrs Bill Stirling. Our party was

115

made up by Atty Stewart, with his enormous Packard, and Geoffrey Wilson, both of whom came to support rather than participate.

Riders came from all over Europe to perform over the steeplechase course at Megeyr which included a stone wall, some 5 feet live-privet hedges which were 7 feet wide, and a solid bar over water. Most fences were about 4 feet 6 inches high and were in fact miniature open ditches with raised rails in front of them. The water-jump was as wide as the amount of water available to fill it, and there was one open ditch that was 5 feet 6 inches high.

I was unable to ride below twelve stone, and in fact only rode once, on a mare called Resista, who was favourite for the Baich Memorial Steeplechase, the equivalent of our National Hunt Chase. I had miscalculated my weight before the race and put up four pounds overweight, riding at 12 stone 4 pounds. When eventually I was beaten by one and a half lengths the public showed their displeasure more violently than I would have expected. As I returned to the paddock I was showered with clods of turf and one stone, which fortunately hit my crash helmet. This made me a little cross, so that after I had weighed in I went in search of the man who had thrown the stone. Wisely, he had decamped.

Mark and Tom were able to do lower weights and therefore had more rides, while in one of the ladies' races Susie Bligh rode a horse which ran away with her down to the start and shipped her off into an eight-foot wall at the bottom of the course. This courageous and beautiful lady leaped back into the saddle and finished just behind the placed horses.

Having been fêted, quite wrongly, as the champion amateur riders of the world by our kind Hungarian hosts, we set off for Munich where I had been asked to ride in the Brown Band Steeplechase for amateur riders. We stayed at Munich's Hotel Vierjahreszeitten and found ourselves going up in the lift with Dr Goebbels, whose wife's hat was so big it nearly covered the top of him as well. Always closely watched by two beefy SS men, he was a small man with a limp and large, innocent-looking eyes. Yet he was to prove that everyone would believe a lie if told it often enough.

We spent two days watching the show-jumping for the Brown Band at Riem over a typical international course, the Rumanians being the chief opposition to the white-jacketed SS riders. A most impressive dressage display was given by a team of regular Army officers with a dozen horses circling the ring at the 'Spanish Trot'.

There were few security restrictions and I was able to photograph

Himmler (Head of the Gestapo) and Fegelein (Head of the Riding School), as well as Weber, reputed to be Number Six in the Nazi Party and then President of the Congress and responsible for all equestrian affairs in Munich.

The night before the Amateur Brown Band Steeplechase I was told by Ernst Hasse that my horse was lame. When I expressed my disappointment, he explained that it was 'politically lame'. As a British rider, I was obviously not welcome. I should have liked to have ridden over this course, which resembled Megeyr, although it was more severe. A piebald hack led the horses round on the race-course, while Goya, the favourite for the Brown Band, was guarded by a dozen SS black-shirted guards.

Goya won by a length from Antonym. Sir James Nelson was representing the British Thoroughbred Breeders and we were shown round the steeplechase course with him. The course included a soft, live-privet hedge which was 7 feet 9 inches high and 12 feet through. The plain fences were about 5 feet 3 inches high but all soft at the top so the horses could go through them quite safely at about four feet.

That evening we were guests at the *Nacht das Amazones* in the beautiful setting of Nymphenburg, where we were asked to join a galaxy of bemedalled German generals, all of whom were armed with binoculars. Through these they examined every detail of the nude ladies who were then paraded in interesting positions on various conveyances in front of us. The human form divine with the back-drop of the Nymphenburg fountains was very effective.

In the middle of this visual orgy, Herr Weber came up to us and said, 'I am a Nazi, you are British, but we are all horsemen and are therefore friends. My advice to you is to go back to England as soon as possible tomorrow morning.'

At that time we did not know of the serious plans that the Germans had for invading Poland, but Weber was fully aware of our position and he did not want us to get caught in Germany. We left the party, went to our hotel, packed up and were away before daylight. We drove as fast as we dared to the frontier at Saarbrücken where we passed through the Siegfried Line; I must have taken about the last photographs of the concrete tank-traps before the war started.

We were closely questioned at the Customs but were soon released and cross the Maginot Line near St Avold, where the tank-traps were mostly up-ended railway lines and the gun-turrets were easily dis-cernible. We continued along the Maginot Line near Thionville where there were vast areas of minefields, and within a few hours we were in Luxembourg. Tourists to the end, we took photographs of the Houses of Parliament, the beautiful bridge and aqueduct, passing by a fortified Namur on the River Meuse where I was later in the war suspected of being a German parachutist.

My car was soon aboard but David took it into his head to go to the Casino for a last flutter and turned up only twenty minutes before we sailed. We were home on 2 September – a narrow squeak. Whatever political leanings Weber had, he was also a sportsman and I shall always be grateful to him for his warning. I had believed that sport should have no barriers and that the keeping open of the bridges between sportsmen is vital, especially when governments are divided on political issues – at least until the Russians savaged Afghanistan before the 1980 Olympic Games in Moscow.

On 3 September, during our first morning at home, most members of my family listened to Neville Chamberlain's broadcast. We were a sad group as we sat in our billiard-room listening to the fateful announcement that Great Britain was at war with Germany. We realized that the happy family Llewellyn would inevitably be broken up. We would see much less of each other; we would be parted from our dogs and our horses, of which Maza alone would see us through.

Silver Grail, my superbly elegant little horse with a charming nature, was later given to the huntsman of the Glamorgan Hounds. Bombed was sold to Charlie Dodd, for whom he won many competitions in South Wales when ridden by Ivor Richards. Overorthrough went back to the Rhigos Colliery where he was given a cushy time by my head ostler, Dai Jones. And I went to war.

Part Two
At War

9   With the Cavalry in the Middle East

During the Second World War the author took part in several major campaigns. During the first of these his regiment, the Warwickshire Yeomanry, as part of the 1st Cavalry Division, joined with the Royals and Royal Scots Greys in Palestine, where they were training to protect the Eastern Approaches to the Suez Canal. The horsed cavalry regiments were also earmarked to move into Turkey should the Germans have attacked the Middle East through the Balkans or the Caucasus.

In May 1941 the regiment, as part of 'Habforce', helped to form 'Kingcol' (Brigadier Joe Kingstone's Column). After occupying Baghdad this force moved into Syria, then in the hands of the Vichy French; the Australians captured Beirut and the British took Damascus. After Kingcol had taken Palmyra, Homs and Aleppo, Lieutenant Harry Llewellyn was hospitalized in Jerusalem. He served temporarily on the staff of the 8th Armoured Brigade before rejoining his regiment, now part of 10th Armoured Division at Gedera, near Tel Aviv.

He then joined his division as GSO III and moved with it to Qatatba near Cairo before being sent to the ME Staff College at Haifa in May 1942.

It was, I believe due largely to the reputation of Ego that I was able, on the outbreak of war, to secure a commission in the Warwickshire Yeomanry. This splendid regiment, which I joined in October 1939 with the approval of the Commanding Officer Lieut. Col. Percy Wright after an overgenerous recommendation from my former tutor F. J. Dykes, had in peacetime been a volunteer part-time unit of the Territorial Army. Now it was mobilized as a unit in the 1st Cavalry Division and stationed at Thoresby Park in Nottinghamshire.

Here we thoroughly enjoyed some good fox-hunting with the Grove and Rufford packs. We also spent much time in collecting our horses which sometimes broke their lines and roamed the park in droves.

121

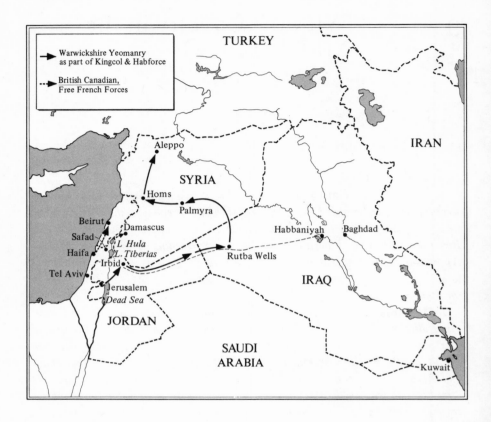

However we very quickly became an efficient regiment. Trooper Ivor Reading (557309) was attached to me initially as my groom and had the care of my chargers, Peter and Prince.

In December 1939 my regiment was the first of several to be sent to Palestine, travelling by train across France then by boat across the Mediterranean to Haifa. En route we lost ten horses from pneumonia near Marseilles, where we spent Christmas and the New Year. Many officers and men were to suffer from the rough crossing; only four out of 'C' Squadron were able to carry out their duties. Ivor Reading did so by slinging his hammock between the heads of my two horses, and was thus enabled to feed them from his eyrie whilst the urine produced by five hundred and fifty animals washed to and fro beneath him.

'C' Squadron spent a month in Tiberias while the rest of the regiment pushed on to Rosh Pinna between Lakes Hule and Tiberias.

We trained hard, but most of us had cars which enabled us to get into the gayer cities of Haifa, Tel Aviv and Jerusalem. There was no blackout. When France fell to the Germans in 1940 Syria sided with the Vichy French and 'C' Squadron was moved up to the frontier at Safad. My troop spent several weeks at the Quarantine Gate. As we were on our own we had a good time, on occasions riding bareback, follow-my-leader style, over stone walls. No hostility was shown by the Vichy French but the Staffordshire Yeomanry, who followed us up on the frontier, were involved in some shooting incidents.

On one occasion near Metullah, I drew up my troop, the third troop of 'C' Squadron, into line and we charged four Spahis who were trying to run off with Palestinian cattle. Surely this must have been one of history's last cavalry charges! There were no casualties but our farrier, Alan Cole, later champion blacksmith of Great Britain, could not stop his horse as his anvil and tripod were beating against the animal's sides. We had to retrieve him after he had carried out a solo 'hot-pursuit' into Syria. I thoroughly enjoyed my time in Palestine, especially when we moved to Naharya near the sea and I was sent on numerous courses.

I first volunteered for the field hygiene course at Sarafand, passing out with full marks; the final paper was on the Anopheles mosquito and I had become very interested in that malaria-carrying insect. I was then sent on a course to the Middle-East Weapon-Training School where I became a qualified instructor in the rifle and pistol; followed by another course to study aerial photography at Heliopolis (Cairo). When Oliver (now Lord) Poole left the regiment, his place as HQ Squadron Leader was taken by Michael Verey, whose place in turn as Signals Officer was taken by me.

About this time I visited Damascus, Baalbek and the Djebel Druze with Bill Allen and Mark Pilkington, shortly before they left for Abyssinia. We spent a most interesting week, passing through the annual migration of the Ruwalla tribe who were on the move to better feeding-grounds. It seemed as if the horizon was filled with camels ridden by all members of the family. Most of the Sheiks and senior men had falcons on their wrists. Not even a couple of world wars would affect their way of life.

I next went on two courses at Abbassia and a signals course at Nathanya. Here the subject interested me very much and I had an excellent signal troop, all of whom became officers before the end of the war. On one occasion we carried out Allenby's famous march against the Turks when he covered sixty-two miles in eighteen and a half hours, having crossed the river Jordan en route. On our return Percy Wright told me that my father had died. I grieved for this wonderful man to whom I was devoted and who had been more of a close friend than a father.

Another time, being in rather a hurry I gave Percy Wright the wrong map-reference for some place. He said, 'If you sometimes took a few steps back and *thought*, you would be a good officer'. He and I had never been friendly, but these were wise words. I tried to do as he said throughout the rest of my military career and always checked, double-checked and checked again. Later in the war I was often called Colonel Double-Check for this habit, which has since not always been enjoyed by my family.

At this stage the regiment did a lot of show jumping. My pack-horse Saracen won the open show jumping at the brigade show and was acknowledged the best show jumper in Palestine, ahead of such horses as Teddy, formerly ridden for the British team by Mike Ansell. Sadly, Saracen died before I could get him back after the war.

In May 1941, the regiment took part in Kingcol, and so we had our horses taken away from us. Using trucks together with the Household Cavalry and the Royal Wiltshire Yeomanry, we were set the task of relieving Habbaniya air force base. The Household Cavalry did this within a few days and then we were able to capture Baghdad.

Life at Rutba Wells, which was held by the Warwickshire Yeomanry, was enlivened by trips into the desert to shoot gazelle to provide fresh meat for the squadron. On one occasion, after an hour's stalk, I shot a trophy head of which I was very proud. Also at Rutba I became, temporarily, the Signals Officer for the Arab Legion, known as 'Glubb's Girls' and at that time commanded by Colonel Lash. One day I caught a man talking on the telephone to Baghdad, whilst two of his sergeants were pointing rifles at his heart. Somehow, although we had removed the wire, he was able to talk to his family about his newly born child, and would indeed have been immediately shot had he talked about anything else. It did not seem wise to put him on a charge. This story was obviously related to the remainder of the Glubb's Girls, who always greeted me in a friendly fashion thereafter.

The Brigade's next move was to turn left, rolling up Syria and capturing Palmyra en route to Aleppo. But all was not plain sailing.

At T3 the pumping-station was held by the Iraqis. Some armoured cars operated by Rashid Ali approached the fort under white flags which coaxed some of our men out of their trenches; eight were promptly killed while the remainder of the troop were taken prisoner. They had the unique experience of being sent to a prison camp in Germany before being returned to the regiment after the Vichy-French capitulated. Possibly the most frightening experience during this campaign was being machine-gunned by Vichy French Dewoitine fighters; two of my signallers were killed as the bullets tore into the ground around us. We had prepared slit trenches before being bombed by Glenn Martin bombers, and although a huge bomb landed about eight yards from my slit trench, no one was badly hurt.

In Aleppo I was taken ill with a fever, and was hospitalized in Jerusalem whilst the regiment proceeded to Iran without me. I was able to rejoin them at Gedera as Signals Officer, training our signallers for tank warfare. General Clark then asked me to join, as GSO III, the 10th Armoured Division, which was the name now given to the former First Cavalry Division, also known as 'Hitler's Secret Weapon'!

Then, after three months as G III Chemical Warfare, when I was stationed with the 10th Armoured Division at Qatatba, I was asked to go to the M. E. Staff College at Haifa from May to October 1942. Naturally I was sad to leave the Warwickshire Yeomanry, a wonderful regiment where I had made many friends, but I was thrilled by the wider prospects now opening up. Later the regiment was to fight with great distinction at El Alamein, where my dear friend Geoffrey Wilson was killed; after fighting at Monte Cassino in Italy, it returned home to become a training regiment near Newmarket.

At the Staff College were many experienced professional soldiers; from them one learned, almost automatically, the art of making war. The work was not arduous but it was interesting and the many operations and exercises were fascinating. It was the first time that I had seen the complete picture.

Monty, who had just been appointed to the command of the Eighth Army, came and spoke to us and, rather cynical though I still was, I was completely bowled over by his address – he inspired everyone with confidence. He told us what he was going to do, how he was going to do it, and how he was going to knock Rommel for six. He started by coming to the front of the stage, looking rather belligerently at everybody and saying, 'I shall be talking to you for forty minutes. During this time I shall expect no personal discussion, no smoking and no coughing. After a short rest, in which you can indulge in such matters, I will then proceed for another twenty minutes.' The spell had been cast. What sort of a man was this who could even stop us coughing? But he did. He spread this personal magnetism throughout the officer corps, which did not like him, and amongst the men, who did. We had all become used to lies, more lies and election promises, but he said that we would win the war and we believed him.

Early in the course we were set a paper to show how we would defend Palestine should the Germans get to Alexandria. It was a lovely day and I wanted to go swimming, so my paper was a short one and took me only ten minutes. Having written this I went down to the beach and had a long swim, being shortly joined by Denis Blundell. He had written a slightly longer paper but we had agreed that Palestine could not be defended. However, he had not come to the same flippant conclusion as I had – that the valley of the Jordan should be flooded through a fifteen-mile-long canal from Haifa refinery in the direction of Beisan. We were both in the dog-house as a result. Though Denis had a lot of red ink on his paper, he was to have a distinguished career with the 2nd New Zealand Division before becoming High Commissioner in London, and later Governor-General of New Zealand.

I survived rather less well at this time and was told by Colonel Jackson that if I wished to return to duty he would not offer any objections; but I believe that during the subsequent conversation he realized that I had studied the Dead Sea in rather more detail than I had divulged. If the Jordan valley were to be flooded, many historical places in which biblical names figure prominently – the Sea of Galilee and Tiberias, as well as Jericho and the Dead Sea with its valuable chemical products – all would be submerged. At the southern end there would have to be a sixty-mile-long escape route for the accumulated waters to flow down to the lower level of the Gulf of Akabah which leads into the Red Sea. Jerusalem and Amaan would become ports, and the water-table would be raised in Palestine, in Jordan and the northern part of Saudi Arabia, where new ports could be established. It could become the busiest inland sea in the world, providing an alternative to the Suez Canal and eventually creating fruitful coastal areas of trees, plantations and crops.

Of course, the political difficulties then and possibly even more so now, would have prevented such a plan; but this apparently harebrained scheme would have been more practical, valuable and far less expensive than the creation of a cross-channel tunnel between France and England. An idea which had started off as a leg-pull finally had me arguing like mad in its defence! So I survived the incident and my work improved as the course continued. The directing staff increasingly put green ink for 'approval' on my papers whilst red ink, for 'disapproval', was annotated far less generously.

For my final exercise I was the head of a syndicate and chose a very able staff officer, a Captain Ekserdjian, who subsequently became a top man in Shell Oil. As a result the administrative side of what Patton referred to as the 'logistics', was first class, and even my conduct of the operational side received the approbation of the authorities' tick in green ink. Until then, I believe, nobody at the Staff College realized how much I had in fact tried, or that I had developed a less light-hearted approach.

During my life I have learned that those who are clever in some ways may be totally inept in others. At one end of the scale are rich men who often survive to a great age without being able to read or write, whilst at the other end are impoverished dons. Those who are intent upon learning enough to be able to teach others to teach are vital members of society but even such capability can bring with it a most unattractive *magister* complex – their very ability minimizes their acceptability.

Many people I met in commerce before the war believed that most soldiers were boneheads. Yet some of the regulars seemed to me to be amongst the ablest men I have known. However, some distinguished soldiers who have since successfully taken up academic or commercial pursuits are apt to pass judgement on fellow human beings whose achievements, in practical terms, greatly exceed their own. Others fall into the trap of making cutting personal remarks to their friends, so that to reply in similar vein could imperil a friendship. People's talents vary; it is the manner in which those talents are applied that really matters.

10 From El Alamein to Tunis

The newly named 10th Armoured Division joined the Eighth Army in the Western Desert at Qatatba. At El Alamein the Nile Delta was defended against the German Afrika Korps, and in July 1942 Rommel was repelled at Alam Halfa. Under its new Commander, General Montgomery, the Eighth Army counter-attacked on 22 October. After a great victory it drove Rommel's forces across Cyrenaica; El Agheila was captured in mid-December, the Army then fighting westwards to take Tripoli.

Rommel's 'savage rabbit' counter-attack was significantly defeated on 6 March at Medenine, part of the Mareth Line which was later outflanked when the Army moved through the El Hamma gap. Under attack from the west by the First Allied Army, reinforced by some Eighth Army divisions, the Afrika Korps finally surrendered after the capture of Tunis in the Cap Bon peninsula in May 1943 when 350,000 German and Italian prisoners were taken.

During my time at Haifa I realized that I was very much on my own. My father had died and, moreover, any post-war career I hoped for in the coal business was in jeopardy as my colliery was not doing too well. I could look forward to no especial privilege, and would not be able to get married unless I could earn enough money. And certainly not least, Monty's address had inspired me.

At the end of the course, to my surprise I was given one of the plum jobs – that of GSO II (Ops) at Monty's Eighth Army headquarters. The directing staff had generally been helpful to me, especially Gerry Duke, eventually the army's top 'sapper', and George Baker, later Field Marshal Sir Geoffrey Baker, Chief of the General Staff. Andy Anderson, later Sir Andy, Chief of the Royal Corps of Signals, George Baker and I were dispatched to Monty's headquarters at Alamein. We could not claim that we helped to win Alamein as the breakthrough was taking place when we arrived, and we caught up with Monty at Fuka, halfway to the Libyan frontier.

Above: My father (left) near Crows Nest Pass, South Alberta, 1902

Below: St Fagans, 1924 – back row (left to right) Rhys, our Mother, myself. In front Rhidian (left) and David

Above left: 44 Ranch, South Alberta, 1930
Above right: World Record Tsessebe Bull shot 1932. Gold Medal, Berlin 1937

Below left: Silver Step. Jumping five feet 1934
Below right: Lloyd George opening the Pit-Head Baths, Mountain Ash, 1934

Above: Cambridge University Steeplechases, Cottenham 1932.
Left to right, HL, Veronica Whitehead, Elaine, Cenydd
Traherne, Derek Evans, my Father

Below: Cambridge University Steeplechases, Cottenham, 1932.
Theorem winning the Stewards Cup (four miles)

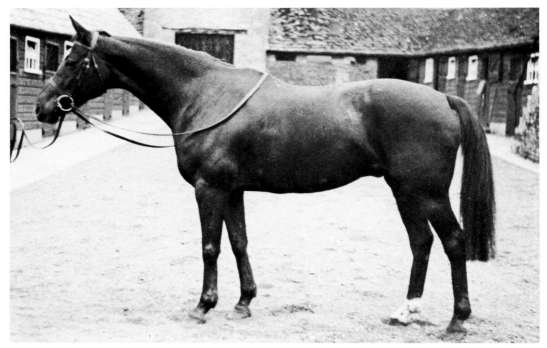

Above: Silver Grail, 1934

Below left: Ego going down to the post for the last time – Gatwick, 1938
Below right: Senior GSO2 Ops (Liaison) 8th Army, Sicily

Above left: Tom Cooper and Billy, 1938

Above right: Trooper Ivor Reading at the Middle
East Staff College, Haifa, 1942

Below: Saracen winning the 6th Cavalry Brigade
Open Jumping. Palestine, 1940

Above: Our wedding at St Margarets Church,
Westminster on 15 April 1944. Leading bridesmaids
(from right to left), my sisters Joyce and Clare and
Mary Rose Fitzroy

Below: Eighth Army L.O., Italy, November 1943

Above left: Kilgeddin winning the Victory Cup at the White City, 1946

Above right: Bay Marble (left) winning the first John Peel Cup at Manchester, 1947

Below: Monty (HL) and Maza (Teeny) winning the open pairs class at the North Hereford Hunter Trials, 1949

Above: Foxhunter wins his first King George V Gold Cup at the White City, 1948

Below: State Control jumping Becher's Brook, Aintree in Foxhunters Steeplechase, 1948

Above: Olympic Games 1952. I nearly fall off
Foxhunter in the first round of the Grand Prix
des Nations – finally won by G.B.

Below: Off to America (left to right) HL, David,
George Legge, Roddy and Nanny see Foxhunter
off from Penpergwm station

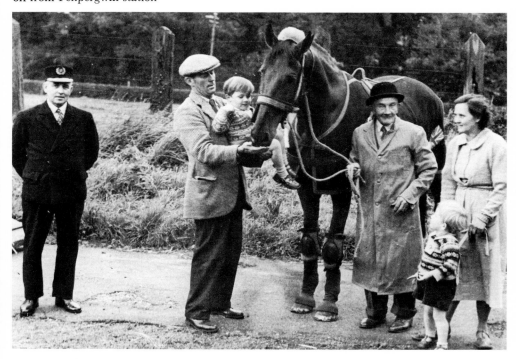

Above: Foxhunter wins Harringay 1950 – HL,
H.R.H. Princess Elizabeth, Col. 'Mike' Ansell

Below: Firm friends, Gobion, 1950

Above: H.M. The Queen presents HL with a bronze model of
Foxhunter – a gift from the BSJA for being Leading World
Rider for three years. Badminton, 1953
H.R.H. Princess Margaret on right

Below: H.M. The Queen presents me with King George V
Cup 1953 – Foxhunter's third win. (centre) Duke of Beaufort

above left: Teeny on Snowdon at Gobion, 1952
above right: Swimming at Ostend, 1956

opposite page: Teeny and myself with Dai and Roddy at Gobion, 1952

below: Davenco Engineering Ltd, Llewellyn Works at Ebbw Vale, 1972

Above: General Freddie's Reunion dinner
Army and Navy Club 1963.
Standing (left to right) Gerald Templer,

Below: Monmouthshire Hounds meet at
Llanvair Grange 1963. Left to right: Cyril
Longsdon (joint-master), Jack Shannon
(whipper-in), George Holder (huntsman), HL
and Mrs Cyril Longsdon (joint-master)

Bill Bovill, Geoffrey Keating, Frank Byers,
Nap White, Ricky Richards, Sir James Grigg,
Bill Williams, Johnnie Henderson, HL,
Sandy Galloway. Sitting (left to right)
Miles Graham, Harry Broadhurst, Oliver Leese
Master (Monty), Freddie de Guingand,
Oliver Poole, John Harding

Above left: High Sheriff of Monmouthshire, 1966

Above right: Anna, 1975

Below: Llewellyn brothers, 1969, (left to right) David,
JL, Rhys and Rhidian

Left: Penny, Tiger and Fluffy, 1977

Below: Roddy, 1977

Above: H.R.H. Prince Philip The Duke of
Edinburgh opens the first Cardiff International
Show, 1974

Right: Meet of Llangibby hounds, Usk, 1977
on Kathy

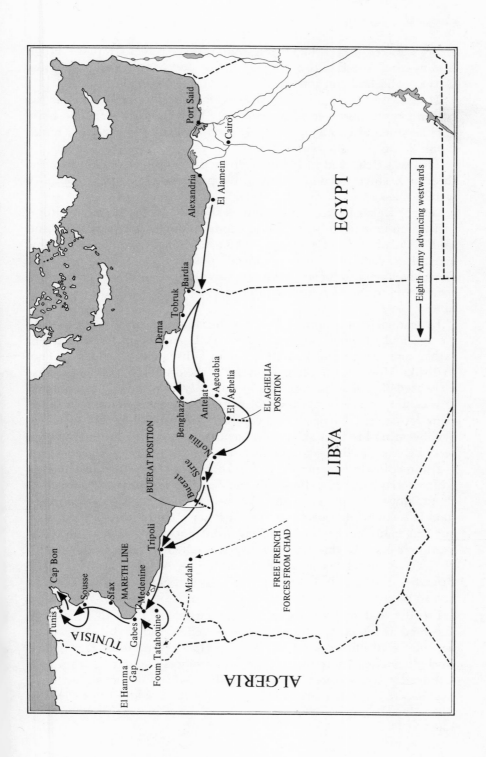

George Baker and I had been sent respectively to replace Hugh Mainwaring, the Eighth Army GI (Ops) and Monty's stepson, Nick Carver, who had run into an ambush near Mersah Matruh.

Monty lined us up in his caravan for our interview, as was his custom, repeating everything he said. 'You are very welcome here; if I like you and you do a good job you may stay. On the other hand, if you do not like me, you can go.'

This was delivered in his high-pitched, querulous voice, while the three of us stood uncomfortably in the presence of the great man. We were not asked to sit down.

George Baker looked over Monty's shoulder at the picture of Rommel which he had in his caravan. Monty immediately perked up and said, 'Ah, ah – I see you are looking at General Rommel – a fine general, a very fine general indeed, possibly the best general the Germans have produced in the last two wars' – and then after a long pause, and in an even higher-pitched voice – 'but, I beat him, I beat him!'

Instead of being appalled at the bumptiousness of such a man, George had the good sense to laugh, while Andy and I followed suit rather more respectfully. This incident subsequently helped me not to dislike Monty as much as so many of the other officers did because I realized that his manner was in fact a type of gauche buffoonery. It was simply one of his ways of being funny: he delighted in delivering 'groaners'. However, his conduct of his own life was strict. He liked wearing his 'hair shirt', but basically he was not an unkind man to those close to him – although I never was.

I immediately became GSO II Operations (Liaison) in company with cheerful Douglas Baker of the Somerset Yeomanry and Peter Paget, my former boss in the Cambridge University OTC. George soon left us and it became the job of Peter Paget and myself to carry out the main liaison between the front-line units and main army headquarters. By this time Monty was already taking forward his tactical headquarters as near the battle as possible and it was to Brigadier Freddie de Guingand, as Chief of Staff to Monty, that I had to report.

Freddie had realized early on that he would have to be as well informed as his commander, who was well served by his ADCs and personal staff officers such as Johnny Henderson, John Poston and Noel Chavasse. There were other young officers operating from tactical headquarters who could be described as 'Monty boys', but those working at the main army HQ were really 'Freddie boys'. In this way we duplicated roles and it was up to us to see that Freddie did not get caught out by receiving information later than Monty did.

This type of internal espionage has often been criticized and the 'Monty boys' derided, but in fact they did a good job. Apart from the armoured-car units such as the 11th Hussars, the 12th Lancers, the King's Dragoon Guards and the Royals whose radio network always worked efficiently, communications in battle, once the infantry were involved, were often non-existent. We achieved a great deal in maintaining communications between other units such as the French formations who normally only reported their positions about twice a week. Reports from the armoured-car units reached brigade, but there were often delays between brigade division and corps HQ and army HQ. Moreover, amongst some formations there was sometimes a reluctance to tell headquarters more than was considered good for them. So we had to ensure that the Army Commander was as much in the picture as the forward Brigade Commander. Also operating in the Eighth Army at this time was J Service, which performed a similar function reporting the movement of our forward units; while the rest of the British Army relied on a system called 'Phantom', again a type of internal espionage. Interception of communication between enemy forward units proved invaluable. We called this 'Yorker', nowadays referred to as Y Service. In this way both tactical and main headquarters were able to become well informed and up to date.

The Eighth Army was now on its way from Egypt to Tunis – always pressing westward. In the Jebel Akbar we were given a tremendous reception by the Senussi, who hated the Italians and were the only Arabs I met who preferred tea to coffee! Apart from 250 Italian Jews, all Italians had been evacuated; it was sad to see how badly the towns had been knocked about and were being looted.

At this time, Freddie the BGS (Ops), who was pale faced and obviously ill, asked me to go down to the 7th Armoured Division near Agedabia as soon as possible. So I went back as far as Tmimi and commandeered an Auster plane piloted by a red-headed Australian bush-pilot. He was not quite sure where to go but put me down near Agedabia at Antelat airstrip, from which the sapper units were just starting to clear the mines. Fortunately, we did not hit one but a Baltimore which arrived just afterwards had its back wheel blown off.

Transport had been laid on for me at the landing-ground by the 7th Armoured Division and I was soon sitting in the division's ACV

(Armoured Command Vehicle). They had just heard that they were to go under command 30 Corps, General Oliver Leese, from being under command 10 Corps, General Herbert Lumsden. I confirmed this, then hunted out their staff officers, to enable me to take back any information or requirements to Eighth Army main headquarters, for onward transmission to 30 Corps headquarters. It took me about an hour to find what I needed to know, during which time we were attacked by low-flying aircraft.

As I was leaving I stopped General John Harding and explained what I was doing. He, in the way great generals always behaved, treated me kindly and marked out my map; he showed me what news he had and told me what his intentions were. Army liaison officers did not always get treated quite so well!

Back at the Antelat landing-strip I saw my Auster take off. My pilot had waited only long enough to allow me to get back to Tmimi in daylight, so I was now confronted with either sleeping on the ground or joining the crew of the Baltimore. Then, who should I find but my friend Douglas Darling, my former instructor at the Middle-East Weapon-Training School, in attendance upon his general, Herbert Lumsden – Commander of 10 Corps, and winner of the Grand Military Gold Cup on Foxtrot in 1926.

Douglas knew that I had been riding under National Hunt Rules before the war, so soon General Herbert Lumsden and I were talking about his horse, Silver Grill, and my horse, Silver Grail, agreeing about everything except my conviction that my horse was three stone better than his. To which his reply was, 'Good God, what is a chap like you doing as an Army LO?'

Of course, this was a job that suited me fine. I was independent, able to move about a lot and fill a job that no professional soldier would have envied. It was not the type of experience that would qualify anybody for command and a great future in the army, but this did not worry me because I hoped that I would be going back into business when the war was over. We talked well into the night, racing men together – a great general and a dogsbody LO on equal terms. The duck, donated by an officer who had passed by, was delicious, and nobody was talking about war until the General turned to me and said, 'You realize I am leaving?'

I said I knew that he was and that I was very sorry. His reply was typical.

'This desert is not big enough to have two such shits in it as Monty and myself at the same time.'

Lumsden, of course, was a thrusting cavalry officer who believed in independent tactics which involved small, fully integrated columns roving round the desert carrying out left and right hooks; whereas Monty repeatedly said he did not wish to disperse his strength in penny packets. He was determined to act as one closely integrated, concerted army whose stamina was not sapped by the dispersal of its strength. He wanted always to be 'balanced'. This was the fundamental difference between two generals, both great in their own way – but of the two Monty was the boss. Lumsden soon went out to the Far East where he was killed on the bridge of the *Prince of Wales* when it was sunk in company with the *Repulse* by the Japanese. Many grieved at the sad death of a great general and soldier-rider.

On my return to base I was told that Freddie wanted to hear my news so I went straight to see him. I had had time to prepare a pretty extensive report to which he listened, fixing me with a half-smile. When I stopped, expecting the sack for my inefficiency or inadequacy, he said, 'Thank you for a good report,' and then suggested that I should have a meal and rest up. Half an hour later he sent for me and said, 'I have had a word with Master (as we called Monty) and General Leese. You are to collect your gear and proceed immediately to General Oliver Leese's headquarters to act there as the Army Liaison Officer and feed us with full reports, such as the one you have just made concerning the 7th Armoured Division.'

I had made it! And this was the beginning of an association and friendship which was to endure until he died in 1979 – thirty-seven years on. From this time I had only three bosses: Freddie de Guingand direct, David Belchem and Charles Richardson – all brilliant men. Freddie, however, was unwell at that time so had to have six weeks' leave.

On 20 November Benghazi was captured and by 22 November the 7th Armoured Division had reached the Agheila defences. The weather, furthermore, had held up the establishment of two fighter wings at Msus. I therefore embarked on a round of reconnaissances, which took place nearly every day. Trooper Reading and I established a little base north of the road facing between Agedabia and Agheila, in some Italian trenches which we had found well stocked with dehydrated vegetables!

This same stretch of road had already become famous, for it was here that 'Bill' Williams, then our brilliant GSO I (Intelligence) and now Sir Edgar, Warden of Rhodes House, Oxford, had been the first person to make contact with the Afrika Corps a year previously. A member of a most distinguished regiment, the King's Dragoon Guards, he was motoring down the road when an armoured car came towards him; it was only after he had passed it that he noticed that it had the German cross on its side. The story goes that he lost a bedding-roll in the encounter. When he reported back to the KDGs, he was not believed, because he was known by them to have poor eyesight. It has since been proved that this was indeed the Eighth Army's first contact, apart from those of the LRDG (Long Range Desert Group) and the SAS operating under David Stirling (the Phantom Major), who was always exploring on the Army's open left flank.

Eventually, the New Zealanders achieved a magnificent left hook with the Scots Greys in the lead and nearly caught the bulk of the Germans near Nofilia, but they slipped through during the night. So Reading and I motored up through the Marble Arch, a huge stone archway erected by the Italians, and I arrived at Sirte with the 4th Light Armoured Brigade ahead of the 7th Armoured Division. Here the Germans had put up a spirited defensive, possibly to give them time to get back to strengthen the position they were planning to hold inland from Buerat.

The speed of our concentration forward depended on what tonnage could be sent up the only road. A thousand tons per day were being sent from Tobruk and soon after Christmas 3000 tons were being sent up daily from Benghazi. Christmas Day itself was warm and sunny. Ivor Reading and I went for a long swim, to commemorate which he calls his present home 'Villa Sirte'.

By this time I had done a deal with Brigadier 'Slap' White, who commanded the Eighth Army Signals. He was short of jeeps so I swapped mine for a Dodge signal van, with four-wheel-drive and double tyres behind. In this we were never stuck. Normally we had three jerry-cans strapped to each front wing, carrying a total of twenty-four gallons which enabled our front wheels to grip that much better and helped to distribute the weight. Occasionally, armoured cars got stuck and had to use sand channels; but we only once had to resort to those, in the bed of the Wadi Buerat itself which I tried to cross when out on a solo recce. I had not liked the look of an adjoining crossing which I thought might be mined. It was!

We had made our camp just east of Sirte near the coast, as was our custom, and we were alarmed that night to see lights out at sea, thinking that raiders might be trying to come in behind our lines. We later identified the boat as being that of a local fisherman who was getting on with his job and not bothering about the war. This outlook was extraordinary – I remember seeing Arabs walk through the minefields despite the bodies that had been blown up and lay browning in the sun. They took the view that the Germans meant the mines for us and not for them!

The next stage in the campaign was Montgomery's attempt to out-flank the German positions east of Tripoli and capture the city – the capital of western Libya. The leading reconnaissance regiment, the KDGs, found their way down off the high coastal escarpment but were then dispatched in the direction of the Tunisian frontier, thus by-passing Tripoli. Monty and Oliver Leese had laid bets as to who would get there first.

As soon as we could move the 11th Hussars sent out a troop and I tucked in behind them in my Dodge truck. As the cars approached Tripoli, one car stayed behind as a link while the other two probed forward with mine sitting behind them at a comfortable distance. There were very few people about – just some startled eyes at open windows. The crescendo of high-pitched voices soon told us that the German 90th Light Division had gone. Nevertheless, we darted across any main thoroughfares because the enemy had developed a nasty technique of leaving behind 88mm anti-aircraft guns to shoot at anything that appeared on a long stretch of road. The Germans were expert at pulling out at the right moment and this was a skilful withdrawal.

The 11th Hussars reported that they had reached the port and I was able to send word back straight to the main army that Tripoli was in our hands. My message reached them an hour before it came through the proper channels – from regiment to brigade, from brigade to division to corps, and then back.

I drove into the yard of the Grand Hotel where I was greeted rather as a distinguished guest would be received on the steps of the Hôtel de Paris in Monte Carlo! The manager asked us if we would care to have lunch in the hotel, so I dumped a few rations on him, telling him to add these to what he had already, and that we would be pleased to have lunch with him. By this time the crowds were cheering and starting to loot, but the New Zealanders had been quick to follow up and they had everything under control in a very short time.

About three-quarters of an hour later Monty's lot from Misurata and Homs arrived. I was able to confirm that the 11th had got there first so that Monty lost his bet and Oliver Leese won his! There was a great scramble for suitable billets but Monty decreed that all headquarters should be under canvas out of the town.

I returned to the hotel for an excellent lunch, insisting that the Italian manager sat down with us. He spoke good French and he confessed that the night before he had been sitting in the same suite attending the farewell meal of the German generals. Business is business!

Our lunch was later surpassed by a most wonderful five-course dinner. For some reason which has never been explained to me I had virtually become the boss of that hotel, so that if anybody arrived it was really up to me to decide whether they were to be allowed to enjoy the comparative luxury of spending the night in a bed, even if the sheets had not been changed since the German generals left.

I told them at the hotel that anybody wearing a red beret was admissible – which meant that the 11th Hussars, who had done all the work, could come – but to be very careful about anybody else. I believe that whilst I carried out a reconnaissance that afternoon some quite distinguished 'rubber-necks' had been turned away and been sent off to the inferior Delmahari Hotel down the road.

During my first night I was disturbed by an enormous thief who had entered my room. I chased him down the marble steps of the Grand Hotel and achieved the best tackle of my life just before he got to the front door. No one has ever done better at Cardiff Arms Park. As we stood up I tried to knock him out under the chin but merely succeeded in dislocating my thumb. At that moment the thief received a smashing blow to the chin from a British officer who turned out to be Major Jefferies of the Catering Corps – a former army heavyweight champion. We handed the thief over to the New Zealand Police who had had seventeen cases of rape to deal with that evening. Monty, surprisingly, said that the men deserved these fruits of victory.

Within an hour my thief had escaped and when he was recaptured at the Delmahari Hotel, where he had taken a room, it was filled with enough rations to last six months. Apparently he had been a stoker on a warship and had spent many months in the 'hidden army' in Alexandria before taking off into the desert posing as a member of the Long Range Desert Group. He had pillaged his way westwards. He stayed with army units, stealing many rations, watches or any loot that came his way. I offered to go back to Alexandria to his trial but apparently this was considered unnecessary, and I believe he was locked up for the rest of the war.

Charles Richardson then asked me to make contact with the Free French under General Leclerc. Air recce had reported the movement of armoured cars and MET (soft transport) about a hundred miles south of Tripoli. I felt this was a long journey to make on my own, but Peter Paget was busy and jeeps were short, so Ivor Reading and I set out alone armed with only .303 rifles. We climbed the escarpment south of Tripoli and set off due south through Gharian, a hundred kilometres away. There was little 'trade' on the road but occasionally we could see vehicle tracks crossing it, no doubt those of the LRDG or the KDG.

I have never disliked a mission more than this one. We were making for Mizdah about fifty miles to the south of Gharian. The country was open, really nasty stony desert with the wadis almost dry in spite of the recent rains. From some fairly high ground we saw three black dots moving on the skyline about ten miles away; one of these was undoubtedly a half-track and therefore German. We moved even more cautiously down towards Mizdah.

Suddenly we heard a tremendous babble of voices which we identified as a loud gramophone, so we dismounted, crept over the skyline and saw clearly members of the French Foreign Legion walking around, and two French flags flying. An assortment of vehicles was gradually moving into the town but they apparently had no scouts out on our side, so we beat a hasty retreat before they sent somebody out who might mistake us for hostiles. After all, my job was just to find out where they were. Leclerc was then asked to see Monty and they got on famously together. Leclerc's troops and the KDG shortly afterwards gave the Germans a hiding when they raided them in Southern Tunisia.

The enemy had by now retreated to Ben Gardane which was just beyond the frontier about a hundred miles to the West. The harbour was not cleared for several days. As soon as it was open, however, we started pushing 2000 tons of supplies daily through the port as this was vital for the build-up for our next objective – the Mareth Line inside the Tunisian frontier.

Our stay in Tripoli was badly needed. We all wanted to clean up, and Master soon organized a victory parade where the Eighth Army showed it could be really smart if it wanted to be, although it had acquired a reputation for dressing rather informally most of the time.

A joyful, often tearful Winston Churchill came out and spoke to us. He said, 'When anybody asks you what you have done in the Great War, it will be enough to say that you marched with the Eighth Army.' Then he continued, 'We all draw comfort from the fact that every night you are pitching your moving tents you are a day's march nearer home.' This particularly moved the men of the Eighth Army, many of whom had been away from their homes and loved ones for many years. I organized a group at one corner and made them all shout out 'Viva Churchill' – I think he was a little surprised when he found out that the cheerleader was a British officer!

Shortly afterwards, at one of Montgomery's conferences, I met General George Patton, of whom I was to see much later. I heard this great American cavalry officer say, 'I may be old, I may be dumb, and I know I am "deef", but it don't mean a thing to me.' This is what he actually said, although there have been other versions.

As we came out of the conference, David Yates (later General) who had been a friend of ours before the war and was then GI in 1st Army Headquarters at Le Kef, turned to me and said, 'We all knew that Monty had the Almighty in support but this is the first time that I have realized that he has had Him under command!'

In spite of difficulties, we recognized Monty's ability as a commander. Usually there are two types of leadership. Either you lead by example with a sharp edge, and hope that everyone will swirl in behind you, or you lead with a blunt edge when you keep your nose in front and allow those on a broad front to provide much of the initiative and do nearly all the work. Monty was the only man I knew who combined both methods! He led with both sharp and blunt edges.

We were told Rommel planned a lightning 'savage rabbit' to capture the Medenine Feature – a main pivot of our defences – and I soon found myself buzzing up and down the road between main army headquarters and 30 Corps. Naturally, I preferred straightforward liaison, but often there were occasions of great importance when documents were passing between the generals and an officer of field rank was entrusted with the vital facts. As the resident Army Liaison

Officer at 30 Corps, it was my job to do this daily run for five days on end. Ivor Reading and I took it in turns, one driving while the other slept in the back of our Dodge van.

On one occasion I delivered a package from the hand of General Leese to the hand of General Montgomery at six o'clock in the morning, not having shaved since the morning before. Without even saying 'Thank you', Monty took my package. I told him it was from General Leese whereupon he looked at me and said, 'I always like to see my officers shaved! Get a shave and then go and have breakfast.' If he had only said 'Thank you' I would have stood on my head.

I then went to see Freddie de Guingand to tell him about how the reception for Rommel, which he had planned, was going. He was most thankful for our efforts and later I learned that this rather energetic programme had earned me a mention in dispatches. This was the difference between two great men. No one could dispute that Monty was a war-winning general, but there was a part of his character which the Americans would classify as being 'rude aggressive'.

Making daily recces and returning to main headquarters kept me fairly busy. It now appears possible that all this information concerning Rommel's proposed attacks could have come from Ultra when our code-busters broke the Enigma code machine.

I had learned from experience that no liaison officer was very popular if he made any dust or showed himself, so usually left my vehicle well back. On one occasion I walked halfway up the Medenine Feature and had hidden myself between some rocks to take a good look for any movement. Suddenly, I was alarmed to hear a tremendous lot of chattering and to my horror saw Monty, Leese and others walking up the side of the mountain in full view of the enemy, to hold a conference on the top, their maps and everything flashing in the sunlight. Robin Hastings, on the HQ of the 7th Armoured Division, had quite a lot to say about this and asked me in no uncertain terms to tell my bosses to be more careful in future. This I did, through Freddie. I am interested to see that he mentioned it in his *Operation Victory*.

The enemy attack came in at the Medenine Feature on 6 March. I was lying up in front of 7th Armoured Division headquarters when I heard the most frightful howling noise, which in fact was the *Nebelwerfer*, a German six-barrelled heavy mortar. The noise was quite awe-inspiring but somehow I never had much respect for what one might call blind shelling at anything. I was much more wary of the bullet and the machine gun. They were so personal. I suppose I would not have been a very good liaison officer if I had exposed myself to much rifle fire, and this comparatively seldom took place, although we all took many doses of long-range shelling. Rommel threw 140 tanks on to our guns and morale was high when he lost 52 of them, while we did not lose a single tank. The savage rabbit had been given a bloody nose – 'a bloody nose', repeated Master.

Our next job was to get past the Mareth Line, which had been established by the French before the war to meet a threat from Italians stationed in Libya. First we tried to batter away at the Line itself from Medenine to the sea but it became obvious that we would not succeed. The Wadi still had water in it and we were unable to get our supporting anti-tank guns across. I went forward to look at this battle and got pinned down by a lot of metal flying about; eventually I just managed to get back to my vehicle about half a mile away in the rear.

I was able to report back to main army headquarters that our anti-tank weapons had not crossed over to the other side. Confirmation of this unfortunately was not available from Brigadier 'Crasher' Nicholls, who was also stuck down somewhere without communications. However, enemy intercept, the 'Yorker' Service, confirmed from the German forward units that our assault had been unsuccessful.

The battle of El Hamma which followed has often been referred to as 'The Grand National', or as the 'left hook of all time'. Our troops having failed to cross the Wadi Zig Zaou between the mountainous part of the Mareth Line and the sea, a tremendous operation was launched from the area of Foum Tathouine by the 10 Corps and the 2nd New Zealand Division.

In the late evening of 26 March the main force charged through towards El Hamma, completely disrupting the 15th and 21st Panzer Divisions en route. This exhilarating charge had the advantage both of the sun behind and clouds of dust flying in front. It was a great military feat that can rank with any famous charge in history. There were comparatively few casualties but sadly my fellow LO, Peter Paget, was one of them.

This superb blitz took the New Zealanders and 10 Corps to El Hamma but another battle had to be fought at the Wadi Akarit. It was vital to know how this attack went and I went forward to see for myself what was happening.

At one time it looked as if the Italians were forming up for a counter-attack but I saw that the bustling about was in fact the enemy packing their bags; very soon it was obvious that they wanted to surrender. Shortly afterwards an endless file of Italians, most carrying two suitcases, moved to our rear. They seemed to be in a hurry – as who would not be after having the Ghurkas literally at their throats. The 4th Indian Division reported back 'ammunition expenditure – nil'. The long trail of prisoners was led by a tall white-haired Italian officer, whose bearing was, to say the least, theatrical.

On my immediate front there was an eerie silence. We could however hear a tremendous battle going on for the Jebel Romana to the north. Here the wonderful fighters of the 51st Highland Division were having a rough time before the enemy was forced to leave, enabling this division to pursue its other reputation as 'Highland Decorators' across the plains into Tunisia – HD in a circle was plastered on every building.

Just after this Akarit battle, General Eisenhower paid us his first visit and Freddie and Charles Richardson presented me to him in the tented Ops room at main army headquarters. He asked me to outline the functions of army LOs and the build-up of information coming through to higher command, including our integration with J Service (own troops) and 'Yorker' (enemy intercept). He was surprised that I was about to motor off to Le Kef – he had not yet fully realized that a deserted battlefield is the emptiest (and safest) place in the world. He was formal, polite and commanded respect, but gave me the impression of a senior member of the Cabinet visiting a marginal constituency.

I had been asked to take dispatches and outline the general battle position to First Army at Le Kef. David Yates, the GSO I was told to expect me. I thought I was going to be able to motor straight there but a few miles short of a big feature called Fondook, a tremendous battle was going on to my right. This meant, in fact, that Fondook was not in our hands as I could see some enemy traffic on a road about a mile to the north. Ivor and I hid the Dodge van in a depression in the ground, put up our camouflage net and laced it with palm fronds so that it was difficult to spot; and of course we put a lot of sand over our 'roundel' to hide us from the air. I had no idea what was going on so we settled down for the night.

In the early morning we noticed German troops leaving the position, some of them motoring by only a quarter of a mile away which was uncomfortably close. I then saw them setting up an '88' to wait for any British troops following them up, and rightly assumed this was their rearguard. After the '88' had also been removed, I waited for a couple of hours and then moved forward towards Fondook where we could see and hear no one. Complete silence. It was astonishing to me that there had been no follow-up or any scouts sent out to see what had happened to the enemy. No mines had been cleared, so I erected a sort of white flag and went very gingerly down the middle of the road, looking carefully to see that there were no mines.

We went completely unchallenged through the gap and after about a mile we saw some American soldiers sitting disconsolately by the side of the road. Although later in the war we recognized some of their divisions as having been the finest, these soldiers had been flung into a battle for which they were not prepared. All they were concerned about was that their rations had not come up. They were unshaven and highly indignant about everything – I never saw troops with morale so low. It is no secret that in fact the Americans had not even reached their start line, and the Welsh Guards had taken Fondook after a bloody battle in which Glyn Rhys Williams, thought to have been recommended for the VC, was killed.

I was naturally anxious to find out where my brother Rhidian was, but I had to press on to Le Kef as instructed. My journey was through the most beautiful part of Tunisia. There was not a single vehicle moving one way or the other but occasionally one came across brewed-up armoured cars and transport vehicles, both British and German. The Germans had tried to punch their way through to Le Kef and were only just held up a few miles to the south by the heroic efforts of a mixed group of British troops.

David Yates, whom I had last seen in Tripoli, told me I would find the Welsh Guards in the Kessera Forest, so without dallying I went straight up to them. Rhidian's tent was pointed out to me. I quote from a joint letter we sent back to my mother: 'Today was the first day back in my battalion after ten days. To my amazement, in walked Harry whom I did not recognize.' I wrote, 'I had no idea who Rhidian was until he came forward with an amazed "Good Heavens!" After all, we had not seen each other for four years and I was at least able to congratulate him on the Military Cross he had won at Dunkirk.' Rhidian then writes, 'I cannot imagine why I did not recognize Harry as he has not changed at all. He looks fitter and harder than I ever thought he could. His eyebrows are completely bleached as is his moustache and he is looking a little heavier, but he hotly denies this.

'We both send our fondest love to the most wonderful mother in all the world and her wonderful family. Signed, Harry and Rhidian.'

On returning I found that the Eighth Army had come to a standstill. I therefore spent a few days with my friends in the Staffordshire Yeomanry of which Jim Eady, later Chairman of Bass, was the Colonel. Jim Eady was credited with besting Monty when he had addressed commanding officers before the Medenine battle. Monty was well known for repeating himself and so he confronted his staff officers with, 'They tell me I repeat myself. I cannot believe this. What do you think, Colonel Eady?'

Jim replied, 'Only when you wish to emphasize a very important point, sir.'

Most of the senior commanders had gone to Cairo, leaving Colonel John Oswald in charge. Since our role was static there was little for me to do so I asked John if I could go and see my brother in the Welsh Guards, and then report back on any progress. When I was released the Welsh Guards had got across the Cap Bon peninsula to Hammeimat, and Tunis was in the process of falling; Von Arnhem had agreed to capitulate with the loss of 350,000 troops.

As I motored up the road I noticed the 90th Light Division, whom we had chased the whole way from Alamein, marching down in column of threes, led by their commanding officer, whose request to surrender to the much-respected New Zealanders had been granted. They were a first-class formation. As they reached the road I involuntarily saluted them, whereupon the whole regiment gave me, a dogsbody major, the eyes-right. I learned later that they had destroyed every single item of equipment and all spare ammunition before surrendering. They had been told to report to the Welsh Guards, so I motored up the road ahead to warn them that the 90th Light were on their way.

The first member of Rhidian's regiment that I spotted was Captain McVitie, the former racehorse trainer, sitting on a hastily-improvised loo. Here again, there appeared to be no forward points. He told me where regimental headquarters were and I was given the bad news that Rhidian had been nastily wounded at Hammam Lif. His company had had a very rough time on this high hill overlooking the Bay of Tunis. His batman, Bishop, who was beside him, had had his head shot off, and most of his company were casualties.

I went on in search of Rhidian, and was directed to Thibar monastery near which there had been a casualty clearing-station, but found he had been sent back to Châteaudun. I spent an hour in the beautiful monastery, known for its red wine, but now taken over by the press who always achieved the best billets.

I then pushed on to Constantine, passing columns of unescorted German troops on their way to prisoner-of-war camps. I was the first Eighth Army man that anybody had seen. A party was thrown in the officers' mess within a few minutes of my arrival; a collection of beautiful French ladies and English officers accumulated and we had a great evening.

At dawn the next day I set off for Châteaudun where I found my brother Rhidian in hospital in the next bed to David Gibson-Watt, also wounded at Hammam Lif and later awarded the Military Cross. Rhidian's elbow was painful, but he was not to lose his arm as was at first feared. He still refers to the feeling of relief after he had been shaved by Ivor Reading.

I suggested to him that when he got out of hospital he might like to come as a staff officer to Eighth Army. He agreed, and this set in motion the procedures which led to him becoming GSO III at 13 Corps under Tony Sugden, of the South Wales Borderers, a great personal friend.

I then motored to rejoin main army headquarters south of Enfidaville. The fields of poppies and other wild flowers in Tunisia were really beautiful and it was a pleasant drive except that suddenly, both Ivor Reading and I had become tired. We seemed to have been driving for months on end. Somehow, not being in danger any more had taken the zest out of our job.

When I returned to Eighth Army headquarters near Enfidaville I found John Oswald, who was displeased at the length of my absence but was human enough to understand that I wanted to see my wounded brother. I was forgiven.

I had written by airmail to my mother explaining exactly what had happened to Rhidian, to receive a reply from her some weeks later: 'It is very comforting to know you were so near Rhidian when he was wounded'. I had travelled a thousand miles to see him and nearly got the sack – but as far as she was concerned I was 'near' him!

11

The Invasion of Sicily and Italy

From North Africa the Allied Armies crossed the Mediter-
ranean, to Sicily which was occupied by the end of August 1943. On 3 September
the Eighth Army landed on the toe of Italy; this was followed by the First
Army landing of British and American troops at Salerno. The two armies
advanced up the Italian peninsula, but by winter no progress had been made on
the west coast by the First Army against the German defences, which were
particularly strong at Monte Cassino. The Eighth Army had reached the Sangro
River on the east coast.

During this campaign Major Llewellyn continued as Senior Liaison Officer
at Eighth Army main headquarters until December 1943, when he was sent back
to England on a confidential mission.

My next instructions were to go immediately to Zuara west of Tripoli,
and I lost no time in doing so. There 'Shrimp' Coghill, the Military
Secretary, told me to report to Freddie in Cairo, so I wrote myself
out a priority pass which read, 'Please give Major Llewellyn priority
at all road-blocks, airfields, etc. Signed. H. M. Llewellyn, Major
GSO II (Ops)'. This immediately got me a seat in a bomber from
Castel Benito back to Cairo.

Freddie said I was now to call myself GSO II (Plans) to a bogus
Twelfth Army; another of his brilliant ideas, this Twelfth Army was
supposed to be planning the invasion of Turkey. Monty really *needed*
Freddie. He had been a brilliant Director of Military Intelligence in
Cairo and was to prove outstanding as such at the War Office after
the war. He thought in terms of what the enemy would do, what his
reactions would be and therefore there was always a cover plan at
the back of his mind.

Our headquarters were in the Semiramis Hotel which had the
code-name of 'George'. This was where we planned operation 'Husky'
for the invasion of Sicily and I became GSO II (Plans). We had

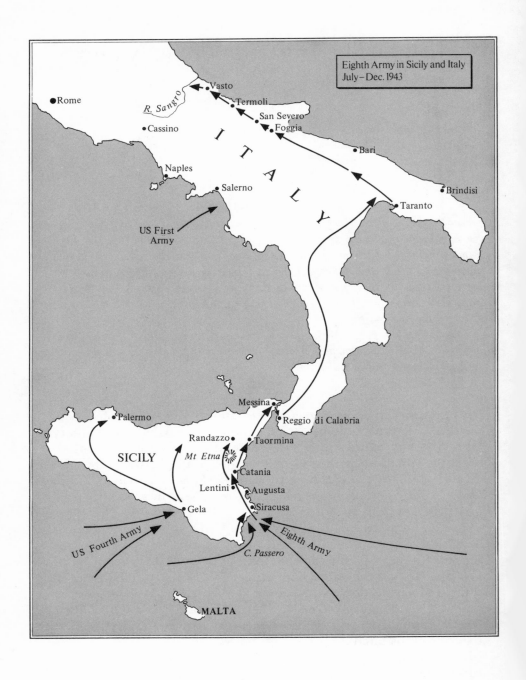

Eighth Army in Sicily and Italy
July–Dec. 1943

Rome

R. Sangro

Vasto

Termoli

Cassino

San Severo

Foggia

Bari

Naples

Salerno

Brindisi

Taranto

ITALY

US First
Army

Messina

Palermo

Reggio di Calabria

SICILY

Randazzo

Taormina

Mt Etna

Catania

Lentini

Augusta

Gela

Siracusa

US Fourth Army

C. Passero

Eighth Army

MALTA

responsibility for building up the invasion map: this function was really an extension of the gathering of information, from all sources, that became a major feature of our headquarters.

The primary object of the map was to coordinate information mostly received from the Staff Duties Branch. We planned the rough location of every ship carrying troops and arms from a vast network of ports; we would thus be able to know where our reserves were at any given moment and we practised this exercise often. This was of particular importance nearer the date of battle, for which we needed to know the availability of the reserves, and how long it would take for them to get up to the invasion front – in our case, the south-eastern corner of Sicily. The naval operations room daily monitored with us the exact position of every ship.

After I had flown down, Ivor brought the Dodge 'bread van' back to Cairo by road. We had both planned on going to see our friends in the regiment, but I became too involved and so Ivor Reading went back alone. The brunt of the driving had fallen upon him and he was very tired. We had planned that he would come back to me after about a month, but I was suddenly whisked off at a moment's notice to fly into Malta with John Poston, Monty's ADC. This gave me no time to organize the return of Ivor Reading which meant, sadly, that I did not see him again until after 1945. He had been a wonderful friend and companion, and without him I certainly could not have moved around as much as I did. I am sure the same has applied since his return to me after the war!

John Poston and I took a flight in a Baltimore bomber to Tripoli before setting off for Malta, still a besieged island suffering from many air-raids. The air trip from Tripoli to Malta was uneventful except that one engine went on fire as we landed.

Before the rest of our staff arrived, I brought up to date the map which I had prepared in readiness. So when Freddie de Guingand walked in to our tunnel headquarters, he had all this information presented to him, and it proved invaluable for putting the rest of the staff in the picture. The naval and air-force operations rooms which worked closely with us were nearby.

I now reverted to liaison again and was appointed Senior GSO II Ops (Liaison) having a dozen officers in my section for which, in fact, there was no room on the Eighth Army headquarters establishment. But this did not stop me from building up a nice supply of vehicles in order to keep my boys mobile.

On the night before the invasion many of us accompanied Monty and Freddie to the northern tip of Sicily, where we saw Colonel Hopkinson's parachutists flying overhead to be dropped along the coast from Augusta down to Cap Pasero. The 101st American Airborne Division was also due to be dropped on our left. Unfortunately, a strong westerly wind got up and both units of parachutists had their gliders and parachutes blown off course. Many of Hoppy's men were lost at sea, while many of the American division landed in our area.

That night, Monty and Lord Louis 'Dicky' Mountbatten went aboard the former channel-steamer SS *Antwerp*, taking a few people with them, including myself. We landed south of Syracuse and everything seemed to be strangely quiet, although we were strafed by a lone German fighter. I acquired a nasty cut across my shin, which could have been from a bullet but was I think from a very sharp stone, or a part of it, which had been flung in my direction as we landed.

Our transport was laid on and we arrived at Monty's mess where I had tea with him. During our conversation he asked me if I would ever consider being a regular soldier after the war, to which I am afraid I replied, 'Good heavens, no!' This was a very unwise thing to have said. From that point onwards I was never referred to as 'Harry' but always as 'Llewellyn', and it later cost me one very good job.

I had been swanning about a certain amount with Brigadier John Currie who was Commander of the 4th Light Armoured Brigade. George Luck, Warwickshire Yeomanry, who had been his Brigade Major, was leaving and Currie had asked 'Shrimp' Coghill to ask for me. Freddie gave permission and I was actually setting off to join the 4th Light Armoured Brigade when Freddie again asked to see me. He explained that Monty had finally decided that someone else was to have that coveted job. He gave as the reason that having recently been a GSO II (Plans) I was too much in the picture, but really Monty had a high opinion of Miles Fitzalan-Howard and had not forgiven me for telling him a few weeks earlier that I did not want to become a regular soldier. I was infuriated but I suppose Monty was right. Miles Howard, now the Duke of Norfolk, told me recently (when my son Dai was lucky enough to marry his niece Vanessa Hubbard) that he had a frosty reception from John Currie; but he did a wonderful job and subsequently had a distinguished military career.

After my fateful meeting with Monty, I set off to find some of my

LOs, and found myself mixed up with a bunch of Americans, British, Italians, and finally a few Germans as I moved west. Trying to avoid some of the latter I drove round a corner to be confronted by an advance American dressing-station, manned by some beautiful ladies in khaki trousers. One of them dressed my leg and started taking my details. I asked her why and she said I would qualify later for a Purple Star. I did not think that my scratch deserved this distinguished medal, so terminated the proceedings and headed back to the beach; but not before noticing that there were more Italian customers than Americans at the dressing-station – some of them were deliciously tight.

On returning to SS *Antwerp* I was put in charge of a dozen Italian generals, each carrying, as usual, two big suitcases. After I had locked them up and relieved them of their Beretta pistols, the senior general, who had been in command at Cap Pasero, asked to see Dicky Mountbatten. So I marched the general up to him and was as surprised as Mountbatten was when he asked to be given the Military Cross. He gave as his reason the fact that he gave up as easily as his father had done in the First World War, for which gallant act he had been awarded the MC. Dicky Mountbatten was at first appalled, then angry before audibly chuckling. Shortly before this superb man was killed he discussed this incident with me and his archivists have since been in touch with me about it.

After Patton had triumphed on the southern beaches of Sicily, where he met strong opposition, he was given the task of going left to Palermo and then along the coast road to Messina. This involved the meeting of British and American troops at Randazzo to the west of Mount Etna. It was possible that the British might mistake the Americans in their coal-scuttle hats for Germans, so I had to ensure that a radio link was established at Army, corps, divisional and brigade headquarters level.

To make doubly sure, Freddie sent me over to see Patton. I could not get past his staff to see him. After waiting an hour I found out where his tent was and walked straight up to it and announced, 'Major Llewellyn, Liaison Officer, sent by General Montgomery.' Without any formality, a soft voice said, 'Come inside,' where I found Patton stripped to the waist. He said, 'Excuse me Major, but it's kinda hot.'

I then outlined my business, and he learned that I had been in a horsed cavalry regiment. As a horse-lover himself he was motivated to ask if I knew the Llewellyn who rode Ego second in the National in 1936 which he had seen. When I told him I was the same person, he forgot all about the war and we had a gossip about Americans and steeplechasing – Pete Bostwick, the Grand National, the Maryland Hunt Cup; rank made no difference when talking about horses. I told him I wanted to go and see his forward brigade and he agreed to this. When I asked him for written permission he said, 'Just say, "I am a friend of the General's" ' – this was the accepted password. Again, when I returned to his headquarters I would have to use the same code words and walk straight in to him, which in fact I did.

Our meeting happened shortly after Patton had received much publicity for slapping in the face a soldier whom he thought was malingering while claiming to be shell-shocked. He was a very thrustful 'all-around cowboy' sort of general, who often carried a pair of pearl-handled Colt revolvers, and who 'got things done'. He told his generals that if they had not taken a certain objective by a certain time he would sack them, and he did. I believe there were two Pattons, the really tough, thrusting cavalry officer, and the soft-spoken, gentle man – perhaps I was lucky to see only the latter side.

On 18 July, which was my birthday, I looked across the plains to see Mount Etna mildly erupting, and felt inspired then to write to Teeny Saumarez and ask her to marry me. She asked all her friends to read my letter as she could not understand my writing, but none of them could understand it either. No one could decipher what was in fact a proposal of marriage. As, in her next letter, she did not turn me down, this seemed an encouraging sign, and I took it that she was at least examining the proposition of which she now claims she was unaware.

As we were then about to take Catania I went up to the leading units in accordance with my daily task and soon found myself driving through the streets of that city where most of the shops were being looted. As soon as the Germans had disappeared the inhabitants had set about getting all they could until law and order were restored. I pushed on to the northern outskirts of the town and I suddenly had that instinctive feeling that all was not well. Everything was too quiet and only one or two elderly Italians were walking about. So I dived into an open gateway, closed the gates behind me and put my jeep in the garage, while Walker, my driver, and I went into a charming, four-storey house. As we were doing this a battle broke out all round me and I later learned that a poor old woman was killed on the road just outside the house.

The firing went on for half an hour while we kept absolutely quiet. We then heard voices coming from the basement so we stalked down, pushing the door open to find three nervous Italian officers, one of whom was shaking and pointing a Beretta in my direction but who then gave it to me willingly. As soon as they discovered we were British there were tremendous cries of 'Viva Churchill!' Apparently they were more afraid of the Germans than the British and had resolved to stay behind to become prisoners-of-war.

I was then told to seize the best buildings in Taormina for use as army headquarters. Having signalled David Belchem, I took over the bottom floor of the Vista Mare Hotel. David, who had a great nose for a good party, was quickly on the scene and soon a cheerful gathering was proceeding on the bottom floor of the hotel, with someone banging away on a piano. We suddenly heard the whine of shells going over our heads. The Germans were lobbing them over Taormina into our troops on the southern side, but we soon realized they had no intention of trying to stop our party. Afterwards David said to me that I was not going to be able to keep a new car. Two days later Freddie said to David, 'You will never be able to hold on to that,' and took it for himself. Monty then did the same thing and used this car throughout the campaign.

Our sappers repaired the road and eventually we were able to cross over from Messina to Reggio on the toe of Italy. I would remind readers that it was the men of the Eighth Army who first stepped upon the soil of Europe again on 3 September – four years after war was declared.

The landing was not seriously opposed and we were soon chasing the enemy up the coast road towards Salerno where the First Army landed a week later. This was beautiful country and I always placed my vehicle under a fig tree. There were grapes aplenty and we lived off fruit as we pillaged our way forwards to Catanzaro. I was then told to make contact with the First Army, so Major O'Brien Butler, an experienced gunner, and I set off up the coast road through Cetraro. It was soon evident that no Germans were in the area but we leap-frogged and went along very carefully. I did not get any shivers down my spine and by this time I had come very much to rely on my instinct. Armoured-car regiments in particular developed this instinct through long practice. There were one or two bridges which I tested with my mine detector, and using extreme caution we then pressed on.

There were high mountains to our right as we approached the Gulf of Salerno but we received rather a rude shock at Cetraro where there was an American outpost who asked us for our dog-tags. Having identified ourselves he asked, 'Does the Eighth Army always send a flock of journalists twenty-four hours ahead of it whenever it makes an advance?' Apparently, Christopher Buckley and his fellow war reporters had slipped the leash and taken off ahead of us; but this was the first time we had learned of it and we felt rather silly. I am not sure whether our headquarters heard through the BBC or ourselves that the road was clear, but certainly this was one up to the press.

I carried out many rather hairy forward recces before we reached Termoli – some into the mountains which were really 'no man's land' until 13 Corps (with brother Rhidian as GSO III) moved up. On approaching San Severo I found three carriers knocked out and no Italians in the fields, so I went back and returned in an hour by which time the Italians had re-emerged. The three were carriers of the Royals, and had been knocked out by an '88' gun on the long road approaching the town. It was obviously quite safe for me to go on and I was given almost a civic welcome. Walker, who liked putting on a cowboy act, had acquired two lots of bandoliers which he wore criss-crossed, and carried a pistol in each hand. I persuaded him to put the pistols away. Everything was thrown at us – flowers and fruit – but I was soon informed that there were a couple of Germans in the hospital in the town. Sensing that they had stayed behind on purpose and could be useful for interrogation, I went to the hospital.

One had gone, but I found the other, who said he would not come out of his room unless he could have my word of honour that he would be protected from the Italians. To loud booing, I brought him out with my hand on his shoulder in true police-fashion and put him on to the front of the jeep where Walker stood with a pistol in each hand, which made the crowd quieten down. As we drove away, the German turned to me and said, 'You know, they were cheering for us yesterday, asking us to come back soon.'

We then went back to Foggia where the SAS were camped on the edge of the town. A menacing paratrooper stopped me and said, 'Where have you been?'

I said, 'San Severo – you can go there now, it is quite safe.' This did not please him or Shan Hackett who was the boss there and heard of the incident later. It was a silly, boastful thing to say to these people, who were running far greater risks than I every day of their lives.

At Foggia we also took part in X Force activities, helping to rescue escaping prisoners from behind the lines, and one or two of my officers went off in boats. When we had reached Termoli there was an escape-route down through Italy for prisoners from camps in the north, and quite a few of them had come out by boat before the system was blown. Dermot Daly and Simon Ramsey (now Lord Dalhousie) sought to get out through Termoli. A heroic American had been operating a radio contact from the top of a mountain but the Germans caught him, so that Dermot and Simon had to do the remainder of the journey on foot. I helped Dermot to get a plane from Foggia which flew them to Algiers.

I had gone up to see the attack on the cemetery north of Termoli and yet again was struck with admiration for the PBI. In open order the Royal Ulster Rifles and the Lancashire Fusiliers were launched across three-quarters of a mile of open ground while they were being shot at from and near a cemetery. The Germans could not have been very good shots because there was a spatter of bullets behind me as I observed the battle from the top storey of a *pension*. Only in the last fifty yards did the men start to run and after a short, fierce battle, rooted out the Germans.

The Eighth Army then set about taking the Sangro while 5 Corps moved into Vasto. My old Dodge van, still working for G (Liaison), was fairly near the Sangro position when it received a direct hit and was brewed up within a few minutes. I grieved over the demise of my old friend which had carried me so gallantly through the desert.

Almost immediately, however, Freddie, Chief of Staff, asked me to see him. He knew that my father had died at the end of 1940 and that my Uncle Bill had recently died, which meant that my colliery at Rhigos would welcome a brief visit. I did not know if this was his real reason, but he immediately handed over a document to me and said, 'Pack up your things, leave them here and take these documents to General Jock Whiteley in Algiers. Then, take them, and whatever else he gives you, back to England. These documents must never leave your person until they are delivered at the War Office.'

I asked what they contained and he said, 'Top secret, I cannot tell you.'

I never liked having this sort of courier job but as the documents were obviously of importance and had to go back to England, I packed within a couple of hours and was on my way to Algiers. I was met by a car and a motorcycle escort, and taken up to Whiteley, who read some of the documents, re-sealed them and gave me some of his own.

They were securely strapped to my vest and I literally wore them. A special flight was then laid on for me to go from Algiers to Marakesh where I spent the night. There was a party going on downstairs and as I was going to my room some French officers asked me if I would like to join in. After a pretty rigorous time in Italy I would have loved to have done so, seeing an abundance of decorative civilian ladies as well as those in uniform. It must have been a wonderful evening judging from the clamour as I confined myself in my locked room and tried to sleep, on my last night after four years abroad.

12

North-West Europe

Early on 6 June 1944 (D-Day), the assault divisions of the British and American liberation armies landed on the coast of Normandy. After being closely involved in preparation of plans for the invasion, Lieutenant-Colonel Harry Llewellyn, commanding a team of liaison officers, arrived in France overnight. Their task was to inform Major General Freddie de Guingand, Montgomery's Chief of Staff at 21 Army Group, of the progress of the battle.

After a two-month struggle the Germans were almost surrounded in the Falaise pocket, from which they escaped across the Seine. Harry Llewellyn's team was in the forefront of the pursuit to Brussels, and kept de Guingand informed during the disastrous Arnhem airborne operation in September and Rundstedt's counter-offensive through the Ardennes in December.

The author returned to England shortly after VE Day in May 1945, when 21 Army Group main headquarters were established in Germany.

From Marrakesh I flew over the Atlantic to Prestwick. Having delivered my documents to the War Office, I then telephoned my mother in Wales. She was astonished to hear my voice. As I had been given a week's leave I was able to be home for Christmas.

I was greeted by a row of flags round our front door, and my dogs, Lancer and Fury, all dressed up in ribbons, on either side of my darling mama. Lancer, who had waited for me under a large nitida bush every day since I had left home four years before, gave me a tremendous welcome and would not leave me for one minute. Fury's reaction was to jump up at me and try to knock me over. It was a wonderful homecoming.

I was then sent a signal by Freddie, telling me to stay in the United Kingdom and to take instructions from the War Office. My suspicions were thus confirmed that my secret documents were connected with Monty's appointment as the Commander of 21 Army Group, charged with the invasion of the mainland of Europe.

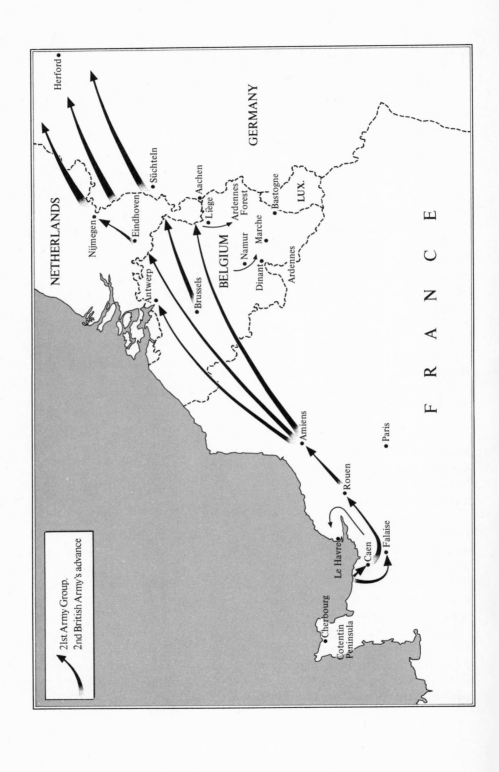

21st Army Group.
2nd British Army's advance

I was told to report to St Paul's School, Hammersmith, and that my job was first to be personal assistant, then military assistant, to Freddie de Guingand who was himself to be Chief of Staff, 21 Army Group. I was told to 'scrub the hutch', so I visited the headquarters and made sure that everything was right for the arrival of my superiors.

On arrival, Freddie confessed that sending me back to see my colliery had only been his own cover plan for me, although he had not had definite news until Christmas Day. He said he wanted somebody he knew to be his assistant. My job would be to sit in his office using his telephone to listen in to and record all telephone conversations. We had a blue light outside our door and when this was lit no one was to come in. There was also a connecting door to Monty's office where Kit Dawnay was to prove his worth as his MA. Freddie promised that when the planning period was over he would return me to my work in G Operations (Liaison).

Various members of Master's team then filtered back. David Belchem became Brigadier General Staff (Operations) and Bill Williams BGS (Intelligence). George Baker came back to be Brigadier (Staff Duties) but said he would serve under Bert Herbert, who was doing the job well. Frank Byers (now Lord) and Gerry Duke also came back immediately; but, most important as far as I was concerned, Sergeant Harwood, Freddie's personal clerk, was there. Few realized what a wonderful contribution this modest and above all super-efficient man made towards winning the war.

I had charge of the Allied Order of Battle map, the key for which was suspended on a chain round my waist. Apart from my main task I had another important function which was to brief some senior officers about our plan. After they had been briefed they were put on the 'X' list.

Another of my jobs was to see Master if Freddie was ever too sick to continue to do his duties properly, and he said he would accept my judgement on this.

He worked me hard! I had to be there by 6.30 a.m. and stayed nearly every evening until anything up to ten o'clock. However, he was generous when it came to a question of visits for me to see Teeny, now a Wren at Westgate, near Southend.

After a month of what could be called a 'whirlwind courtship' I was at Westgate one night when I asked Teeny for a 'Yes' or 'No'. It was

'Yes'. My initial reaction was to feel sick – the shock was greater than anticipated! (I record this with her permission.)

After most of the staff at the Connaught Hotel had inserted me into my beautiful boots (worn with my uniform for the last time) we were married at St Margaret's, Westminster, on 15 April 1944. She promised 'to obey' but has since said she had her fingers crossed! My father-in-law, Vincent de Saumarez (the fifth Baron) had arranged for a carriage and pair of beautiful horses to take us from the church and, as we drove up the Embankment, everybody waved. The wedding reception at the Savoy allowed us to catch up with many of our friends and this day was memorable for two other incidents. I kissed, for the only time in my life, both my old cook, Mrs Stinchcombe and my mother-in-law – a double which has never been repeated.

General Freddie had given me a week's leave for our honeymoon, which was generous as no one was getting much leave at that time. We went to Cauldhame, a beautiful lonely house near Stirling, lent us by Bernard Bruce's mother.

We had a wonderful week. Every night, while Teeny wore in turn the new dresses from her 'bottom drawer' I wore my blue patrols. We dined by candlelight. Teeny is half Swedish and I soon got used to living by candlelight. The house bordered on the moors so we went for long walks; only occasional aircraft reminded us that there was a war on, and the absence of the hustle-and-bustle of the last few years was much welcomed by us both.

On returning from our honeymoon, on the 22 April, we moved down to Portsmouth. I quote from Freddie's book *Operation Victory*: 'At Portsmouth I made a change in MA (Military Assistant). Harry Llewellyn, who had acted in that capacity since my return to England had run the Liaison Staff in Eighth Army and I had promised him that nearer the day I would return him to his old calling. I was sorry to see him go.'

The planning for 'Cossac' the codename for our part of Overlord, the overall invasion, was over. A staff-trained officer was not essential any more and in any case Freddie had the superb Sergeant Harwood. He knew that I felt the urge to go 'swanning' again. This meant that I went back under David Belchem, who had been a good boss in Eighth Army and was the same until the war finished. People who worked for him liked him better than those who had not, and to whom he appeared rather too clever by half. He more than once protected me when I made mistakes and his brilliance, grasp, deduction and memory were only equalled by Bill Williams, and he was surpassed only by Freddie himself.

I had then few contacts with General Freddie; I felt that as GSO I could claim no special relationship with the man to whom I was devoted and without whom Monty could not have achieved what he did. In a rare generous moment, Monty once described him as the best Chief of Staff the British Army ever had. However, he resented my keeping him to his promise and also the fact that I seldom went to see him. I have always believed that when you leave a job you should cut clean and in no way compromise your successor.

Joyfully I went back to my own job, and good regiments were asked to supply officers for my section. I interviewed something like fifty. Unfortunately, many of the people that I chose such as David Burgersh (now Westmorland) and Charles Irwin (now Halifax), were not vouchsafed unto me, but I managed in the end to get a good gang round me. Some of my officers were Americans, and the Unit was fully operational before D Day on 6 June.

Whilst looking through X list (the roll of those who had been briefed), I noticed that Superintendent Curtiss was the only Wren on it. She was the boss-lady at Portsmouth so I went off to see her; I told her that I had just been married to a Wren stationed in Westcliffe-on-Sea, and without Teeny knowing how, she was transferred to Portsmouth as a driver. 'Soupy', as she was affectionately known, also helped other people – even senior officers in the Women's Services had kind hearts.

This change meant that I was able to take a bedroom in the Grand Hotel at Southsea where Teeny and I spent any spare time we had. From then on she thoroughly enjoyed her job of driving admirals around. Although she herself was not able to say, 'Deddy is an Edmiral,' she could in fact claim that the first Baron de Saumarez was Nelson's chief Captain at the battle of the Nile and later, after Nelson's death, commanded the *Victory*. Her father's mother was descended from the Captain Broke who, in command of the *Shannon*, took the *Chesapeake* from the Americans in 1813. This was the last American man o' war to be taken on the high seas before the *Pueblo* was taken in the Gulf of Korea. Hemy's picture of Broke boarding the *Chesapeake* is now in our hall. Teeny, however, had no ambition to be anything but a driver. I did have limited ambitions for her because I would have liked to have been able to introduce her as 'Leading Wren Llewellyn'.

She and I had a fine time with Maza, the only horse to see us through the war. She was brought to a farm near Petersfield where Teeny, as a natural horsewoman, soon learned to jump. She had hunted only once and that was when the meet was at her home, Shrubland Park. On this occasion she and her sister Vicky turned up without hard hats and were sent 'home' by the Master, who was then informed that they were already home.

Our hotel room was on the top floor and the V1s continually flew over our heads or up the Solent. They never disturbed Teeny one little bit but I had always trained myself to look at any potential source of danger, such as an aeroplane, before diving for cover. While she slept I was irresistibly drawn to the window when those ominous missiles were passing by. One could trace their course by the tail flame at night but only once did one come above the hotel, having first appeared to be coming straight at it. I ducked while Teeny slept on.

When I became GSO I Ops (Liaison) the new establishment of my section provided for a clerk, and I was lucky that this coincided with the calling up of Mr Wilkins whom I had inherited when I bought C. L. Clay & Co. in Cardiff Docks in 1936.

He had kept the wagon book which dealt with the movements of and repairs to our 800 Rhigos coal-wagons, before becoming my assistant private secretary. He was a superb keeper of files and a skilled shorthand-typist. I managed to get him straight to G (Liaison) without him having to go on a clerks' course. He arrived at Southwick and there was no better clerk in the headquarters. As a private, and later lance-corporal, he had great presence. As neat in his appearance as he was in his work, he was always called Mr Wilkins by all ranks. He was to stay with me until he retired in 1974. No one was ever better served – and for thirty-eight years!

While we were at Southwick, I twice had to see De Gaulle, and found him austere and unfriendly whereas Leclerc had always been charming, although militarily correct. De Gaulle was a hero-figure and impressively tall. He did not want people to think that he 'owed anyone a bob', and if anyone from my section had to go and see him I sent someone other than myself.

Far different, however, was my encounter with Winston Churchill, our 'glorious' war-winning Prime Minister. Colonel Eric Boles, of the Special Air Service, and I were sent down to meet his railway-coach, to ask him what he wanted to do and help him with transport or warning people to be visited, and so on.

We were first confronted by Captain Lang RN, his personal aide, but had to wait an hour before being ushered in to the great man's presence. Apparently he could not decide what to wear and we learned that this performance took place daily on such visits. He recognized me immediately, in spite of my moustache, from pre-war days at Chartwell and the first thing he did was to offer me a very stiff whisky to drink to old times. I had been teetotal until I was married and had never tried to handle a drink as powerful as the one that I was presented with and obviously had to drink.

Monty had particularly said that he did not want Winston to go to the east of Portsmouth or anywhere near Pluto, the underwater line ready to be laid on the bottom of the channel to supply our troops with the necessary fuel when they landed in Normandy. David Belchem had laid on a road-block somewhere near Southwick to stop him there and prevent him going to Portsmouth and Littlehampton. Winston set off for Southampton with one of my officers, Doug Robertson of the Calgary Highlanders, in the lead. Doug was motoring down a long stretch when he looked behind him to find that the cortège had turned round and was scorching off in the other direction. I alerted headquarters and the decision then became Monty's.

In the event he called off the road-block. He realized that even he was not the immovable object to meet Winston's irresistible force. As a result, Winston was soon parading down the front at Southsea, giving the famous V sign; he turned round, and in no time at all was inspecting Pluto at Littlehampton. Obviously it had been his intention to do this the whole time. In his dealings with Eric Boles and myself and, of course, much higher up with Monty, he had been a naughty boy – a type of youthful intransigence which made him so lovable to most people. Security on Pluto was not in fact breached and no harm was done.

I had been at Chartwell when Winston had had his sixtieth birthday. He thought it was the end of the line for him and was very depressed. History has since proved how wrong he was. He was going seventy when he saw victory in Europe in 1945.

I was now charged with going to France as soon as possible to establish a headquarters site for the main 21 Army Group. I had under me a Colonel Jones, Camp Commandant main army, with

Eric Spencer of 2 TAF (Second Tactical Air Force) to see that his headquarters were put in their proper place near ours. We went over in an MTB towards the evening of D Day, and at first light landed at Arromanches where jeeps were available. Six of us scoured the whole Allied beachhead. Having fully covered the area, I decided on Le Tronquay as this had a good network of roads and lanes around it, plenty of water, and was 'on the copper' (i.e. the electricity and telephone wires passed near the site). It was ideal.

I had been told to see Monty to get his approval before coming back. On arrival at his caravan I found General George Patton sitting on the steps whittling away at a stick.

'Harry! Hullo – how are the horses?' I then asked him if I could help him but he replied, 'Your general won't see me and I am staying here until he comes out.'

This was at the beginning of the problems that arose between Patton, whose army at that time was under Monty's command, and Monty. Patton was always in a hurry and by nature wanted to press on; for example, he wanted to plan that after we reached Paris he would set off for Frankfurt. Asked about his supplies he replied, 'I have a logistics guy to take care of those things.'

I left Patton on the caravan steps and returned an hour later to find a frigid Monty who told me that I had put his main headquarters within range of the enemy cannon. I replied that I doubted if they had a piece far enough forward to sustain fire at our headquarters. This drew a hostile look and a couple of throaty, highly pitched 'Ahs'. We then looked at a map together and he pointed a finger to an area just north-east of Bayeux, saying, 'Why cannot we put the head-quarters there?'

I said, 'Only yesterday, Sir, you were present at the conference which decided that this would be the Field Maintenance Centre.'

A few more throaty 'Ah's. He pointed to a place further north-west. I said that only yesterday he had decided that that would be the alternative FMC. Obviously this was silly of me but we had been constantly on the move for forty-eight hours and we had done a very thorough recce. I thought he was trying to catch me out.

When I returned with the plan to General Freddie in Portsmouth he was very perturbed. He asked me what I had done to merit Monty's strict instructions that I was not to go to his tactical head-quarters again. I told him what had happened and he gave me a tremendous rocket saying it was not for junior officers to get in the hair of the commanders at such a crucial stage. Of course he was right. Nevertheless I immediately wrote off to Brian Franks, a pre-war friend, to see if I could join the SAS. Such an application was far too late. When I went to Jack Gannon, the military secretary, he told me to calm down, saying it would be impossible to find me a more active role than I already had and that I was in any case too much 'in the know' about future plans. Moreover, Freddie and David Belchem had been extremely good to me and it was really my job to carry on working for them.

I had previously been in charge of the phase line map in Freddie's office in St Pauls, and so knew how the invasion battle was meant to go. Initially, however, our progress was slow round Caen where the British Second Army held most of the German armour. Fighting in the dense *bocage* delayed us, but reaching our targets was helped by the Germans launching a blitz to cut through the Americans at the far end of the bridgehead to the coast, towards Avranches.

Their blitz was a disaster. The Third US Army came round in a big right-hook almost to close the pocket in the Falaise Gap. Many Germans escaped but left behind a vast amount of equipment. Paris was now open and our friend, General Leclerc, was accorded the honour of capturing that beautiful city.

At this time I found I was less able to 'swan' than I had been in the good old Eighth Army days. I had to control and coordinate a team of LOs whose reports kept flooding in to keep Main Army Group very much in touch. Freddie and David seemed satisfied and I was told that I had been awarded the OBE for the hard work of my officers and the battle-pictures painted in our reports. Although Monty made us all cut paperwork to a minimum I had asked that reports should include the reaction of civilians, damage to towns, loss of livestock and condition of roads. In his report Thomas Pink surpassed himself by stating that he was pinned down by enemy fire between two dead cows. He had difficulty in deciding which of the two smelt the worse.

The further TAC headquarters moved away from the main 21 Army Group, the less contact we had. I managed to escape from the responsibility for their vehicles and the 'Monty boys' were run quite independently by Monty himself. A rivalry unfortunately existed which, however, in some ways spurred my people on to greater efforts. I had LOs at each army headquarters, splendid men like Tom Bigland and Ben Hutchings whom I was able to retain. The

163

junior officers were often used on courier work, and a plethora of facts was produced throughout the invasion and all battles up to the closing of the Falaise Gap.

Distinguished Senior officers on the way from or to the battle often worked with me for a few weeks, amongst them Pat Patourel (VC), John Lawson, John Congreve, Bill Fyffe, John Bowlby and so on.

One day I went into a deserted camembert factory, selected a dozen cheeses and sent them to my new father-in-law. A month later he thanked me for 'the camemberts which had walked in that morning.'

When initiating LOs I went over to look at the ever-bustling Americans a few times and observed many battles near Villers-Bocage and later on the way to Vire. I had to show my team what was expected of them. The principle was that they should actually see for themselves, without drawing fire by putting up dust or moving around. No marked maps or notebooks were to be taken into the forward areas and they were to call in at divisional or brigade headquarters on their way back to exchange information. The communications of the armoured-car units were uniformly good, but our infantry battalions' radio links often failed.

As soon as the Germans were in full retreat towards the Seine it was all go. Now there was a race to cross the great river. A few warcorrespondents and I crossed the lowest Bailey bridge and were about the first to arrive in Rouen. I had been asked to check out the Nazi SS Headquarters which already the locals had started to loot. At least they had made sure that the place was not mined so we had a good look through the establishment.

The situation was now fluid and we occasionally passed a few groups of apparently unguarded German prisoners by the side of the road. I had been told to establish the main army headquarters at Amiens and had with me again Colonel Jones and Eric Spencer of 2 TAF. Naturally we put up at the best hotel, but the following morning David Belchem sent me a signal to press on to Brussels to establish our headquarters there. I quote from Freddie's book, *Generals at War*:

During the great advance to Brussels and the Dutch border, Llewellyn and his party moved with the Guards Armoured Division, which was leading Dempsey's spearhead. He arrived in time to take part in the hectic festivities that took place in the Belgian capital. It must have been a memorable experience, for the people went quite mad with joy, and the celebrations started as the enemy were still leaving the city . . .

Harry Llewellyn carried out his task with great efficiency. He claimed, in the name of Army Group Headquarters, the buildings that had just been vacated by the German High Command. There was, of course, no official hand-over in the terms of King's Regulations!

In fact it was not all that easy to take La Résidence in the Rue de la Loi as the local authorities were trying to move in at the same time. I told them that if they interfered not only would my King be displeased but so would General Eisenhower and, even more fearsome, the great Montgomery himself. We took possession only just in time as looting had already started. As we were entering one of the larger rooms they were removing a rather nice painting which I made them put back; I was subsequently most interested to learn that this picture had given Freddie, to whom we had allocated the room, much delight. The colour-blind Freddie recorded:

When I arrived in Brussels I was shown up to my office. What riveted my attention was a picture which I took to be a Parisian boulevard in the spring. It had the composition of a Renoir. It affected me profoundly. I never forgot this occasion and whenever I felt depressed or downhearted, I turned in my chair and looked up at the picture, to experience a return of my faith in ultimate victory.

Nearby I took over another house which I renamed 'The Maison Liaison' for my greatly enlarged staff. This was run by three Russians, who had been working for the German TODT Organization which had been building the Western Wall, and whom we had acquired in Amiens. My gentlemen were looked after by gentlemen-drivers, who now required gentlemen to look after them – and these Russian gentlemen filled the bill. They were splendid, and were soon called Omsk, Tomsk and Minsk.

Since we always held three times as many people as we were entitled to it was no great problem to dress my Russians up in British uniforms, with the head-badge of a Swan which had been accepted as the insignia for my section. All our vehicles had this stamped on them. When Tomsk collected his army boots, however, he found them too small but could not make anyone understand his problem. So, dressed in his uniform and his cap, he ran barefoot into the headquarters, only to be accosted on the bottom floor by General Meade Dennis, Monty's gunner adviser, who had come back with us from the Eighth Army. Confronted by a British soldier carrying his boots, General Meade asked him, 'What the hell are you doing?' to which the excited Tomsk replied rapidly in Russian. No one could understand him so he suddenly bolted from this confrontation with the General, still carrying his boots, flew up to my office, and burst in through the door, pursued by two clerks. A message went back to Meade, who had ridden in the first race I ever won, the Tredegar Point-to-Point Open Race, on Pentyrch. He was pacified when he learned that Tomsk was one of 'Harry's boys'.

Omsk, Tomsk and Minsk had beautiful voices. Lady (Edith) Kemsley, a great family friend of pre-war days, very soon appeared and stayed with Maori Cunningham in the Avenue Louise. I asked her to dinner at Maison Liaison. It was a five-course affair and I brought in a Belgian chef from the Villa Loraine to produce the meal. As we had our coffee, the Russians started singing Russian songs from behind a curtain. It was pretty high-class singing and very moving, and we all felt that somehow they were mourning for their country. Edith Kemsley sent me round a dozen bottles of Bollinger the next day. Shortly afterwards she also sent us a vast quantity of war comforts – balaclava helmets, gloves, scarves, socks, etc. – which equipped my section for the rest of the war. These had been produced by the *Daily Sketch* Comforts Fund.

After a breather, 30 Corps set off on 17 September up the Eindhoven road in an attempt to link up with the British Airborne Division; this was landing north-west of Arnhem with the object of capturing the bridges over the Dutch Rhine at Arnhem and the River Waal at Nijmegen. Although Ben Hutchings was officially covering Jorrocks (General Horrocks) and his 12 Corps, I went down to see them off. There was a tremendous clatter but after a tough start the Guards Division passed on with great dash. I wondered then if they would get to the bridges soon enough to reach the 1st Airborne Division – in the event the outcome was tragic.

Monty had always been accused of going too slowly; now he was blamed for taking too much of a risk. However, the decision whether or not to go, after information had come through two days beforehand that two Panzer divisions were present, was in fact made by General 'Boy' Browning. He was the immaculate battle-proven Commander of 1st Airborne Division; his troops were straining at the leash – too brave and no doubt impatient at the passive role they were playing

166

in Britain. But for the presence of these two German Panzer divisions, the plan would have worked. At 21 Army Group their presence was clearly marked on the map in my information room and was held to be ominous. It might be argued that Monty or Miles Dempsey could have stopped the operation. Years later, the latter told me that he took the chief blame; perhaps this was a little too characteristic of that modest and delightful man.

Some time earlier, Tommy Bullitt, star of the Americans in my section, had been sent off to inspect Breendonk. This was the SS camp near Antwerp, and the first such torture-chamber and human abattoir to fall into our hands. I sent his report to David who passed it to Freddie, Monty, the War Office and then Churchill, who sent Duncan Sandys out to examine the place. The forerunner of Belsen, Auschwitz, and Dachau, Breendonk was now being used to house captured SS; Duncan Sandys had it closed down.

When we reached Brussels, we found that signals units had been scattered around the Stockel racecourse. Encouraged by Tommy Bullitt, and the Baron 'Zizi' Leclercq of the Belgian Jockey Club, I persuaded General 'Slap' White to move his signallers out; in return for which Baron Zizi arranged that all members of the Allied forces would have their racing free until the end of hostilities. Tommy rode work most mornings and competed in 'bumper' races. He was also our advance liaison officer during the Ardennes campaign, a week before Christmas.

In effect the Allied Armies were now caught with their trousers down. For some time very little information concerning the enemy had been coming in from the area south of the Roer Dam. I went to David Belchem on 15 December and pointed this out, adding that our experience had often shown that 'no news was bad news'. He agreed so I sent off Tommy Bullitt to Bastogne to find out what First US Army thought about this 'blind spot'. Colonel Robinson, Bradley's LO at our headquarters, was also told of our nagging doubt. David said he would give me his telephone number when he was off-duty and I stressed the importance of my LOs doing the same.

The Germans had, in fact, stealthily built up the Fifth and Sixth Panzer Armies and had imposed the strictest wireless silence. When they attacked on 16 December, thick fog covered the Ardennes and we did not know where their leading troops were. Freddie was fog-bound on leave in England, but David Belchem acted quickly. Philip (Lord) Hardwick already had his SAS squadron at instant readiness.

My officers were each allotted a bridge over the Meuse; with an SAS armed jeep they each set off through the thick fog. By first light each LO reported that no Germans had reached any bridge. It was a great feat for Bernard Van Cutsem, later the successful trainer, to find his way through the fog and traffic to reach five miles beyond the bridge at Liège.

Early on 17 December, Tommy Bullitt telephoned from Namur to say that ten miles from March on the road to Bastogne he had been confronted by a Tiger tank. He and his driver had jumped from his jeep and dived behind a pigsty. The Tiger blew both jeep and pigsty to pieces with high-explosive shells, by which time Tommy had escaped into the thick woodland behind; he then walked for seventeen miles before getting a lift back to Namur.

This was the first recorded contact between 21 Army Group and the enemy in that area. It appeared there was nothing between the German spearhead and the bridge over the River Meuse at Dinant, from which the next day a few German motorcyclists were seen. I told Tommy to come back to Brussels, made out his report and, after a couple of hours, we set off together back through Namur. We had difficulty at road-blocks where we had to establish our identity, as many German parachutists had been dropped, some wearing US uniforms. Near Spa, fifty US troops had had their uniforms removed before being shot.

First we tried to reach March but the enemy was holding it while their thrust line had turned south-west through Leignon towards Dinant. As we motored back to Ciney, the 2nd US Armoured Division from Hodges' First Army suddenly appeared; this was a fantastically efficient, warlike unit 'on the prod' – the opposite to the US troops sent to Gafsa in Tunisia. As they arrived they were hull-down to units of Roscoe Harvey's 29th Armoured Brigade which had been refitting before being called forward to the battle. We first told the US tank-men, then motored over to the British and informed them that the German tanks were to their right near Leignon. Tommy and I returned to Brussels and learned the following morning that they had brewed up eighty-two German tanks. The German tanks had, in fact, run out of fuel, and so ended Rundstedt's Ardennes offensive of which the objectives had been Brussels and Antwerp.

Monty was in good form throughout this battle. He was reported as saying that he wanted the Germans to get as far as Quatre Bras, so he could win the war at the second Battle of Waterloo.

A few weeks later, General Omar Bradley decorated me with the US Legion of Merit, saying as he did so: 'Colonel Robinson has told me about your section's activities and I am delighted to give you this personally.' The citation was signed by President Theodore Roosevelt. Poor Tommy was given nothing!

I took the next headquarters recce to the lunatic asylum at Suchteln. Whilst there I was told to take the headquarter recce to Herford but found there was no room for us so I pushed on to Bad Oeynhausen where we arrived in the dark. Our vehicles laagered in the main square while I moved into a nearby hotel overlooking our camp for the night. During the night I heard troops passing and on looking out of the window saw a German unit pussyfooting past the hotel. Fortunately everyone kept quiet and no harm was done. Our main headquarters eventually moved to Bad Oeynhausen (Bad O) as recommended by me, by which time I had returned home.

I had been asked if I would like my name put forward as Brigadier Allied Forces Liaison as Chris Peto was at that time anxious to get back to parliamentary duties; but I said I would like to get back to my bride of one year, my business – and of course my horses! I turned down an immediate 'B' release (offered for business reasons), and was then given an immediate 'A' release – much better as it meant a set of plain clothes and some cash!

Operations now being over and operational liaison as such ended, my section was due to be disbanded and was 'wound up'. I went home on the aeroplane that followed Freddie; but not before he had called in a small group of about a dozen officers who had been in his team in the desert and north-west Europe, to say goodbye – and, at the end, a barely audible 'Thank you, gentlemen.' Such was our respect, admiration and affection for our boss that not one of us could say a word as we left.

Part Three
Post-War Activities

13   Back to Horses – and Coal

During the winter of 1945–46 I managed to buy a beautiful, small Elizabethan house called Gobion Manor, five miles east of Abergavenny, and we were to have ten happy years there. When David arrived in 1946 on 2 April, and Roddy on 9 October 1947, we were cramped for room but we managed surprisingly well. The house was standing on about two acres of land so I had to lease fields for turning the horses out and for training the show jumpers.

At the back of the house I built eight boxes and a saddle-room. This dealt fairly adequately with our requirements for hunting during the winter, hunter chasers in the spring and show jumpers in the summer. I also erected a large oblong schooling-lane which proved invaluable for making jumpers.

I was well placed too as far as business was concerned. When I returned home in May 1945, my office at C. L. Clay & Co. was only an hour away in Cardiff docks; it took me about the same time to reach my colliery at Rhigos in the Glynneath Valleys via the Heads of the Valleys road.

I enjoyed seeing all my business friends again, but my visits to Rhigos colliery stood out. Each time I went there it was with a feeling of adventure as we were developing the Peacock and Yard seams, which were proving profitable. My Uncle Bill (known as 'W.M.'), who had died in 1944, had improved every aspect of this colliery, which consisted of four drifts going into the northern outcrop of the South Wales coalfield. By developing work on the lower seams we were producing a 'bastard' anthracite which was very much in demand all over the world, and the profits started to come in.

I was most grateful to Uncle Bill, whose gold cuff-links I still wear almost daily. As a family we loved him. He was a first-class shot, but basically he was a foxhunting man. He was Master of the Bwllfa Hounds which he ran at his own expense for twenty-three seasons and at times had a hundred couple in kennel at Nantmelyn. Before the war he had hunted his huge country – from the Brecknock Beacons to the sea at Margam – six days a week. In order to do this he had established kennels also at Glyncorrwg. Uncle Bill had re-established the Welsh Hound Stud Book with his friend Willy Rees, Master of the Pantyscallog. Without doubt he was the inspiration of the Banwen Miners' Hunt in their post-war years.

He was immensely popular with all the men and time and again he would see to it that the hounds were in the vicinity of one of the collieries around 2.30 p.m. when the morning shift was coming up and the afternoon shift was going in.

For no personal reward my uncle had kept a very tight control at the colliery while I was serving abroad. Some people had said, 'Let's keep our most profitable seams until after the war'; but he refused to do this as our policy had been to put our best foot forward. In fact this had paid off because we were already developing our most profitable seams. During the war the company made a small profit which enabled it to cover the debenture charges and to contribute to the sinking fund. It meant that I was able to redeem them all soon after the war.

Thus without encumbrance I owned the Rhigos Colliery and C. L. Clay & Co., Coal Exporters, and seemed well set for the future. In the years ending 31 December 1945/46 we made £111,000 and £120,000 profit respectively and were going on to better things with plans to plough all our profits back, when the Socialist Government came to power in 1945. Sadly, the two years 1945 and 1946 qualified for the Cripps Levy, and after I had paid pretty stiff income tax, the 'special contribution', as Sir Stafford called it, obliged me to cough up £85,000, leaving me practically no financial reward for two successful trading years.

The Socialist Party had expressed 'the will of the people' and dispossessed me of what was to turn out to be a substantial profit-maker for them—legalized daylight robbery! Naturally, I felt this was unfair because I had taken risks, worked hard, and with the help of Arthur Lewis, our Managing Director, had built up a really good business. I had a wonderful team. We had not had any stoppage at the colliery itself as every one of my thousand men knew that he could approach me personally. I had become fond of so many of the employees over the ten years, and it meant that my business career had come to a full stop – worrying for a newly married man starting to raise a family.

174

I was so frustrated by all this that I even thought of taking up a political career. But I rightly decided against it. Apart from the Wavertree by-election in 1935 when I canvassed for Randolph Churchill, I have seldom involved myself in politics. It is not my scene. I had been a Liberal at Cambridge but soon became a staunch Conservative. At elections I had made only a couple of speeches to small audiences in halls at Caerphilly, where one man kept interrupting with questions like, 'What about the old age pensioners? What about the Means Test?' and so on. Eventually my chairman lost control and shouted at him. 'I have had enough of you, you Caerphilly bastard!' 'Ah,' replied the man, 'I knew I'd have you in the end – I do come from Maes-y-Cymmer!' This was the next-door village!

After the war Jim Thomas, who had been First Lord of the Admiralty and was our Chairman on Television Wales and the West, became Lord Cilcennin and gave up his seat for Hereford. David Gibson-Watt stood in his place in the 1960 Election. Robin Day was his nearest rival as a Liberal and I was asked to climb on David's wagon in the market-place at Hereford. He had won gallantry awards and I emphasized how good he had been as a soldier. Unfortunately I had seen rather more in North Africa of David Watts-Russell. I kept on referring to David Gibson-Watt as David Watts-Russell. After repeating myself several times, in spite of kicks from Jim Cilcennin, a loud voice from the back of the market place shouted, 'Get back on your 'orse.' David's majority was reduced from 10,000 to 2000 and he swore he would only employ professional politicians in future!

My offer to help was again taken up in the 1973 Election when I considered myself to be an expert on the Eurodollar and international finance generally.

Unfortunately, there was little interest in my carefully prepared speech when I toured Merioneth. My audience of six in Towyn dwindled to two and the other four became bored and went off to have a swim. In Dyffryn I had the slow hand-clap from two ladies from Bradford when I said I could not guarantee that Enoch Powell would become Chancellor of the Exchequer.

I had some success in the main square at Dolgellau when, loud-hailer in hand, I found only a handful of Conservative supporters there. I turned the instrument up to its maximum volume and welcomed what I termed 'this vast throng' in a voice that must have been heard all over the town. Gradually, people emerged from the shops and came down the street, so that by the end of my speech,

175

which had nothing at all in it about international finance, there must have been a thousand people there, I was able, quite truthfully, to boast that local interest in the Conservative cause had recently increased a hundredfold. Half of my speech consisted of Welsh jokes – the rest was taken out of a little blue book which outlined the aims and objects of the party. This was my only political success.

It seems to me that alone among the European countries, we are rich in coal, gas and oil, and when the average Briton works hard enough he deserves the life-style he covets, instead of trying to survive on national largesse he will be able to regain his self-esteem. The Tories must be right when condemning maximum reward for minimum effort – but there is no instant remedy for the *maladie Anglaise*. Thank heaven we have a superb Civil Service which succeeds in righting successively rocking boats.

We need more than two main parties and coalitions would provide governments which would have well balanced ideas and avoid committing themselves zealously to extremist policies. The Trades Unions are now such vital component members of our society that they should not be permitted to govern the country through the left wing of the Socialist party.

It must be quite obvious why I would make a poor party politician. I have been totally non-political in my public jobs and have found my bosses of both parties fair and reasonable, and enjoyable to work with.

Those were happy days after the war. The horses that I had bought cheaply at Newmarket had been sold, mostly because they could not remain in training as there were no feed-coupons available for horses that had not been placed as two-year-olds. These were kept on one of the farms at Rhigos in a large twenty-acre field, well-fenced by discarded wire haulage-cables, and with an old shed which gave the animals shelter.

Any oats left by the pit-ponies, of which I had 120, had been swept out and put on the muck-heap. Dai Jones, the head ostler, collected all those sweepings for me and fed them instead to the horses who, as a result, looked nearly as fat as the pit-ponies themselves. Amongst them were such well-bred horses as Bay Marble, by Donatello, Fair Times by Fair Trial, and Sunstone by Solario. These aristocrats literally lived on the crumbs from the pit-ponies' table in those days.

Cooper was not happy as a bailiff at the Llanyravon farm, which

I sold. Compulsory purchase would have applied had I not done so. Then Cooper went as head lad to Tom Hanbury, who trained some nice horses; he worked there for ten years before retirement and eventually went back to join his family in Weymouth where he was 'pot-man' in the Black Horse.

Tom and I used to go and see him sometimes and went down when he was very ill in hospital. He was very pleased to see us and said 'Goodbye, Master Harry,' and 'Goodbye, Captain.' We had his bed moved so that he could look out over the lovely countryside that he so loved. Finally he just put his index finger to his forehead as he always used to do when he saluted us, and a couple of days later he died. He was a marvellous man; much of the fun I have had is largely due to him and I know that Tom and his family gave him a happy time and a good job.

In 1946 George Legge, who had been my father's stud groom and who, on my father's death in 1941, had left to look after the horses at Hancocks' Brewery, came back to me. I was delighted to put him in charge of the racehorses as he had been a superb feeder, and in his late fifties was still a good horseman. For five years he turned out my horses beautifully and his feeding improved their performance.

Once established in Gobion we soon had five horses in training, but I was unable to ride them in 1946 as I could not do less than fourteen stone. Tom Hanbury rode for me and won the open race at the Berkeley Hunt Point-to-Point on Bay Marble. I realized I had a very good horse again so set about getting off my weight, which meant running every day, dieting strictly and cutting down on liquid. I took too little liquid and had some bleeding from the kidneys which was frightening. I then went off to see Dr Nander at St Briavels, on the Wye; he was an Edinburgh-trained Indian who was a brilliant diagnostic. He told me to increase my liquid and gave me some thyroid pills which helped me to keep losing weight.

I managed to buy back Bachelor's Gown, who had won the Cheltenham Grand Annual Chase for me in 1938. Ridden by Tom Hanbury, he won the open race at the South Hereford point-to-point. I often hunted him with the Beaufort and the Duchess of Beaufort referred to him as my 'Munnings' horse.

At this point I will outline my post-war racing activities before returning to my main concern, show jumping.

By 1947 I was able to do twelve stone and the first horse I rode was Bay Marble at Manchester where he very easily won the John Peel Cup with its beautiful solid-silver trophy, later to be stolen from Llanvair. Later that year I leased State Control, a six-year-old gelding bought for fifty pounds in Hereford market by my neighbour Tom Jenkins. He had been a moderate point-to-pointer but in 1948 he won the Foxhunter's at Cheltenham for me amongst other races, while Bay Marble won the United Hunts Steeplechase. I am told this was the only time that the 'Hunter Double' has ever been achieved by the same rider and, on this occasion, by the trainer as well. Now the United Hunts Chase is held at the April meeting so the record is likely to remain.

State Control was nearly brought down early on in the Foxhunter's. We were twenty lengths behind coming down the hill at the back of the stands, but he stayed on well to go into the last fence three lengths behind the leader, Mighty Fine. I had my whip out before jumping the fence and was forced to ride at it as if it had not been there. Fortunately I met the fence right and jumped past Mighty Fine to lead by two lengths and held this advantage to the finish.

State Control was made 5 to 2 against favourite for the Liverpool Foxhunter's which was then over the full four-and-a-half-mile Grand National course. He gave me a superb ride in the front group all the way. After the Canal Turn second time round I could not get anyone to come with me, and was ten lengths ahead with a double handful coming to the fifth fence from home. He met it a bit wide but I let him put in a short one. He hit the solid plain fence halfway up, turned right over, just missed me and broke his back. Tom Jenkins came down before he was destroyed. It was a pitiful sight seeing that splendid animal trying to get on his feet. I make no excuses to anyone who saw two grown men in tears. We loved that horse and admired him for his fantastic guts. He always drove forward – no need ever to kick on. Why should a horse want to serve his master so selflessly? In this case he gave his life.

Later, before my weight began to get the better of me again, I rode my last winner under National Hunt Rules when David Wills's King Karl won the Hunter Chase in March at Chepstow in 1948 by fifteen lengths. I rode him twice in the following year for Andrew Hartington (now the Duke of Devonshire), on the last occasion being beaten by a short head by fellow show jumper George Hobbs, on Waymark, at Wincanton.

Probably the best steeplechase horse I ever rode was Lord Stalbridge's Red April (by April the Fifth); I rode him in my last race under Rules at Fontwell Park on 23 March 1949. Fighting Line, ridden by Atty Corbett (Chief Scout Lord Rowallan's son) and Red April came to the last fence together. We met it very wide but as I felt I had the race won I let him put in a short one. He was a specialist at standing back and really hurdling fences but not at putting in 'short ones'. He could never have been a horse for Aintree, although he was tremendous on the Park tracks and was third in the 1946 Gold Cup. He hit the fence hard and lost three or four lengths. We were catching Fighting Line fast and were beaten only by a neck. I had only just been able to do 12 stone 12 pounds so I retired from the fray after this thrilling ride and then concentrated on show jumping, a sport in which the rider's weight is less important.

Since I stopped riding under Rules in 1949 I have never trained horses for other people to ride except for River Picnic in 1954. He was seventeen hands, long-legged and 'tubed', so made a noise. Under George's care and good feeding he improved greatly. I ran him in a race and he did no good. I had him tubed again and he then won at the Llangibby point-to-point by a distance, after which he won six races off the reel. As a result of his open race wins, the National Hunt Committee brought in a rule stopping a horse from winning more than three open races a year at point-to-points. Wyndham James rode him in all his races but he was not good enough as a hunter and I sold him.

Having been made a member of the National Hunt Committee in 1946, and a Steward from 1948 to 1950, I wish I had been able to spend more time steeplechasing. Apart from occasionally stewarding at Cheltenham I have taken a close interest in Chepstow, of which I have been a director and steward since 1950. I like to think that by introducing the two sponsored races – the TWW Champion Novice Steeplechase over two and a half miles, and the Rhymney Breweries Steeplechase – I helped to start off this pattern of sponsored races which George Francis, the Managing Director, and John Hughes, the Clerk of the Course, have pursued under the very able chairmanship of Colonel Roddy Hill. It has been a happy show which has gone extraordinarily well. During 1978 and 1979 we had bad luck with many meetings abandoned because of bad weather but we have survived and will survive. It is a well-appointed racecourse and its members are well-served.

Meanwhile, the versatile Maza was taken round some of the show-rings in South Wales where she proved herself well up to international standard; she was then eighteen. When I took her down to a competition at Christchurch, for which the then huge sum of two hundred pounds was offered as first prize, she was second, and later became a member of the first British civilian team ever to travel abroad when she went to Nice and Rome in April 1947. She was the best speed horse we had at the time on the team and on two occasions finished third in Nice.

It was Maza who really established me in show jumping after the war and inspired me to acquire Kilgeddin, which I bought for the princely sum of two hundred pounds from Father McCarthy who jumped him as Kilbragh in Ireland. He was a 16.3 powerful dark-brown gelding, probably the boldest I have ever met. He was keen, so keen that he used to rush at his fences and then 'dingle dangle'. He would not fold his front legs and consistently had one or two slats off under our old rules. I used to jump him a lot over parallel bars to make him use his head more instead of sticking it straight up in the air, and also to make him round his back. Much of the time I rode him in a hackamore – a bitless bridle.

Although Maza was my number one horse, I took Kilgeddin to the Victory Show at the White City in 1946, which was the first big show organized by Mike Ansell. Much to everybody's surprise, including my own, he won the Victory Cup with Douglas Bunn second on Rahin. From then on he was recognized as a team horse but more of Kilgeddin later.

Meanwhile, although Maza had gone through the 1947 season well, her age was beginning to tell and I withdrew her from show-jumping in 1948. She proved a supreme hunter and Teeny was hard to catch out hunting. I am afraid Teeny was much too brave which resulted subsequently in her breaking so many bones that she must be acknowledged as the female rival of Terry Biddlecombe. The published picture of his skeleton, marking his innumerable breaks in red, shows that he had over two hundred injuries.

The Puissance which Kilgeddin won in Rome, in 1947, was the first event won abroad after the war by a civilian. I rode in the green coat of the Talybont Hunt of which my brother Rhys and my sister Betty had been joint-Masters. There was tremendous feeling about this green coat; some people thought it was not smart enough. But it was very smart. It was made by 'Huntsman' but sadly someone objected to the colour. The English are great traditionalists – it had to be a red coat, and so it was for me thereafter.

On our way back from Rome we went by train as far as Nice where I had left my pre-war Jaguar car in which I had travelled out with Teeny. We arrived in Paris rather late in the afternoon and were lucky to get in the King George V Hotel. On our way to our room we noticed a poster which said, 'Come to see International Show Jumpers at Le Palais des Sports'. It was rather like a circus poster. We thought this might be fun. We did not know what to expect, so changed quickly and went off to the Palais des Sports.

We saw a horse show taking place in what was best known as a cycle-track in the winter. It was not a proper arena, but there was a white ribbon round the ring and people could walk between the ribbon and the seats. There was plenty of tan down and the horses seemed to respect the white ribbon. They had speed competitions over the fences and we were quite amazed at the spectacle. One of the stars was a coloured rider on a beautiful big chestnut horse called Roi Réné. Then there were our friends d'Oriola and d'Orgeix, who had been in Nice in the French team and were going like bombs. It was a thoroughly enjoyable show and very exciting.

We travelled to England the next day and as soon as I got home I told Mike Ansell about it. I gave him full details and said that he should come and see the next show as it was just the sort of thing we should put on at a London exhibition hall.

Mike and Victoria Ansell came over to the show in Paris in October 1948, after the Olympic Games. Ruby Holland-Martin and I gave Mike a birthday party – he has since returned our hospitality a thousandfold.

That is actually how the Horse of the Year started. Mike talked it over with Tony Collins in the first place and planned with him to have a fully-balanced show with jumping and show classes – this is, in fact, the formula that still exists. It was dreamt up by Mike Ansell and Tony Collins, then received enthusiastic support from Colonel Vivian 'Pudding' Williams, who was a very distinguished supporter of all our horse sports in those early days.

'Pudding' was a delightful person to deal with and his contribution to all horse events, especially dressage, was immense. He was the father of Dorian Williams, famous broadcaster and now Chairman of the British Horse Society.

The show was to be staged at Harringay and Mike soon organized supporters who became foundation members and had to guarantee

£100 each. Of those foundation members only 'Pug' Whitehead and I are now alive. Mike delights in recalling that at the first Horse of the Year Show in September, 1949, there were only £27 worth of advance bookings at the start of the proceedings!

Another important event in the post-war history of horse shows was connected with the Royal International Horse Show. In 1945, Guy Cubitt and Stanley Palmer, representing the Institute of the Horse, and myself representing show jumping and the syndicate which in fact owned the Horse Show, went to the White City. I had been delegated by Mike Ansell, and we were to meet Frank Gentle and Wally Ayres of the Greyhound Racing Association with a view to moving the International Horse Show from Olympia to the White City.

I should add that early in the war Ruby Holland-Martin had formed a syndicate of nine to buy the International Horse Show. We purchased its goodwill, some of the uniforms that were available, the jumps and various other accoutrements.

As a result of our meeting we decided that the Royal International Horse Show should take place at the White City. As far as the nine owners were concerned, of whom I believe there are only five left now, we had the right to a box for life. But more important, Colonel Cubitt, Stanley Palmer and I decided to go to the White City basically because there was infinitely more room and many more spectators could be accommodated. It was to prove a wise decision.

14   Foxhunter

After the success of Kilgeddin in winning the Premier Campidoglio in Rome, the Puissance, I felt I now had an opportunity to enter the field of international show jumping with the best horse that I could afford to buy.

The vesting date when the Government took over the collieries, which included my Rhigos Colliery, was 1 January 1947. Although I then knew that in four or five years I would be getting some money, I realized I could not get into business again until I had the cash. This meant that I would have a few years in which I would be able to go show jumping and have enough time to dedicate myself to that pursuit.

The chief difficulty was to find the best possible horse. So I examined, very carefully, the records of *every* single registered show jumper on file at the offices of the British Show Jumping Association at 43 Montague Square. I reduced the number of potential animals to about twelve and then made further inquiries about this short-list. As a result, two horses stood out. One was a roan animal called Victory Boy and the other was Foxhunter. So I went to see both of them jump.

I was particularly impressed with Foxhunter when I saw him jump at the Bath and West show near Cheltenham where he was placed and later when he went to Blackpool. I felt instantly that there was a feeling of friendship between us. I noted that when I went up to him he examined me carefully; possibly he was just looking for sugar, but he had those charming, kind eyes which were always a feature of the horse. He was, quite obviously, a gentle, affectionate animal and I felt a little flattered by the interest he showed in me.

He was a big, upstanding rich golden-bay gelding, 16.3½ hands with dark points and a white sock on his near hind leg. He had rather a long, straight head and there was no dish below the eyes. He was

naturally overbent and his ears were constantly pricked, giving him
a cheerful, happy expression.

Having thus examined him and having had the advice of many
people I determined I would try to buy him but I first discovered
what the price would be. I can now disclose it was £1500, which was
quite a lot of money for a show jumper in those days. But I knew the
horse would be worth that. He was obviously a great athlete and well
up to my weight, and apart from his temperament out of the ring I
could see that he was basically cooperative when ridden in the ring
by his owner, Norman Holmes.

I rang up two or three knowledgeable people. One of them was
Fred Foster, who said I must be mad to buy a lame horse. I had
noticed that he had been shod with very thin iron and that possibly
he was footsore as he had flat, sensitive feet and clearly did not relish
jumping on the hard going. When he walked he looked as if he was
lame in both his forelegs, but I felt sure this was because of the way
in which he had been shod. I did not have a ride on him but sent up
Harry Steel-Bodger, the father of the England rugby footballer,
Micky, to examine him. I could not have chosen a more knowledgeable or wise man.

He had the horse out when he went to see him at Norman's farm
at Thrussington, in the Quorn 'Friday' country just north of Leicester. He appeared not to be quite sound, but then he was not quite
lame but just shuffled along. He was examined for heart, eyes, lungs
– everything – and Harry Steel-Bodger asked if he could go for a ride
on him. So he took him up the road which passed the farm and when
he was about half a mile away he started to gallop him down the
hard road. He then walked him home, but even at the trot he did not
seem any lamer or more footsore so Harry went in and had lunch
with Norman Holmes. Just before he left he said he wanted to see
the horse trot out again. In fact it was to see if he was any worse
after being 'hammered on the hard, high road'. In the event he was
no worse, so he sent me a telegram to say that the horse was sound.
I immediately telephoned Norman Holmes, said I would buy the
horse, and put a cheque in the post.

I was now the owner of this magnificent animal and will outline his
background.

He was born on the Corporation Farm at Hethel near Norwich.
His dam was Catcall, a throughbred Clydesdale cross. Her sire, Step

Forward, was successful on the flat and over hurdles. Catcall was a brilliant hunter, credited with having plenty of sense in a trappy corner when hunting with the Norwich Staghounds.

Foxhunter's breeder, Mrs Millard, recalls that his sire, Erehwemos ('Somewhere' spelt the wrong way round), who also had a gentle and friendly temperament, was a beautiful dappled bay in brilliant spring coat when he came to call on Catcall in his capacity as a Hunters Improvement Society premium stallion. Mrs Millard said: 'He got his marvellous friendliness from his sire and grandmother Kitty – a very active pure Clydesdale mare.'

She records he was foaled on the evening of St George's Day on 23 April 1940. On that day, according to the following day's edition of *The Times*, Sir John Simon, Chancellor of the Exchequer, introduced purchase tax and 2½d. postage for the first time. A penny a pint was put on beer and Queen Mary was inspecting the FANYS at Salisbury. There was a violent earthquake in Eastern Germany; but in a quiet stockyard at the Corporation Farm, 'Catcall gave birth to a good colt', as recorded by Knyvet Millard.

He was given the odd name of 'Eelskin' but this was changed when Norman Holmes bought him as a four-year-old. In Norfolk barns they used to keep a 'throssle-board' at the stable-door entrance to stop straw spilling outwards, and within a day or two Foxhunter was nimbly jumping over this. He was an active foal with long, spindly legs. He was impudent with the other animals. As a yearling he was playing with a cart mare over a gate when he was caught by the ear, resulting in a distinctive split which he kept throughout his life. He also took a delight in jumping a white 'gash' or stream in the bottom meadow of the farm and had the habit of jumping over the road fence, or into any field he chose; he would gallop round it and then jump back to join his friends. He obviously 'jumped for joy'. Man-made barriers or fences meant little to him.

In January 1944, Norman Holmes met Knyvet Millard in the Corn Exchange at Norwich. They record the deal was made in the bus after Norman had seen the horse and they then 'wet the bargain'. The kindly influence of the horse-loving Millards had a lasting effect on Foxhunter. They gave him, to a great extent, his cheerful view of life and helped him to tackle any task with the confidence and know-ledge that man was there to help him.

Norman took him to the Manor Farm at Thrussington, just north of Leicester, and changed his name from 'Eelskin' to 'Foxhunter', which proves that changing names does not bring bad luck. Norman told me: 'He was the kindest and most knowing horse I have ever handled. Within four days I had longed him over a three-foot-six-inch pole. I was driving him round the farm in long reins, jumping him over every fence or gate. Within a fortnight of his arrival I backed him and rode him six miles to the meet of the Quorn Hounds at Six Mills. Later, I gave George Barker, the huntsman, a lead over a four-foot-six-inch post-and-rails.'

Oscar Wilde described foxhunting as 'the unspeakable in full pursuit of the uneatable' but Norman Holmes says, 'I was intoxicated with the performance of this young horse out hunting.'

The following December an army lorry ran into his hindquarters which damaged his back tendon and joint. He was given a year's rest and it was not until Foxhunter died that the extent of the damage was realized. His skeleton now rests next to Hermit's in the Royal Veterinary College and this shows that the appendage to which the muscles over his quarters should have been attached was completely removed. Vets wonder how the muscles ever managed to re-attach themselves to what was almost a flat bone.

The affection that Norman felt for this young horse and his constant care and attention undoubtedly saved his life. It took fifteen months of patient nursing before he went hunting again with the Quorn when he again proved to be brilliant.

At Newark Show he was second in a strong middleweight hunter class before having one fence down in a novice jumping class the same day. He then won first prize at Peterborough and the Beaufort Hunt Show. Then he went to Newark and won the open jumping before I bought him.

Other experts like Ted Williams, who lived in the area, wanted to buy him but his stilted action in front, and the fact that he had been lame for over a year, stopped them from making an offer.

For many years to come this unique animal ran our lives.

I picked up Foxhunter from Norman Holmes' farm at Thrussington and took him straight to the Royal Show at Lincoln.

When I first rode him in the collecting-ring I was amazed at what a short-striding horse he was and how, when he jumped, he seemed to make no effort and just picked his legs up. It was as if he was in a hurry to get back again to the ground, without over-exerting himself by pushing his body up into the air more than he needed. I very nearly did not jump him in the open class but did so and had four fences down.

I was appalled, particularly as there seemed to be little contact between my brain and his. He wanted to jump everything in his own way. I found that he had his tongue over the bit and therefore had to be ridden on the very lightest of pressures – if any pressure at all. Norman rode long, had a very secure seat and had only the lightest touch on his mouth, leaving a good deal to the horse who adjusted his own stride. That system would not have worked out in international classes where the optimum effort is often required at large fences.

The winner of this competition was Victory Boy, who had been number two on my short list – a touch of irony.

When I brought Foxhunter home I tried everything that I could to get him to accept the bit above his tongue and for some time did his early schooling in a plain snaffle with two sideshanks to stop the bit going through his mouth. I also put a crossed noseband on him to stop him opening his mouth and kept the bit rather higher than was usual. However, when we started jumping this only lasted for a few minutes, then his tongue was back over the bit. I eventually acquired a snaffle bit with a 'gate' in it. This gate was much too big and too high, so I had it cut down to about one inch long and five-eighths of an inch wide and inserted it into a piece of rubber tube one and a half inches long. I also restricted the movement of the gate so that it would not damage the roof of his mouth nor dig into the sides underneath his teeth. I then put an ordinary drop noseband on him and within a day or two he was accepting this kind of bit on top of his tongue; he stopped trying to curl it up because he knew he could not get it back over the bit.

Basically, the importance of a bit is that it should be comfortable in a horse's mouth and accepted by him as the link with the rider's brain, down through his arms to the reins, to the horse's mouth and then up to the horse's brain. This meant, therefore, that a new system of communication had to be set up between Foxhunter and his rider. Being the trusting, placid, cooperative horse that he was, he soon responded and this then enabled me to proceed with his ground-training.

Every day I kept at him, asking for obedience. Never once did either of us get angry with the other; but I soon realized that to keep his head in the right place and have him accept about one pound per square inch pressure from me, we had to proceed slowly and for short periods. I was soon able to make him obedient at all paces.

Halfway through his training we went to Ostend and Le Zoute and here he showed that he had exceptional athletic ability. We were placed in some events but were unable to win a competition and we had not, on my part dominance, nor on his part complete obedience.

Nevertheless, we were able to tie with the Swiss for second place in Ostend in the Nations Cup, behind the number one French team. The team then went on to Le Zoute where he was second and fourth. Twice in Le Zoute I was trying to make sharp turns in speed competitions when, instead of turning to the right he got his tongue over the bit and the signals that came through made him go to the left.

I then took him to many local shows but he did no better than second at Bridgend and a third place in the International Show at Newport before winning a competition at Abergavenny. Throughout this period he was being schooled by me every single day for periods up to two hours. The ground was pretty hard so I turned him out on 7 December before sending him to Colonel Joe Dudgeon's establishment at Merville, near Dublin, basically for schooling over banks, and secondly for a course of dressage in the capable hands of Mr McMasters.

Mr McMasters did a marvellous job on him. He was selected as a member of the 1948 Olympic squad and was then sent straight to Aldershot, arriving there at the beginning of March. He had put on a lot of weight and I was thrilled when I rode him. Although I could not make him really extend himself at a trot, he did the remainder of what could be described as dressage up to three-day-event standard with great ease.

What was most evident was that he enjoyed this type of obedience-training. Noticeably he went far freer when people were watching. I always felt that he was a bit of a show-off. When he was being schooled in the big riding-school he would quickly become bored – but not if he had a crowd of admirers. This certainly applied later in life when he was jumping in front of a big crowd. He seemed to sense the occasion and responded to claps and cheers, which he took as much as a pat on the neck from me as signifying the approval of his human friends.

At Aldershot, Joe Dudgeon was in charge and we trained the horses intensively. Kilgeddin had been chosen as well as Foxhunter, so I took both of them on the official Olympic trials at Windsor, Bath and West, and White City when they both went well. We practised over a wide variety of fences and ditches and it was soon evident that Foxhunter was, in terms of being athletic, our best horse, although rather less experienced than the others.

During the whole of this time we were based at Aldershot and I stayed at the Bush Hotel at Farnham. I often used to run the four miles to Aldershot; not only was I in those days a fitness crank but, when I was riding steeplechasing, I had a weight problem, which meant that I had to weigh less than 11 stone 9 pounds stripped.

After being equal-first at the Bath and West trial, it was apparent that Kilgeddin was our second-best horse at that time so I agreed to give him up. He was ridden first by Bobby Hall but went better for Lieutenant-Colonel Henry Nichol, who rode him in the Olympic Games. The huge arena at Wembley Stadium over-impressed Foxhunter and he never went freely enough, hitting four fences to be placed equal-seventh with Kilgeddin, whose impetuosity and strength caused him to hit fences towards the latter part of his round.

The third British horse was Eddie Broad's Monty. Whereas Foxhunter and Kilgeddin had sixteen points each, Monty had thirty-five and a half faults, being given a heroic ride by Lieutenant-Colonel Arthur Carr. In this event the scores of all three horses counted and Arthur was told that whatever happened he had to get round. I look back upon Arthur's determination to fulfil this order as one of the gutsiest performances I have seen in show jumping.

Monty was a horse who shortened when going into fences and would stop at wide obstacles; but after he had refused at the first fence, Arthur drove him round at the cost, of course, of hitting many fences. The result was that the British team, in spite of its high total of sixty-seven and a half faults, won the Bronze Medals, the first to be won by a British team in the Grand Prix des Nations.

There was a water shortage in London at the time which meant that towards the end of the competition the water was turned off, so that the ditches were empty for the second part. An empty ditch will stop many horses whereas one full of water can be jumped with great confidence. They look into an empty ditch as if the devil himself was going to pop out of it. This resulted in the high penalties created throughout; the Mexicans won the team event with thirty-four and a half points, Spain was second with fifty-six and a half points, and Britain third with sixty-seven and a half points.

The Bronze Medals, I believe, put British show jumping firmly on the Olympic map at a time when many people said that this should be a test of only human beings' prowess without involving other mammals to do the main work.

A few days later I took Foxhunter to the International Horse Show at the White City where, for the first time, he showed everyone what a super horse he was. He won the qualifying event for the King George V Gold Cup with two clear rounds – the second one against time – and beating d'Orgeix on Sucre de Pomme by several seconds.

On the following day he won the Gold Cup itself. Foxhunter had certainly arrived.

However, we could only finish third behind the American and Spanish teams. Henry Nichol again rode Kilgeddin in the team event, Ruby Holland-Martin rode my Talycoed – about whom I will say more later; while I rode Billy Llewellin's Night Bird to be third in the *Daily Mail* Cup.

After we had won the King George V Cup (£30 to the winner), the Duke of Beaufort received a telegram from his Majesty which read: 'Very pleased to hear Lieut. Col. Llewellyn has won the cup for Great Britain. Please give him my warmest congratulations.'

The royal family, by their support and interest such as this, have encouraged us to feel that we were jumping for our country. I believe that this was why we have always stressed the importance of sending *teams* abroad and most of us feel that winning international team events is far more important than winning individual events. Sadly, the big money that people jump for nowadays is usually considered more important than the team event. Both owners and riders often try to keep their horses fresh for the big prizes, rather than compete in the team events for which no prize-money is offered. Many of us feel, in these days when it is so expensive to buy and keep horses, that there should be some reward for each owner in a British team.

After Wembley in 1948, the team all jumping in army uniform, we went to Dublin where Foxhunter won the military and civilian competition but was unable to jump the courses, which included banks, with any great freedom or skill. For this reason I rode Kilgeddin in the Aga Khan Cup when we finished second. This was the first of many thoroughly enjoyable visits to Dublin where our hosts and spectators do not care a pin for politics and always give the British team as warm a welcome as their own.

We finished the season by going to Paris in October where Foxhunter was second in three competitions – the speed event, won by Sucre de Pomme, the high jump and the Puissance. Teams of two jumped for the International Trophy which Foxhunter won, with Ruby Holland-Martin on High Jinks.

In 1948 I took Maza to some hunter trials for Teeny to ride. She won the ladies' class at the Golden Valley hunter trials and later was first, with Monty, in the pairs event at the North Hereford Hunt hunter trials.

We went round together at quite a pace, both horses jumping beautifully and as we were coming into the last fence Teeny said to me, 'Don't you think it would be rather nice to hold hands?' It was a tender thought, but I replied, rather ungallantly, 'Let's hold hands after the fence.'

This we did as we passed the post and of course we were delighted to be placed first. This was a great farewell for Maza – in her twentieth year to be retired on a victory. She was a really brilliant all-rounder; I only wish that three-day-eventing had taken place before the war and had been open to civilians, because having been a champion hack, good across country, and an international-class show jumper, this type of competition would have suited her well.

Early in 1947 I had bought a nice big quality Irish hunter which I called Talycoed. We won classes at Bridgend, the Royal Welsh and Kington, and then in the following year, 1948, I lent him to the three-day-event team as he was obviously a potential cross-country horse. He did not make the team but he won the show jumping sections at Hastings, Imber Court and the New Forest trials. I then had him back and lent him to Ruby Holland-Martin who was very successful with him. He rode him for the British team in Rotterdam and at the White City where he was placed. Then I lent him to Ruby again and he won on him in Cologne, and brought him on to Paris where he was third a couple of times, jumping six foot six inches in the high jump.

I then had a marvellous season's hunting on him. He was a wonderful 'visiting' horse and I took him to Leicestershire where he was absolutely in his element. On one occasion Teeny came with me but rode a hireling which unfortunately gave her rather a nasty fall and she could not remember what happened during the rest of the day.

At that time she was not accustomed to foxhunting. The Lady Allendale of the day cried 'Ware harrow!' Instead of avoiding it Teeny gingerly picked her way through the harrow and on arriving safely at the other side, turned to Lady Allendale with a sweet smile and said, 'Thank you very much!'

During the 1948 winter I also bought from Northern Ireland a horse which I called Strathmore. He too was a super hunter and I took him visiting all over the place. He turned out to be a good competition horse for Teeny. In the following year, 1949, she rode him at the White City where she was second in the Princess Elizabeth Cup, dividing Iris Kellett on Rusty and Pat Smythe on Carmena.

I mention these horses because their careers were developing at the same time as Foxhunter was making his mark and they were to play their own important roles in our lives at that time.

Foxhunter started the 1949 season with a great flourish. He won the Grand Prix International in Paris and then the Parcours de Doubles with Monty, who alone won the Prix de Gentlemen. After this we went on to Nice where he won his first big foreign Grand Prix, the Grand Prix de la Ville de Nice. He also won, jointly with Monty, the Grand Prix de France which was a competition in which the scores of both horses were added together.

In Rome, later, he was second in the Puissance but I did not want to push him in the speed classes so early in his career. He jumped a beautiful round in the Victor Ludorum and was placed fourth on time.

Also in Rome I had Kilgeddin, which really meant that half the team belonged to me. I might add that this was quite an expensive item in those days when we had little outside help. Pat Landsberg in his good book, *Foxhunter*, drew attention to the fact that there was no international fund in those days. He said that those riders sufficiently keen had to contribute an unknown sum towards our international prestige. 'Colonel Llewellyn,' he goes on to say, 'upon whom the severest strain was inflicted, for he was almost perpetually on tour, had made it clear that he could no longer afford either the time or the money to satisfy his love for continental tours.'

He said that all the expenses of the visiting team should be paid by the visiting country. 'Foxhunter does attract a considerable public abroad and it hardly seems right that Colonel Llewellyn should, of necessity, have to pay for the privilege of thrilling the crowds on the Continent.'

I do not regret having spent so much on helping to send our teams abroad – the results were worth it. We did have some help from the

BSJA, and under the rules our hosts had to pay for our hotel bills and the expense from the frontier to the show itself and back. This was some contribution, but when you added it up the total actual expenses must have been twice what one was allowed. For instance, later in Nice in 1951, five of the ten horses were mine. They were Foxhunter, Monty, Kilgeddin, Strathmore and Polish-bred Snowdon. Incidentally, Snowdon caught pneumonia and Ivor Reading came out to take him home to Wales. In the devoted way that he has with animals he slept with Snowdon the whole way back to this country where, in the hands of our capable veterinarians his life was saved. He was then exchanged for a horse called St Teilo, about whom more will be said later, and was ridden by young Michael Scudamore who was to win the 1959 Grand National on Oxo.

On leaving Rome, the team went back through Paris and took part in an outdoor show in Le Zoute. The horses were rather tired but Duggie Stewart was able to win the High Jump on tough old Kilgeddin – another great victory for him.

Foxhunter was then taken to the Royal where he won the FEI competition, and also a competition at Lydney; but in the main class Teeny, on Strathmore, beat Foxhunter, Monty, Kilgeddin and such good international horses as Niblick. This was really quite remarkable as she had never jumped a fence until 1944 when Maza had taught her how to do it.

At the White City at the end of July, Foxhunter started off in great form. He was second in the *Country Life* Cup and in the King George V Cup was equal-fourth. However, he was part of the successful British team again in the Prince of Wales Cup. In the next competition he was asked by me to stand off too far at a spread fence and landed in it and hurt himself. It was found in fact that he had some injury to the lumbar regions.

Harry Steel-Bodger took him off to Tamworth. He was kept there for a fortnight, but as a result he had to miss Dublin and Ostend. Monty won four first prizes while Kilgeddin also won four, including the *Daily Mail* Cup for Duggie Stewart. He was also a member of the winning British team for the Prince of Wales Cup.

Strathmore performed very well and was, as I have said, second in the Princess Elizabeth Cup as well as winning the international pairs relay with Kilgeddin.

The team went off to Dublin and I took Monty who was second in the Dublin Committee Cup on the last day. Kilgeddin hurt himself on the second day when colliding with one of the banks which I was trying to jump too boldly and he was lame for the rest of the show. Then we all went off to Ostend and Le Zoute and here Kilgeddin won the first individual in the Prix de Nations; Monty won the Grand Prix d'Ostend and was also first in the Prix Claridge. At Le Zoute, Monty was placed on every occasion but did not win and this applied to Strathmore, but Kilgeddin was first individual in the Prix de Nations. So, even without Foxhunter we were going along quite nicely.

Mike and Victoria Ansell had come with us to Zurich and Geneva and on one occasion I dressed up as a model in one of the shop-window displays, sitting there for half an hour without anyone in fact realizing that I was a dummy. This of course was thoroughly enjoyable to me and eventually I had to laugh and gave the show away. My companions were models of people dressed up in riding clothes and apparently I was so immaculate in those days that they could not tell the difference.

The Nations Cup in Geneva in the Salle des Expositions was a pretty tough affair. Poor Duggie Stewart had broken three ribs in one of the earlier classes and so I had to take over the riding of Kilgeddin which included the Nations Cup. In those days you could ride two horses so I rode Foxhunter and Kilgeddin and we won. Mike Ansell was delighted and I often remember the words of the great man as we went to our rooms at the Richmond Hotel: 'Today, you have struck a blow for Great Britain.'

With those words ringing in my ears I went to my room to be telephoned by Duggie Stewart who said, 'You know, I'm absolutely furious because I really felt that I was fit enough' – he could hardly speak, incidentally – 'but on the other hand, many, many congratulations.'

It was wonderful when one was jumping in teams with people like that and those were marvellous days which I think everyone enjoyed enormously. They may have fun these days, but nobody could have had more fun than we had.

Foxhunter, incidentally, removed the flowers from the hat of the decorative wife of a senior Swiss general, when she presented the prizes – which was amusing for everybody except the general's lady.

I did not take Foxhunter to Nice in April 1950 because I knew he had a hard season ahead, but I did take Monty to Nice, Brussels and

Ghent, where he had a remarkable run, winning six competitions in a row. He won the Prix Buchephale at the end of Nice, then all three competitions in Brussels, and the first two competitions, both speed events, at Ghent. It may surprise British people that Monty had a fan club on the Continent which thought he was a better horse than Foxhunter. Of course he was not, because he could never win the big events like the Puissance as Foxhunter could, but when it came to speed competitions he was unbeatable when at the top of his form, as he then was.

I took Foxhunter out to Lucerne where he had a good show, winning two events including the Grand Prix de la Ville de Lucerne with Craven 'A' second, as well as being part of the winning team in the Nations Cup.

I lent Strathmore to Teeny, and he was second in the ladies' championship behind Michelle Cancre of France. He jumped fairly well in the other competitions, but the classes were really too much against the clock to suit him as he was a very big horse, 17.2 hands, and did not turn quickly.

At Vichy, a little later, Foxhunter was in good form again. He won the Grand Prix de la Compagne during a freak storm. The clouds were being bombarded with silver nitrate which brought down a deluge. Cries of protest from us all went up whenever a gun was fired. He was third, rather unluckily, in the Grand Prix de Vichy. He was winning the event on time, but when jumping over a pole on top of a bank he kicked a sod of turf back from the bank and this dislodged a pole which he had not touched.

Later at the White City, Foxhunter was in tremendous form, winning the Puissance and the King George V Cup, being placed in everything else as well as helping Great Britain to be first again in the Prince of Wales Cup. He then went on to Dublin where he won the first competition. He just cantered round beautifully. I think at that time he was at the zenith of his skill and I was able to place him a long way from each fence. I was paid a fine compliment by Joe Dudgeon who said, 'I see you leave it all to the horse these days!' I could not have been more pleased by that remark. He knew perfectly well that really I was placing him.

Back home at Harringay Foxhunter sustained this terrific form. He won three competitions including the Victor Ludorum at the end, so that 1950 had been a very good season for him.

Now we decided to venture across the Atlantic. Foxhunter was selected for the team to go to the three eastern horse shows – Harrisburg, New York (in the old Madison Square Garden), and the Royal Winter Fair at Toronto.

The horses went on SS *Parthia* while Teeny and I flew to New York. We all went straight to Indian Town Gap which was near Harrisburg, in Pennsylvania. This was an old army camp where the horses were pretty well-housed, whilst we had army huts which were either too hot or too cold. The stoves were always going flat out and one could not open the windows.

Foxhunter and Monty did not need much work after their journey so I left their exercise to the excellent Wendy Jones while Wilf White took charge of the team. Teeny and I went to stay with Tommy Bullitt, my war-time colleague at Oxmoor, near Louisville.

Foxhunter jumped fairly well in every competition at Harrisburg but was only placed. He really did not enjoy himself at all; nor did he like New York where he became quite asthmatic in the stuffy underground stabling in the old Madison Square Garden, so I did not jump him at all for the second half of the show.

Matters were quite different, however, when we went to Toronto, where Foxhunter won three events in the six days to finish on a good note. The American tour had been gay and our hosts spoiled us. Each night after the show there was a party or a ball. All committee members and box-owners at New York and Toronto wore tails or hunt-coats – *and* silk toppers during the evening performance. They still maintain this high standard. To own a box is a status-symbol *plus*.

Foxhunter won the Puissance, after which I only jumped him in one other competition at Nice in April 1951. Rome, however, was one of the shows we enjoyed very much; here, also in 1951, Foxhunter had only to jump the last fence to win the Nations Cup. He put a foot in the water whereupon the Italians shouted 'Bravo' in delight. Hearing the tumult, I politely took my hat off but returned it to my head in time to jump the last fence. This silenced the partisan crowd but soon their hero Piero D'Inzeo came in and jumped a clear round which meant that the Italians just won the Nations Cup.

It was getting dark and the Italian crowd was so thrilled that some of them set their programmes on fire to show their appreciation of their Italian team. The Piazza de Siena was surrounded by a ring of flame, a sight that no one could ever forget.

On the next day the papers were critical of the British Colonel –

didn't the British Colonel know that the spectators were shouting '*aqua*' not '*bravo*'? They described my action as unnecessarily sarcastic. Knowing that it was hoped our presence in Rome would increase the goodwill between the British and Italians I apologized to the Ambassador who in fact was very amused. He reminded me that in the 1940 Rome show, the Italian soldiery were sent to it to applaud the German military riders in the event. They cheered enthusiastically whenever the Germans hit a fence.

I also apologized in a cable to Mike Ansell who replied, 'Do not worry, perfectly all right if you had had your hair cut.' This was a trite answer as I did not have much hair on my head even in those days.

In the remaining days of the show none of the other officers, Spanish, French or Italian, ever saluted me but merely took their hats off when greeting me. Passing back through the customs at Ventimiglia I was greeted by the officers as Colonelo Capello. In Wales this would have been the equivalent of 'Harry the Hat'.

Every year in Rome the riders used to see the Pope. I once complained in *Horse and Hound* that the Pope had kept us waiting two hours for our audience which meant that our riders had little time in which to school their horses. Unfortunately I said that he had been delayed by a 'paid audience' which made the Vatican very angry. In fact, the hotels sold tickets for the audience which were only return bus-tickets, a point which was not made clear – since then it has been.

When I arrived at the show in the following year I was met by Count Pecori, the Chief of Protocol, who said that the Vatican had been upset so I apologized. A few days later the team presented itself for an early audience with the Holy Father. Five minutes before the Pope was due to arrive a small cardinal with his red cloak flowing all over the place rushed in and asked for Colonel Llewellyn. Enrico Luling pointed me out, whereupon he said, 'We are very sorry but his Holiness is going to be a little late.'

Enrico's knees gave way and he had to sit down because he had never heard of anybody having an apology from the Pope. Shortly afterwards, his Holiness appeared, made a beeline for me, and I discovered that he knew a lot about show jumping. He said that as a cardinal he had visited every horse show at the Piazza de Siena.

The riders always appreciated these audiences very much whether they were Catholics or not. The Popes to whom we were presented always commanded great respect and affection.

Foxhunter won a competition in Rome and was placed in others but he was lazy and I felt that he was getting rather bored. Kilgeddin had been ridden by Ruby Holland-Martin to win the touch-and-out competition but on the next day he slipped up outside his stable, fell and broke his femur in three places. This meant that this great horse had to be destroyed, which made us all very sad.

He was insured for £1000, and in due course this was the sum I collected for his death, but not before the agent for an insurance company had approached me and said that if I played the game really properly I would be able to get at least £10,000 of which they would like to take a chunk. If, for instance, I said that the authorities at the barracks were negligent; if I said that there was a loss of profit as far as jumping that particular horse was concerned, and so on. I told him that I had had the horse insured for £1000 and I was not going to put forward any other claims. Whereupon the agent looked at me in despair and said, 'I always knew that the British were bad businessmen.'

During the show Monty was staying at the Embassy in Rome where a party was given for the British team and I asked the Ambassador to make it quite clear to Monty that it was not being given for him, which he did. When we arrived, Monty recognized me. He twice said, 'All roads lead to Rome, Llewellyn.'

I had of course, not made 'Harry' after I told him in Sicily that I would never become a regular soldier. He went out of his way now to be as pleasant as he could to me. Teeny, being tactful, told him that Monty had been named after him, which in fact he had not; but he was in good form. I discovered later that he had arrived with fifty signed postcards of himself, which he had given around to all the staff, which to me seemed rather extraordinary. Anyway, it was a good party and the little man was in good heart. We talked a bit about the war – particularly what fun it had been in the desert. I think he enjoyed that desert much more than he had the rest of it because he was always squabbling with his American colleagues.

Just after that I went to a dinner in London which was organized by Tom Bigland, a member of my liaison team in north-west Europe. He had been attached to 21 Army Group TAC headquarters for some time. At this meeting Monty was again friendly, having just come back from Russia where he had had a meeting with Zhukov. He was telling us what had happened when he came out with a typical Monty 'groaner'. He said, 'Well, General Zhukov had been talking and we had all been listening to him and were very interested in what he said, and we were there, after all, to hear what he had to say – well, then I had one or two words to say and suddenly, everything stopped. There was absolute quiet, absolute quiet, and I realized, of course, that they were not really wanting to listen to Zhukov, they were listening to me, to me!'

Again, that was just the sort of buffoonery he occasionally practised. I was pleased that my last two contacts with him were so congenial.

My Austin horse-box went from Rome to Madrid without any mechanical faults of any kind. In Spain Foxhunter was second in two classes and fourth in another. Teeny rode Foxhunter in one class when she was again second in the ladies' championship, this time to Pat Smythe, and he went very well for her. She was the only other person ever to ride him in an international show. Ruby won the Grand Prix on Aherlow – our main triumph.

Madrid was much liked by the riders. After schooling we all swam at the Campo del Mar and the night life was gay – delicious food, *flamenco* singing and endless dancing. When I came home I practised Foxhunter round local shows but tried to keep him much fresher than he had been so that by the time that the White City came he was in his best form. In fact he won on every single day and every competition for which he was entered, except the King George V Cup in which he was second.

The last competition he won was the *Daily Mail* Cup in which we beat Pat Smythe by one tenth of a second – she has never forgiven me. Great Britain again took the Prince of Wales Cup, the team event, and this really was one of Foxhunter's best shows ever.

We then took him to Dublin where he won a competition and we again won the Aga Khan Cup before going to Ostend where he won two competitions. Monty won the other two, so that between them they won all the competitions in Ostend except for the Consolation for which they were not qualified.

People were often kind to me about these successes, but on this super animal any fault would have been mine. I felt I did not deserve congratulations as it was all too easy. It was only later, on less good horses, that I learned it could sometimes be unbelievably difficult.

We went on to Rotterdam where Foxhunter won the Grand Prix and Britain the team event. More than satisfied, I then did not jump him at all until I took him to Harringay where he won two events.

At this point Madame Tussauds decided to put a model of me in their waxworks exhibition, so we asked many Harringay riders to come to the official function that took place to celebrate my addition to the collection. I went down there half an hour beforehand and with the cooperation of the staff removed the model of me and sat myself right at the back of a group of models which included Jack Hobbs. When the assembled show jumpers all appeared, there I was sitting quietly just as I had done in Zurich. Nobody noticed at all until somebody said something ridiculous, whereupon I smiled, and Madame Roblin, owner of Arlequin 'D' suddenly screamed, '*C'est lui, c'est lui-même!*' – whereupon the whole charade came to an end.

My entry to Madame Tussauds was better than my exit. Years later they wrote me a nice letter asking would I mind if my model was removed. Of course I agreed. Marilyn Monroe and I were melted down together and apparently our wax was put into the model of Hanratty, the A1 murderer!

We next went off to Zurich. Foxhunter was my first horse and Mary Whitehead's Nobbler my second horse. We won a competition on the first day on Nobbler, but later as I was going round a corner rather quickly the matting, which was covering the ice in this big hall, slipped, and Foxhunter and I had a nasty fall. This meant that he could not compete for the rest of the show and it also put me out as well because that night I had quite a bad internal haemorrhage.

In fact we went on to Geneva where I was only able to ride Foxhunter twice. He was second on the first day before having a bad fall at the bank. He landed all in a heap. People who saw him get up said that he did so very gingerly and, with me lying literally between his forelegs, he refused to move. I am quite convinced this was because he did not want to hurt me and everybody who saw it thought the same thing. He just stood there until I got up. I hurt my side again and believing that there was something dreadfully wrong I quietly went back to the Red Cross Hospital in Zurich where a Dr Wolf put me on a scanner and had a look at my innards. This was all done through the kindness of Steinmann who was the head of the Swiss team. The diagnosis was that I had pulled the diaphragm which is the division between the stomach and the chest cavity, and it had become displaced off my lower left rib.

Dr Wolf gave me some Lactiol pills and put me on a milk diet. Although I had discomfort and indeed pain for some weeks, this problem was soon behind me. I told no one about it at the time.

200

Even now, I have a thickening on my rib as apparently the damage was quite extensive.

Foxhunter was then retired for the season after having so far had a very good one. I wish of course that I had not taken him to Switzerland where he had these two accidents; for with a horse like that one does not really want to have accidents at all if he is to be kept at his best.

Foxhunter was sent to Aldershot in April 1952 to be trained by Jack Talbot-Ponsonby in company with Aherlow, Nizefela and Craven 'A'. These were the outstanding horses at that time, although Tankard had flattered, ridden by the always cheerful Brian Butler whom everybody liked so much.

Jack, in those days, left a great deal of training to the riders. The Olympic team went to the Dublin spring show where Foxhunter won three events, and we had trial practices at the Aldershot and Windsor shows.

A vital part of the 1952 Olympic training was at the Lucerne Horse Show which had a reputation for excellent courses. Foxhunter was at his best again and won every single event in which he took part except the last event which was a handicap. As he had won on all the previous days he was set to jump six inches higher than anybody else in a speed competition.

One of these events was the Grand Prix de la Ville de Lucerne which he won for the second time and therefore this meant that we won that event outright, because Lucerne and Geneva alternated in those years. After tackling four barrages we reached the final one. Foxhunter's only rival was Discutido, the Argentinian horse ridden by Jorge Canaves. This Grand Prix had turned, as was the custom, into a Puissance over two big fences. Having jumped a six-foot wall we then had to jump a triple bar, seven feet wide and five feet six inches high, only seven and a half strides away. When you jumped the big straight wall and landed steeply, you ran out of impulsion or forward movement. You then had to kick very hard to jump this spread fence. If you met it right it was fine, but in fact the distance on the first occasion proved wrong for us both. Foxhunter and Discutido had only just made it. When the wall went higher I calculated that the triple bar was almost unjumpable. Therefore, after jumping the wall well we then took a circle to get a really good run and jumped the big spread fence which, by this time, was five feet nine

inches high and seven feet wide. In was a difficult fence on its own
without being related to the previous fence.

Of course, this put poor Jorge into a terrible position. Morally, he
had to 'have a go' to win the class. He jumped the wall and then
immediately attacked the triple bar but, as I forecast, he could not
jump this big spread, even on a wonderful horse like Discutido. He
met it wide and landed in the middle of it. He smashed the fence to
smithereens to incur four faults. Foxhunter for his circle had three
faults – and the Grand Prix!

The reception that I was given was mixed. The riders thought it
was a great feat of arms but the public mainly thought I had been
just rather too cunning. The papers next day referred to me as the
Konkursfuchs (Concours-Fox). The Argentinians had excellent horses,
but as regimes were established and then toppled they had different
riders each year, according to which side was in gaol or not.

We had a lively show with marvellous people taking part. One
party finished up with a challenge between Mary Whitehead (number
two only to Pat Smythe) and Brian Butler as to who could swim the
best, so they jumped into Lake Lucerne and swam from the *Schweiz-
erhof* in the town all the way to the Palace Hotel in the early hours
of the morning. The ball had been started off by Herr Lustenberger,
the President, borrowing the band's drum which we then rolled down
the main street, hitting it all the way with the show jumpers coming
along behind singing 'Glory, Glory, Hallelujah', and other hymns;
'Silent Night' was one of them! They were great days and we were
all friends. We played hard as well as tried hard; things were taken
very seriously as far as the competitions were concerned.

Not such a jolly time was had when we went on to Cologne in 1952
when there was an upset between Oscar Christi, who was second in
the individual in the Olympic Games, and Carlos Figueroa, of Spain.
They had fallen out over a certain lady and it came to fisticuffs
coming home from one dance so they agreed, in the true Spanish
fashion, to settle it the following day. They were to go out a couple
of miles, strip to the waist, take a big stone in one hand and batter
each other until one had submitted or apologized. This was an absurd
thing to happen in the middle of a horse-show and they were both
friends of mine so I said, 'In the name of our friendship will you
please shake hands and make friends?' They shook hands immediately – both were relieved and delighted. Then I suggested they
tossed up for the lady, so they flipped a coin. Carlos won, but by
that time the lady had disappeared!

By the time it came to competing in the Helsinki Olympic Games we had some very fit, fresh horses. Our team included Wilf White (Nizefela), Colonel Duggie Stewart (Alerlow), and Peter Robeson (Craven 'A') reserve, and Foxhunter and myself. Teeny came in the York aeroplane with me and the horses, and we all had a smooth flight from Blackbush Aerodrome to Helsinki.

On arrival there our horses were sent to good, spacious stabling and everything went well except that Foxhunter suddenly decided that he did not like the Finnish oats and hay. Knowing that he had become rather a finnicky feeder we had brought our own Spillers nuts with us. Unfortunately we had not been allowed to get these off the aeroplane so Mike Ansell, Teeny and I went out to the airport saying that we wanted to look at the aircraft. While Teeny and Mike kept the guards busy, I managed to get hold of the nuts and put them in the car which we had parked nearby, without the guards seeing us. We went straight back to Foxhunter and he ate up like a good boy.

The training facilities were good and all went well until the competition itself. It was a muggy day and I rather unwisely did not give Foxhunter much exercise. I wanted him to keep fresh. My feeling in those days was that he always jumped better when he was fresh; but there is a great difference between being fresh and not being warmed up enough and I am afraid that I was guilty of the latter. I only jumped him over about three fences and did very little work with him. I ought really to have got him stoked up, and should have realized that I was going into a strange arena – which would make any horse look about him when he got there.

This is exactly what happened when I entered the ring. Our first round ended in near disaster. He started peeping and looking all over the place, convinced that every fence concealed the devil, and this got him into serious trouble. The course was not big and he only had two fences down in the first two-thirds of it in spite of being sticky. Six fences from home there was a fairly difficult double – two pairs of parallel bars both five feet high and about twenty-four feet apart. Foxhunter jumped these so carefully that instead of putting one non-jumping stride in the middle he put in two. He did not touch a fence which shows what a wonderful athlete he was. Then we went into the wall, at which he had a good stride, but again he put in a short one; he did not stop but just bucked over it and nearly sent me flying. There is a photograph of me with one hand on the horse's knee and

I firmly believe that had my spur not been hooked under his saddle I would have fallen off.

Anyway, he had plenty of sense as usual, and stood still while I got back into the saddle. I circled, which of course was another three faults, and rushed him over the last few fences, hitting one of them, which meant that altogether I had three fences down; one circle – three faults; and 1¼ time-faults; a total of 16¼ faults.

This was disastrous, and meant that our team was standing sixth after the first round so we all went to lunch feeling wretched. I decided that I would go back and rest myself and my shattered nerves. I think that my greatest ever triumph was that I did actually manage to sleep for an hour.

Foxhunter, meanwhile, had also lain down. People had tried to disturb him but George stood guard over him. I got on him a lot earlier before the next round and gave him a thorough preparation. He was really worked up so that when he entered the ring he was a' raring to go and there was no question of his feeling tired because I was at him the whole time. I had him under a lot of pressure and he was what they call 'full of impulsion' – the desire to go forward. He jumped a most beautiful round with great ease which, of course, he would have done in the morning as well if only I had stoked him up enough. But there we were – isn't it – as we say in Wales.

This last clear round, fortunately, meant that our team was placed first. The British Team had 40¾ points, the Chilean team 45¾ points and the Americans who were third, 52½ points.

The result was thrilling for the British and it was a moving moment when they played 'God Save the Queen' for the first time in the Helsinki stadium. Perhaps we could say that he who wins the last battle wins the war. Anyway, it was a particularly satisfying event to have won – the only one won by Great Britain and of course very good for show-jumping because it drew attention to the fact that we had a team that could win Gold Medals. This did more than anything, I think, to raise funds in the years to come.

I might add that although Foxhunter jumped a clear round at the end, when you put together the faults over both rounds the best horse in the team was Nizefela who had only had eight faults including four at the water. In the jump-off he was placed fourth. To this day I believe he jumped the water but the two soldiers, untrained judges, at that fence disagreed. One said he had hit it; the other said he had not. I think to this day that Wilf White is the unluckiest man I have ever known not to have won an individual Gold Medal, as he would have done had he jumped that water. It was not considered 'British' to complain and so no objection was lodged, though in fact I doubt if such an objection would have been upheld.

There followed great celebrations. Foxhunter and I got much more praise than we deserved because Nizefela had had eight faults and Aherlow, ridden by Duggie Stewart, a twelve and a four, making a total of sixteen; while Foxhunter was actually the worst in the team with 16¾ and then a zero. In fact he had the highest faults and did the least well, but such is the way of the press that we got all the praise as a result of his last round, a point that I repeatedly made to everybody.

It really was the most rewarding effort – the whole thing – and we were delighted. Winston Churchill sent me a telegram – 'Warmest Congratulations' – and the Duke of Beaufort had messages from HM the Queen and Queen Mary, who sent congratulations to us.

Asked why the British had succeeded, I replied, 'Because we have the best hay and the best oats and the best horses.'

15   Goodbye to Foxhunter

The 1952 Olympic Games saw the climax to Foxhunter's show jumping career. I went next to Dublin where I rode The Monarch for Bill Hanson and won a couple of events; I then rode him again at the White City. Here I was, in fact, second in the King George V Cup when I should easily have won it. I do not know what happened but I completely misjudged him at the water and the fence that followed, which allowed my Spanish friend, Carlos Figueroa, to win it on his wonderful little mare, Gracieux.

He was so excited that first of all he kissed the mare, then his groom, then everyone in sight, and eventually climbed on top of The Monarch and kissed me – in front of the television cameras! He is a wonderful chap and a good friend of mine to this day.

In order to keep Foxhunter fresh I took him foxhunting quite a lot over the winter of 1952–53. Then during the 1953 season I went to one or two local shows to get him going again.

I jumped him in the National Championship at Shrewsbury for the first time for four years which he won with the only clear round – no problem. He had come to the stage where he was jumping very cleanly, much more cleanly than he ever had done. He was a horse who, particularly when he first started off, used to 'rub' nearly all the first few fences, but in 1953 he stopped this habit and was jumping nearly every fence clean. In other words he had had one or two accidents and he was more careful. He had lost just a little bit of his 'dash'. I knew this so that I felt a bit apprehensive and was already planning on retiring him at the end of the year.

However, I was able to produce him at the White City show in tremendous form where he helped to win the Prince of Wales Cup for the fifth time in succession and, very gratifyingly, won the King George V Cup for the third time.

Before the qualifying event a cloud had burst over the White City and the arena was flooded with rain about two hours before the

206

competition. 'Master' – the Duke of Beaufort – wanted to know whether he had to put the Princess Royal off or not. Mike Ansell did not want to abandon it so asked me, 'Do you think we ought to stop it?' I replied, 'For heaven's sake, don't do that – this is just what we call lovely Welsh weather!'

In fact, it was just the going that Foxhunter loved jumping in. He had big, flat feet and did not mind jumping at all when it was wet. Mike put the performance off for an hour while his regiment, the 'Skins' band played 'Singing in the Rain'.

Foxhunter won the 'qualifier' and then the Gold Cup the next night with the only clear round – in front of the Queen. It was a great triumph for Foxhunter who became the only horse to win the competition three times. The BSJA gave me a wonderful little gold replica of the trophy – St George slaying the dragon – to be stolen from Llanvair twenty years later.

He was then equal first in the Puissance. We had reached the height of nearly seven feet, with three of us left in the contest – Uruguay (Piero D'Inzeo of Italy), Galway Boy (Alan Oliver) and myself. We all agreed that it was not quite fair to the horses to jump those very big fences in such bad going; the judges agreed, so we willingly divided. The public gave us a tremendous cheer showing how wonderful it is on these occasions.

Nowadays I do not like to see the Puissance, but when I was competing I was much keener on it. I suppose as you grow older you soften a little, but when I was show jumping it was my speciality, in spite of my fourteen stone stripped. Including that night, Foxhunter won the Puissance four times at the White City.

He won or was equal-first in all his classes and to complete the 'grand slam' he was called in first on the final day in the *Daily Mail* Cup. It was then reported to the judges that a small brick had been displaced off a one-foot-high 'take-off' wall and we were relegated to second place. Someone said it was 'a good thing that the foreigners should win something.' My reply was unprintable – especially as the winner was Merano, ridden by Raimondo D'Inzeo of Italy, who virtually took over from Foxhunter and was the world's biggest winner from 1954 on for several years.

At Harringay in early October, Foxhunter started well. He won on the first two nights; and then in the Leading Show Jumper of the Year class itself, he got stuck in the middle of a fence when he was, in fact, winning the competition. That did not help his general attitude. At the same show I asked him to stand off too far from a fence,

207

at which he fell and knocked my teeth about. It would have been nice to have been the Show Jumper of the Year as well as winning the National Championship and the King George V Cup in the same year. I remember Seamus Hayes coming to me before the show and saying to me, 'I believe Foxhunter is better now than he ever was.' I made it clear to him that I thought the horse was jumping too clean. I think he thought I was mad.

Looking back, that fall heralded Foxhunter's decline.

I should not have sent him to America. Pat Smythe and Bill Hanson came with me and were as keen as I was to go. I took a mare called Lady Jane which I had bought. She was too small for me but a marvellously plucky little mare and we went off first of all to Harrisburg where she won a competition.

Unfortunately, Foxhunter was completely unnerved by what had happened at Harringay and on two occasions he was refused out of the ring, so I stopped jumping him. He did not like the rounded walls they had over there. They were like coloured mounds and he hated those. He would jump them outside but not in the ring, so I did not jump him for the second half of the show. What was most noticeable about that Harrisburg show was that this was the time when Pat 'arrived' as our number one on Prince Hal, on whom she won five competitions which was a tremendous performance.

We went on to New York and Foxhunter had recovered a bit by then; in fact on the second night we won the Drake Memorial, a major competition. After that I could see he was tiring so I withdrew him from the last two competitions. This was just part of the horse's outlook at that time – he was getting tired and that really should have been the signal for me to withdraw him from competitions. But we were stuck in America and I had to take him on to Toronto where I did not want to jump him. The authorities understood but asked me to jump him in the minor classes. He was placed in two competitions and improved there as there was much more freedom for him. Now he was obviously enjoying himself and became fitter and fresher. He jumped in the Nations Cup where he put in two clear rounds which meant that we won it. This proved to be his last Nations Cup – two clear rounds for a British victory.

I then brought him home and took him hunting. He went brilliantly and I thought that he had regained his zest so I took him to Rome the next year, but when he arrived he said, 'Oh, my God – all these bloody show jumps again – and no hounds!' and I could see from the beginning that he was not going to do any good.

On the first day I jumped a slow clear round on him. On the second day there was a small 'trick' double with fences only fourteen feet apart. I went into it at a fair pace to 'pop' it (i.e. in and out without a non-jumping stride) but Foxhunter decided he would try to jump them in one which was, of course, impossible. He landed with his face on the wall and cut his lip badly and I am afraid that was the end.

I took him back to the Pastrengo barracks and schooled him over very small obstacles but he made it clear he was fed up, so I withdrew him from the rest of the competitions and I did not jump him again that year. I was no longer jumping him for the team, I had given up the captaincy, and my main responsibility was now to my friend. There was no pressure from my Italian colleagues in the show directorate – true horse-lovers.

In 1953 Teeny and I were asked to judge at the Sydney Show in Australia, where they had never jumped under FEI Rules before. I requisitioned a wagon which I called the 'Jury Box', and a hand-bell from the porter at the Australia Hotel where we were staying. This acted as the starting-bell.

Their good horses were accustomed to jumping four-foot upright fences but by the end of the week I had persuaded them to jump spread fences, particularly of the 'staircase' type and these horses were soon jumping over five-foot courses with ease. Good courses make good horses.

Teeny judged many of the other classes such as 'boys over brush', ladies' hacks and riding-ponies. On one occasion she had a class of 120 people; she divided them into four rings, selecting the best four out of each ring to help final placings and this she did in forty minutes. Having painted so well, she has a very quick eye for a horse and made few mistakes. On this occasion, her most difficult task was to judge the best-turned-out girl. This had created tremendous rivalry and she finally had to make up her mind as to whether the girl having the best pair of boots was more impressive than a beautiful girl in a Huntsman's coat with boots only halfway up her legs. She chose the latter but has never agreed to judge any such class since that day.

Our trip consisted largely of lectures and judging at shows in Melbourne and Perth. We flew from the Cocos Island to Mauritius, a distance of 10,000 miles – the longest passenger haul at that time. We judged in Mauritius where Sir Flinders Blood was Governor, before staying with Freddie de Guingand in Johannesburg. Always up to some trick or other, he formed a bogus guard-of-honour as we arrived but looked after us very well while I judged at the Inanda show.

We then went to Bulawayo, Salisbury and Rhodesia. We stayed with General Sir John Kennedy, the Governor who was in fact appointed to the job when Freddie had been the runner-up. We stayed in Inyanga with Colonel Sonny Webb with whom I had been shooting twenty-one years earlier.

Next we flew to Kenya, then unfortunately in the middle of the Mau-Mau problems. We had dinner with Brigadier and Mrs Allen in the Stanley Hotel and everyone in the restaurant was armed. After one night I was dispatched to Entebbe to catch a Comet home. In fact we flew home in an old Hermes as the Comet did not turn up. Later it transpired that this was the same aircraft which crashed into the Adriatic with poor Tony Collins on board.

We would not have been offered this world tour by the various equestrian societies had it not been for Foxhunter – my passport then and, in some quarters, ever since.

At the end of 1953, when the Colliery compensation money came through, I bought Llanvair Grange and seventy-five acres around it, and the Pentwyn Farm, Nantyderry, of 170 acres. I acquired as well as some mountain land at Coed Peggy Shams on the Trevethin Mountain, which gave me the right to turn my sheep to the hill. I was kept busy moving into Llanvair and getting the farms going.

Many alterations were carried out. These included the building of two large barns at Pentwyn and three at Llanvair. The former water-garden at Llanvair was changed into sheds at the back of our kitchen garden to house 400 calves and a forty-yard shed was erected. I have never regretted this wise expenditure which nowadays would cost me twenty times as much. I knew that all this would keep me busy but I did not want to feel committed, at the age of forty-two, to a life which consisted only of horses. I have always had a horror of being dependent upon the owners of any horses for my living, and I had no inclination to deal in them. I made a vague effort to start a hunter stud by acquiring blood-relations of Foxhunter, but none of them bred anything of note. I found I was getting too many young animals round me and I was not prepared to set about breaking and training so gave up the project.

Having bought my house and farms I set about buying a business and bought Davies & Co., General Engineers, a 'jobbing' engineering business in Abergavenny. I had some splendid machinists, platers and moulders. Unfortunately the last-named were a dying breed and there were no young men coming along, so I closed the foundry and installed an electroplating plant in it.

Ivor Reading came back to me to manage this branch. He had successfully developed the Montgomery Plating Company in Coventry and threw all his skill and enthusiasm into the job. Sadly, South Wales had not attracted car accessory manufacturers to provide the volume of electroplating needed to make it profitable. We then moved into another shop in an old printing-works nearby and later built a factory at Cwmbran, but the demand was not there in spite of Ivor's great skill and effort; so I closed it down and sold it to Folkes Hefo of Stourbridge, remaining as a director of their South Wales company.

Altogether I made a small profit on electroplating but it did not justify the amount of capital employed in the business. I do not feel inspired to trace in detail the history of Davies & Co. which has cost me an awful lot of money. This company became Davies Engineering and then Davenco Engineering, Ltd, and our years at Abergavenny were reasonably profitable when we were fabricating and machining only. In 1966 we made a good profit and decided to expand the business by building a factory at Ebbw Vale. But after we closed and sold the Abergavenny works for a good profit, we steadily lost money, and it was not until 1977–78 that it turned the corner and started making profits again.

The year 1954, however, was a pretty calamitous year as far as the family was concerned.

We moved into Llanvair on 18 July – my birthday. It was a little larger than the dream-house I had envisaged, but was in a wonderful position with old trees all round it and was situated between the Blorenge mountain and the river Usk two miles away. It has the largest oak, turkey oak and plane trees in Gwent.

One evening I went for a walk through the area we now call the 'arena' which bulldozers had excavated to make a sixty-by-twenty-metre dressage *piste*, as I was beginning to have ambitions for three-day-eventing – if not riding then training one or two horses for it.

Teeny was taking Dai and Roddy to spend their summer holidays near Chichester. She had set off in her Landrover. It was a peaceful evening and the sun was setting when Nanny said the police from Devizes were on the telephone. The question asked was, 'What was the number of your Landrover that was involved in a serious accident near Salisbury?'

This blunt question from a policeman made me realize there had been a terrible accident as they could not even identify the vehicle. He did not know how the occupants were but I managed to contact another policeman who said that my wife had been taken to Salisbury Hospital and my two boys to Odstock near Salisbury. I was told that my wife was seriously injured and also one of the boys, but not which one. On the strength of this report, Nanny and I took off immediately and motored straight down to Salisbury hospital where my poor Teeny was in a dreadful mess, the Landrover having met a lorry on the crown of the road.

She had broken both her jaws, six ribs and, worst of all, dislocated her right leg, breaking her pelvis in the process. She was hardly conscious and on the drip. At that time I do not think she felt too much pain.

I then went to the unit at Odstock and saw the two boys who had bandages all round their heads but seemed, as the young do, remarkably perky and obviously in no danger. They had been very much cut about the face. Roddy had fifty-two stitches and Dai thirty-nine, while Dai had also suffered a spiral fracture of a lower arm.

Over the next two to three days Teeny gradually recovered; as she felt better she was convinced that her children had been killed and this naturally upset her dreadfully. It was vital for her peace of mind that they should be brought to her bedside and for this I have to thank Mr Sheil, a most skilful surgeon who was also a very kind man; it was he who insisted that the children should visit her, which they did after two days. They had recovered their good spirits although still covered with bandages, and having been reassured that they were not in danger, Teeny was much happier and able to endure her own painful wounds.

The injury that caused her the greatest pain initially was the one to her ribs, as she could not breathe without pain. They did a marvellous job on her jaws, replacing the broken bits with the teeth still in them, almost a miracle; but the injury to her pelvis proved serious and she had to have her leg in plaster for six months.

After six weeks we brought her home. She lived in a downstairs room and it was not until the New Year that she was allowed to sit up and then gradually put her feet to the ground. On Christmas Eve the rest of us had had a good hunt with the Monmouthshire. When we returned from the chase with our eyes sparkling, having had a wonderful day, she broke down for the first time.

Everybody who knew her admired the tremendously courageous way in which she faced up to her terrible injuries; but this period of suffering must have stamped itself on her mind because for years she was conscious of it and the pain she had endured. At one time she almost had an obsession and kept the steering-wheel, which she had broken together with her jaws, under her bed, and showed it to visitors.

Up until this time she had been a first-class horsewoman having, as I have recorded, been second in ladies' championships at the White City, Madrid, Paris, Rome, Brussels and Lucerne. She thoroughly enjoyed it but the accident naturally meant that she had to give up riding for some time. When she did start again she went as well as ever but was far too courageous and had many falls out hunting, breaking her collar-bone three times, an arm, wrist, leg and many ribs. She also had a nasty car-crash when she went to sleep on her way to Hereford hospital where she was going for an eye examination. On another occasion she went out on a young horse called Sir Alec on a very windy day. He started to play up, bucked her off and broke her back, causing a wedge compression of the spine, and she was extremely lucky not to fracture the spinal cord.

To put it mildly, she is 'accident prone', caused mostly by the fact that she is absolutely fearless and has not ever acquired the art of estimating the risk of any of her activities.

In the February after her accident I took her to the Canary Islands and Madeira where the swimming did her a power of good. She went out on crutches, soon changed to two sticks and when she returned she was able to walk with one stick. Those who see her nowadays, so cheerful at a party, can have no inkling of the suffering that she has endured.

So 1954, the year in which I started up in business again, was the year in which my wife nearly lost her life.

I did not jump Foxhunter at all in the first part of 1954 but I brought him up off grass in July when we moved to Llanvair. When Teeny was in Salisbury hospital, I made an assignment that I would jump

Foxhunter in the Olympic trial at Durnford because he had been going so much better. He was fresh and back on form and jumped a simply wonderful clear round over a very stiff course.

Second was Pat Smythe on Prince Hal with nineteen faults – a reminder that Foxhunter was not at his best when Prince Hal had won five classes off the reel in Harrisburg the previous autumn.

So, I took him off to Windsor where he jumped a clear round in the qualifying competition for the Championship. Then I took him in for the Championship itself where there was a queer crossed-poles fence in the middle, a type of fence he had never seen. He was getting more careful as time went on and did not relish jumping strange obstacles. He determinedly refused three times and was eliminated.

I was disappointed and very surprised as he had appeared fresh – almost 'cherry-ripe'. As I went out of the ring, Prince Bernhard, who was then President of the FEI, said, 'Could I have a word with you later?'

After I had put the horse away I came back and he said, 'I am going to ask you *please*, not to jump Foxhunter in competitions again. He has been such a great horse it grieves me and everybody to see him do what he did today which was to refuse.'

I said that I entirely agreed with him and thanked him for his advice. It was marvellous that he should take such an interest. He was a competent rider himself although he never seemed to have good enough horses. In fact once I had given him a ride on Monty at Le Zoute to let him know what a good horse was! He had always been friendly and encouraging to our team and I was most grateful to him.

So I withdrew Foxhunter from all competitions that summer and I had no thought of jumping him again.

St Teilo figures very little in my show jumping life but nevertheless was a supreme hunter and he took me through my 1953–59 Mastership with the Monmouthshire Hounds. He was very bold and would jump anything. When I bought him I noticed he had been hobdayed in the wrong place for his wind – a little too low down – so I had him done again after which his wind became remarkably clear. I only jumped him in two local classes in 1953, but when Teeny was in hospital in 1954 I dropped off one day at Shepton Mallet where, jumping his first two rounds of the season, he won the British Novices Jumping Championship – not many hunters could do that. In fact he was more valuable to me as a hunter and I gave him no chance of establishing a show jumping career.

In that year he was ridden by Richard Meade and won the Pony Club Championship at Tetbury, a further proof that he was no ordinary horse. Richard has told people how grateful he was, as riding this horse helped to establish him. No other three-day-event rider has won three Olympic Gold Medals.

I shared my Mastership with Mrs Milly Somerset, who was a red-hot socialist and the wife of Raglan Somerset, the Recorder for Gloucester, and lived at Raglan. She had tremendous intestinal fortitude out hunting and rode in her first point-to-point at the age of fifty-seven. She was wonderful with landowners and farmers, and I took a lot of trouble in erecting hunt crossing-places so that at the end of our joint-Mastership in 1959 there was not a farm that we could not cross. With George Holder as our huntsman, they were halcyon days.

When I retired Foxhunter from show jumping in 1954 I had two marvellous seasons hunting on him. I could jump anything on him, water, huge rails – you really could have fun. He was not very good during a long hunt because he tired. I suppose it was a bit of age – he was then sixteen, and I was quite heavy. If the going was heavy he would tire after a couple of hours and I never gave him a full day.

At this time the whole excitement of show jumping had worn rather thin for me. I had been several years hard at it and I really wanted to do something else. I had had the best horse in the world for a long time, and I think that we could not have improved on what he then did. What was the point of continuing, at my age – as I was then forty-three – on other horses which were not as good?

Then, in 1955, Ruby Holland-Martin gave me his marvellous mare Aherlow, who had helped us to win the gold medals at Helsinki. Ruby had broken his back and was unable to take part in show-jumping. His Overbury stud had failed to breed from her and nor did my small stud have any success. However, that super stud later produced the Derby winner, Grundy.

I decided to take Aherlow show jumping again. It was rather a risk with a mare as good as she had been, winning so much for Ruby. However we got on well together. Out hunting she was absolutely superb. I schooled her on the flat to try to get her a little more obedient in the approach as she was a bit of a puller, and needed obedience training in order to get her thinking along the right lines.

She did well enough in 1955 to be selected for the short-list for the 1956 Olympic Games and went to Ascot with the squad in May 1956.

At about that time I was tremendously involved in developing my business and could not ride her as much as I should. So it was decided that she would remain as a reserve mare with the idea that Peter Robeson would ride her if anything should happen to his first ride, Dorothy Paget's Scorchin.

I went to Stockholm where the Olympic equestrian events were being staged. Australian quarantine restrictions meant that horses could not go to Melbourne, where the rest of the Games took place. I was Chef d'Équippe of the team and also correspondent for the *Sunday Times* for which I reported on international jumping. Aherlow did not go because she and Peter did not get on well. I never thought they would because she was too indelicate a mare for Peter's skilful riding – he was a great purist who sat and rode beautifully. In those days he did not have the accurate eye in the approach that he developed later. He had that marvellous mare, Craven 'A', which he rode in quite a different way – rather like I rode Monty, who was apt to go to the bottom of a fence and then 'pop' rather than stand off. Craven 'A' made her own arrangements and this did not do Peter's judgement any good.

Aherlow was then sent home and I did not ride her until after those Games, when I took her to the White City and Dublin. When I rode her again at the White City, without any worries about representing the team or anything like that, she went absolutely brilliantly in every class, especially the Puissance. After a ding-dong between her and Wilf White on Nizefela, she won.

Judge Wiley had said that not one of the Olympic Games horses was going to be at Dublin – would I *please* bring Foxhunter along as he had heard he was going marvellously out hunting? So I took him to Dublin and agreed he would not jump any banks or jump in the team. I took him as second horse to Aherlow who won two competitions, one of them over banks.

Foxhunter not only won the first competition but also the last, the Dublin Committee Cup, which was then one of the big events in the show jumping calendar. So, Foxhunter really did go out on a tremendous win beating Nelson (Necko) Pessoa on a horse called Gran Geste by a second; and that was it.

Later I took him to Ostend and Le Zoute with the idea of jumping him as second horse to Aherlow which meant that I would not have to jump him a lot, just a couple of times at each show. It was very hot and when I started schooling him there he was so fed up that I did not jump him in competitions. I hope he enjoyed his seaside holiday. We used to go riding and swimming in the sea with him for fun, and I just concentrated on Aherlow who went extremely well. She won the Puissance at Ostend jumping seven feet two inches, and really gave me some great rides at those two shows.

In fact, Foxhunter finished on that brilliant performance at Dublin and retired at the top. This is something I am always pleased about, and I would advise everybody else to do the same with their good horses. It is terrible to see a former champion go downhill. If a horse has served you well he does not really deserve to be punished by going on when he no longer loves it. Not only do we have to help horses to help themselves, we have got to help them to enjoy themselves.

Aherlow gave me an enjoyable time in 1957. It was not like the old Foxhunter days but we went to Rome as members of the team although I had agreed to go as an individual. They were a bit short so I jumped for the team. She did not jump a good first round in the Nations Cup so I built up a really colossal fence outside. I think I collected nearly every pole in the collecting-ring, which must have been about ten, and jumped her at it at great speed. She hit it quite a wallop. I stood her still and scolded her, then I did not do anything with her at all until I took her in for my second round. She then jumped *the* most beautiful clear round.

This was the last time I jumped for my country.

I hunted Foxhunter for the next two winters but he started tiring so quickly that I did not bring him up off grass for the 1959–60 season, just after I had given up after my first term as Master of the Monmouthshire.

Every night at home, and certainly nearly every night when he was abroad, I used to go to say 'Goodnight' to Foxhunter. It was part of the routine when I was at home. I realized after he had retired from jumping and he was getting on in years that I ought to break myself of this habit because I knew I would miss him dreadfully when he died. So, when he was about seventeen I gave up the habit deliberately and avoided going to see him in the evening. It was a great problem for me because his stable was next-door to the house which made it too easy. I had some difficulty in resisting the temptation to see him, but I managed.

Above all, he was my close friend and he had a lot of funny habits. For instance, when one was riding down a lane or alongside a hedge he always nibbled something or other. He would have a nip at the hedgerow and pull something out of it. I remember him once cantering down alongside a hedge and he just lifted his dock – I thought he wanted to empty himself – but in point of fact he just wanted to take a nip out of the hedge. It was quite a compulsive habit and I let him have his way.

He was an extremely kind horse. Time and again my wife and I would be blackberrying in a field and we would suddenly find Foxhunter breathing down our necks. I let him graze in an area where blackberry bushes grew because he loved this fruit and then having joined in, he would suddenly go and eat the blackberries himself, completely denuding one or two of our favourite bushes!

Sometimes if I walked out of the house and he was two fields away he would somehow know I was there and whinny at me, and all this was very moving. I have known him follow me over a fence when I have walked over and left him in a field. He would run up and down the other side and then suddenly pop over and come and join me again. I have never known a horse quite like that, although we had a horse before the war that could never be turned out without a goose which it adored. They used to graze side by side. But horses do get fond of non-horses, just as lions will accept someone like poor Joy Adamson into their pride. Another person who looks exactly like her but smells different and is different, they would be warlike towards and would not trust. Once they know you and trust you, animals look upon you as one of their private circle of friends.

On one occasion Foxhunter and I came out of the arena at the White City and I saw, when I looked behind him, one very old lady, hugging his hind leg. She was obviously devoted to the horse; but when you come to think of it, most racehorses when they come in after a race into the enclosure will be seen kicking at the fillet strings on their rugs, and certainly no one would be able to catch hold of their hind legs and remain undamaged. Foxhunter saw this as another human approach and just stood still. He would often stand still with children underneath him after a competition when they were coming up for autographs. Very often, as he was leaving the ring, if people started to gather round him he would just stop and look around. Somebody might try to give him a bit of sugar but I tried to avoid that since you never quite knew what anyone was giving him.

When we turned him out with ponies when he retired he would go and join them and stay there as their guardian. I have a picture of him grazing with the ponies. I think he must have been a popular horse amongst other horses, if they could tell you about that kind of thing. He was a naturally companionable, pleasant animal, and perhaps one of the reasons that he was so popular was that he was known to have had a string of successes and at the same time was so gentle. That is why Foxhunter was so special and different from any other horse that I have known.

Foxhunter and I had an extraordinary affinity. I think, on looking back, this is why I understood him so well. I knew when he was not feeling well; I knew when he had a headache. He loathed it when it was hot; and he told me so. Very few things upset him. He was a very calm horse after a competition; I never saw him put his ears back. He was the most extraordinarily docile animal and this endeared him to so many people, and he had those big, beautiful, soft-brown eyes.

I used to talk to him a lot, either to wake him up or settle him down and he understood me very well. In fact he understood me so well that if I wanted to stop I would very often find that he did stop. If I wanted him to check I suppose I must have done something very slight; but at even a very slight touch he would check – he would check to a standstill. At a show in aid of the Commonwealth Games in 1958 we were asked to give an exhibition. I brought him up off grass and he was asked to jump a few little four-foot fences to show the art of control – gallop on, stop, turn sharp left, turn sharp right, jump the fences at an angle and stop. This was two or three years after he had retired and he was just as good as he ever was.

Tom Brake who was watching and who was one of the original team that went to Nice and Rome in 1947 – we called ourselves 'The Guinea Pigs' – came up to me afterwards and said, 'You know, we will never see the like of that again.'

Colin Varder of the *Daily Express* said that Foxhunter was so clever that he could sign his own autograph, and as a result I had thousands of letters. I could not discover what letters were for me and what was fan mail. Eventually I had to get three girls down at the paper's expense to go through suitcases of letters separating my own from those intended for Foxhunter. Eventually the *Daily Express* put a stop to it and they printed a copy of my signature inside one of his so-called 'hoofprints' and sent them to all Foxhunter fans.

Then again, there was his appearance. He was a fine-looking, very big horse. He always had his ears pricked and looked as if he enjoyed

219

life. He was just under seventeen hands and he had a majestic way of cantering into the ring. Mike Ansell drew attention to the fact that in France Foxhunter was often referred to as 'Monseigneur', and he was certainly referred to in the press as 'Monseigneur Foxhunter'. He had this sort of charisma which showed him up either as a great aristocrat or a great film star. His appearance was very much in his favour and this, combined with his skill and gentle nature made him something quite different.

On one occasion at Harringay he was looking around him in the ring when he suddenly spied a little grey wall. It was a funny little fence with holes in it. I believe horses are colour-blind and the density of the colour of this wall was almost the density of the colour of the track. When he suddenly came to this wall he stopped. I turned him round, scolded him and tapped him down the shoulder twice. My goodness me! There was complete silence. People had enough manners in those days not to boo, but I had many letters saying that I was not to do that – in fact I had one saying, 'You must not hit Foxhunter because he does not belong to you he belongs to the nation'! I had to be very careful not even to speak crossly to him after that. He was the chap they liked – not me. I was not a national hero, but he was.

Foxhunter died at the age of nineteen on 28 November 1959, having done something to himself in the field. He was perfectly well when he was put out to grass but he was rather apt to buck around and mess about and I think he must have injured himself falling when jumping the ditch in the middle of our park field. He died of a ruptured artery to his kidneys and went very quickly. I was at home when it happened and saw he kept on going down. He was brought in and the vet, Ken Mitchell, was there almost immediately. He noted from the colour of Foxhunter's gums that there was little or no blood supply to his head. He said he was dying and soon life left that magnificent body. He left us peacefully and without pain. You cannot say he died in my arms but I was holding his head when he died. He had been a great friend to me and to many others who were so fond of him.

I did not tell anybody for a few days, by which time I could talk about him without a continuous lump in my throat. I was to remember how joyfully he had cooperated with his human friends and put so much pleasure into our lives.

Shortly after Foxhunter died we decided upon his burial. I own some land situated on the top of the Blorenge mountain overlooking both Gobion and Llanvair Grange; and on my property right at the top are some rocks. Here we found a cavity into which we put a stainless-steel casket. In this was placed the book I had written, *Foxhunter in Pictures*, and his hide, which we had brought back from the kennels where he had been taken after his death. His skeleton was carefully preserved and this was asked for by the Royal Veterinary College; it still stands there next-door to the statue of Hermit, a famous race-horse who won the Snowstorm Derby in 1867.

Some people have asked why I left his skeleton there but buried him elsewhere. The answer is simple. In the Royal Veterinary College his skeleton will be a constant reminder of a great horse, whilst the burial on Blorenge mountain will remind many people that he was partly trained in this beautiful country of Wales. The Blorenge gives wonderful views of about seventy miles in every direction; it is a lovely place for him to be buried. We often exercised over that spot; and the thought of this great horse buried there means a great deal to me.

Foxhunter has left behind him what are known as 'Foxhunter Competitions'. These were really created by me in South Wales, partly because I did not know how to get rid of all the cups we were winning in those days – cleaning them took such a lot of time and frankly I do not like to see trophy rooms. So we formed in South Wales a competition which we called the 'Foxhunter Competition'. Originally the horses were supposed to jump only three foot six inches over rustic type fences; the main idea was to bring the promising hunter out of the hunting-field into the show jumping ring, and introduce a lot of new horses and new people into the game. I was anxious to do this because there had always been a division between the hunting people and the professional show jumpers who toured the country. I think these competitions have done much to bring them together.

This first competition was a great success in South Wales. Then when Max Aitken came to me and asked how he could put £1000 into show jumping, I suggested that he should extend it to London. He promptly did so and introduced it through the *Evening Standard*. After a year or two the competition was so successful that the *Daily Express* introduced it on a nationwide basis and it is now the biggest in the world, attracting something like 60,000–70,000 entries a year. There is a sensational final at the Horse of the Year Show when all good Foxhunters come out, and some good horses have been produced as a result of first taking part in this competition. Foxhunter classes and trials are now sponsored by Hoechst Pharmaceuticals.

So the competitions have achieved what they set out to do, which was to bring more horses into show jumping; in particular we tapped the huge reservoir of horses that went foxhunting.

Another competition which I initiated was the Area International Trial. In the early fifties when we were trying to introduce the FEI rules, riding on at a cadenced pace was vitally important. The BSJA competitions were very slow events. In every area there were people who knew how to ride in the international style and were able to achieve success in the Area International Trials. If they did so they qualified for the Olympic Trial. It was thus a democratic way for riders to promote themselves if they and their horses were good enough, and these trials still have an important part to play today.

16 Business and Equestrian Affairs

When Foxhunter retired, my life branched out in several different directions. I became established in our new home at Llanvair Grange and concentrated on the development of Davies and Co. which, as I have said, later became Davenco Engineers Ltd.

After one or two good years at Davies in Abergavenny I may have become over-optimistic although work was hard to get. I travelled the country and paid visits to Ireland, Belgium, the United States and Canada, looking for work; in Montreal we made the saddles for the cars on the aerial ropeway at Expo 69.

It is now of little benefit to reflect that the engineering business into which I sank so much of my money should not have succeeded as did all the companies which I helped to run for other people. At least I tried – I tried like hell. It is also of little consolation to realize that nine out of ten similar engineering firms have gone to the wall. Enthusiasm is not enough – one has to go into the right industry at the right time. However, the fact that I had shown an inclination to go back into business inspired others to make offers to me.

In 1953 I had become magistrate on the Abergavenny Bench. I did this for nearly fifteen years before retiring when I could no longer fit this in with my business commitments. I felt I had done my stint. I was also busy in those days with the National Society for the Mentally Handicapped Children, being joint-President with the Bishop of Brecon and Swansea.

My farming interests extended further when I bought the Duffryn and White House farms in 1958 and 1960, together about 400 acres. I set up a single-suckling herd of Black Galloway cattle, initially buying a dozen two-year-old heifers from Nancy (Anne, Duchess of) Westminster from her Lochmore herd. I added to them Barqua Kismet, a yearling heifer which I bought as a real bargain for £160 after she had won at Smithfield.

She and others made up a herd of about fifty cows and I managed to buy two excellent bulls at the Castle Douglas Sales. This single-suckling herd at that time proved viable and was profit-making for about ten years; after that the cost of labour and foodstuffs cut the margins down. So I gradually reduced the herd and replaced it by a multi-suckling operation, which involved buying calves under a week old, then bringing them right through to fatten when they weighed at least 10 cwt. Mil Thayers, who manages these operations, is an expert at multiple-suckling from which we get a good return.

We also built up the flocks of sheep; Welsh Mountain on the top and Clun on the Pentwyn farm and my own land round the Grange. I still had room at the top farms so went back to my first love – the Welsh Mountain Pony. I put up something like five miles of fencing against the mountain and to create large paddocks, as distinct from fields, for the stock.

I started off by buying forty colt foals and yearlings at sales, with the idea of wintering them to see how they suited the farm and how the land suited them. They did well and I sold them all off for a reasonable profit. Convinced that Welsh Mountain ponies would do well on the farms, I bought two winners at Vaynor show, called Vaynor Felicity and Llywela, who had won the yearling and foal classes respectively; and later a few mares from the Snowdon herd in North Wales and the Revel Stud run by the supremo of the day, Emrys Griffiths.

Revel Trinket won the mare class at the Bath and West and this put us on the map. In 1965 eleven of our ponies won in the capable hands of Ann Greey. I also bought Coed Coch Brenin Arthur from Daisy Broderick, whose Coed Coch Stud had really dominated the scene until the popularity of the Revel ponies made the latter stud a close rival. Brenin Arthur did the stud a lot of good and bred some beautiful mares, some of which I still have, and produced good winners such as Foxhunter Morllyn.

As I was building up a really nice lot of mares I obviously had to match them with a good stallion so, in addition to Brenin Arthur I re-imported from the USA Grenington Hynod, a gift from Pete Bostwick who had bought him for £2000 – a then record price – from Lord Kenyon. Possibly one of the best young stallions to be used was Woodend Prince which I owned with my childhood friend, Serena Homfray. She has been breeding Welsh mountain ponies with great vigour since her husband, Harber's death. I enjoyed foxhunting before the war with him when he was Master of the Glamorgan Hunt for twenty-three seasons.

Brenin Arthur won some good classes including the Royal, when I lent him to Jack Edwards of Llangollen. He and his daughters were supreme in the show-ring, winning the most cherished class in Welsh pony breeding which was the stallion class at the Royal Welsh, as well as at the breed stallion show at Glanusk.

I then formed a syndicate to purchase Clan Pip, one of the biggest-ever winners in the show-ring, and the leading sire on points for many years. Serena Homfray, Robina Wills and Claire Hunter were my partners, after which I sold a half-share to the Featherstone-haughs in the Black Mountains before they, in turn, sold him to spend his old age in the milder climate of Devonshire. He left me some beautiful mares. The cross between him and Brenin Arthur mares was a real 'nick'.

I found that I was able to sell the ponies privately very well, so I gradually gave up showing which was becoming increasingly expensive. I did not show mares much; if I liked them at two years old I kept them entirely for breeding. Nowadays I show only a few of my young stock and they hold their own in the show classes.

At one time I had built the herd up to well over a hundred ponies but I had what was virtually a clearance sale in 1973 before the demand for ponies went down. I was lucky. This sale included the twelve-year-old mare Rowfant Prima Ballerina which I sold for £1000 after having bought her for £200; I won the mare class at the Royal Welsh Show with her in 1971, being second the following year.

We have sold ponies privately and all over the world – Japan, France, Germany, Australia, Holland, America – and in 1967 I was President of the Welsh Pony and Cob Society. Gradually, I have now cut down the breeding herd to fifteen of my best breeding mares. There is still a demand for good females but only the exceptional stallion fetches a reasonable price these days. I estimate that they not only make their keep but make a small profit which allows me to enjoy my hobby all the more. I think my Welshness comes out in these Welsh ponies. I love going to shows and seeing old friends, not only from the pony world but those families connected with the colliery days, and other business associations which have close links with Wales.

In 1970 I had a serious loss. Llanarth Hansel caught strangles – severe abcesses burst in his throat. In my absence it was decided to give the other three stallions a dose of serum as a prophylactic. Unfortunately, at that time few people had appreciated the danger of serum poisoning. These three, Coed Coch Brenin Arthur, Gredington Hynod and Woodend Prince, all beautiful animals, were dead within six weeks. It is of little satisfaction to know that the product was then removed from the market and vets of every country were warned about the danger of serum poisoning.

The deaths of these fine stallions saved many others but it was a severe blow to the stud and also to my family. We had grown especially fond of Brenin Arthur who was a gentle horse and had a friendly nature – rather like Foxhunter's.

A new departure came in March 1958 when I was asked by Bill Whitbread and Peter Kemp-Welch if I would like to become chairman of Andrew Buchans Breweries. I agreed. I first went off to the brewery at Hythe where I was taught the brewing process and found it interesting. I then joined the board of Rhymney and became chairman in July 1958. I always enjoyed the brewery business and Andrew Buchans, whose name I changed to Rhymney, was a successful company.

In 1972 I felt that we could no longer go it alone as the national breweries were able to afford much more advertising than we could. We achieved a good deal for our shareholders when we asked Whitbread to take us over. This splendid company treated us well. After sixteen years as chairman I became president in 1974 and consultant to what is now Whitbread Wales. When I was Chairman we acquired the Ely and Vale of Neath Breweries and several hotels, including the Angel Hotel at Cardiff, which we modernized and which has proved a great success. In a way it is our 'flagship'.

In 1958 I also became a founder-director of Television Wales and West. Jim Cilcennin was our first chairman and I thoroughly enjoyed ten 'cut-throat' years in that business. Among other interesting people on the board were John Derby, Jack Hilton, Bill Carr, Mark Chapman-Walker, Launder and Gilliatt, Herbert Agar, all of whom were interesting men. Our solicitor was Arnold Goodman, who became Lord Goodman of Westminster in 1967 and proved to be a great man and a close friend.

Jim Cilcennin, a political friend of my brother, David, always stayed with us at Llanvair for the Cardiff meetings. When he died John Derby took over the post of chairman and no one could have done the job better than this highly intelligent, capable and charming man. He loved the business and the business loved him.

I enjoyed the 'fire brigade' committee which consisted of John

Derby, Bill Carr, Mark Chapman-Walker, representing the big interests, and me, representing the other shareholders. 'Goody' – Arnold Goodman – was our wise counsellor in our deliberations. After ten profitable years we were dispossessed by the ill-will of Dr Hill in 1968. No one has ever given a good reason why we lost our licence because TWW had the reputation of being an efficient, well-run and happy company. Possibly it was the only way that Dr Hill and, through him, Sir Harold Wilson, both from the northern side of Liverpool, could get their own back on Derby, one of the remaining 'Seigneurs', whom they thought was too autocratic. Everyone at TWW – in the office and in the studio – had the highest regard for him.

I cannot go into details of all the other members of this talented board but there was a Welsh board with some real characters – Hugh T. Edwards, who believed in fairies; Sir Ifan ap Owen Edwards, the leader of Welsh Youth; Percy Jones, the builders' merchant who became boss of the Salvation Army in Wales – all served with me under the chairmanship of Jack (Sir Grismond) Phillips, a delightful raconteur.

TWW was very profitable for all concerned and, in my case, it made up for the losses I was starting to make in my engineering firm. In addition these connections, of course, involved me in many other business organizations, and I was chairman of the Wales branch of the Institute of Directors on two occasions, 1963 and 1964. I joined the regional board of Lloyds Bank in Cardiff in 1963 and was Chairman of the Eagle Star Insurance for South-East Wales, later to be all Wales, also in 1963. One thing followed another and I found myself being offered jobs abroad and also in this country, but it meant leaving my beloved Wales and this I was not prepared to do.

Apart from the interest of running these businesses there were other rewards such as being able to inspire the support of both TWW and Rhymney Breweries to sponsor races at Chepstow – the forerunners to the extensive sponsorship which has made racing such a success at that charming course. Then again, I was offered interesting journeys abroad. I was the 'leader' of an Institute of Directors visit to Leningrad and Moscow in 1965 and led a Development Corporation of Wales Trade Mission to the USA in 1969. We visited New York, Chicago, Los Angeles and San Francisco. Altogether we sold over half a million pounds worth of goods and the trip was rated as a success.

When the Socialists put me on the Wales Tourist Board in 1968

I found myself even busier for the three terms I served. At last I was able to see much more of the Land of my Fathers, and spent much time in North Wales. I was chairman of their Projects Committee and of the Hotel Development Incentives Scheme Committee; then I joined the Marketing Committee of the British Travel Authority representing Wales.

All of these jobs were fascinating and I particularly enjoyed the BTA work as this took me abroad to 'Workshops' in Belgium, Johannesburg and Sao Paulo. 'Workshops' was the name given to sales operations which involved the main carriers, hotel groups and tourist companies in a joint venture. Each one of them appeared to be successful as in the following year tourism increased, particularly from the countries we visited.

At the same time I was involved very much with the British Show Jumping affairs and was chairman of the International Committee from 1956 to 1960.

This meant that I was responsible for the British team and their visits abroad. In 1960 I was Chef de Mission at the Rome Olympics for all the disciplines – the three-day-event, dressage and jumping teams, which meant that I could spend little time on the beach at Fregene where Teeny, Dai and Roddy spent a delightful week. This is a job that is very difficult to do and I had not wanted to take it on in the first place. Not one of the disciplines was satisfied. I had either seen too little of them or too much, or they had not got the necessary tickets or passes or something. The only Chef de Mission to do a good job was the Chilean General who made his headquarters at the Ritz Bar and told everyone who wanted him to contact him there!

Meanwhile, I was up at four o'clock and rushing around like a lunatic until late in the evening. Never have I felt so unwanted and unappreciated. Disenchanted, I resigned as chairman of the BSJA International Affairs Committee in 1960 while Mike Ansell took over again until I returned to that job in 1966.

The years 1958 to 1966 had been busy ones and on top of those responsibilities I had become High Sheriff of Monmouthshire in 1965, a job which I thoroughly enjoyed, especially as 1966 was the year in which Her Majesty the Queen opened the Severn Bridge.

During this time we started going abroad again on family holidays without our horses but with our children. These were mostly to Southern France, Fuengirola, Majorca, Ibiza, and Formentera. We later made plans to build a small apartment-house to share with friends, which we used on an interchange basis, providing family holidays at the edge of a lovely warm, clean sea in an isolated part of the island of Formentera.

It was only in the later post-war years that horses did not take a prominent part in my affairs.

After I had finally given up competing in 1957, I went hunting a lot more and again took on the joint-Mastership of the Monmouthshire Hounds, this time with Cyril and Mary Longsdon. We still had George Holder as huntsman and therefore had a lot of fun, even if the country was not as open as it had been during my first term.

When I resigned as joint-Master in 1959, Geoffrey Gibbon then went as joint-Master with Milly Somerset. She was killed jumping a fence with the Monmouthshire in 1961. Loved by everyone, a vast throng at her funeral at Raglan heard George Holder blow briskly, 'Gone Away' – and then sadly and mournfully, 'Home, Home.'

My second joint-Mastership of the Monmouthshire spanned the years 1963 to 1965. After my mare Cathy came Jack de Manio, a big, heavyweight cob which I bought in the Ledbury country and which was known as 'Jack the Tank' – a specialist over gates.

In 1971 I bought a mare at Ascot called Madam Longlegs which I intended to use as a brood mare but she turned out to be a brilliant hunter, if a little nutty. She would often behave quite well until hounds started running and then go mad if there was a check. She would buck and kick like fun but somehow she was not very unseating. Her favourite trick was to do a sort of 'sunfish' like a bronco, landing on all four legs and shaking her head; all very alarming, particularly if one was in a queue. She was a first-class mare when in front or jumping alone as she was so bold. From about 1966 to 1976 I had these three superb hunters most of the time.

I kept one of them at Ledbury with John Taylor, one-time whip to those hounds, and these were ten golden years. Juliet Oram and Archie Smith-Maxwell, joint-Masters most of that time, were both the non-shouting type and showed tremendous sport. In my experience, quiet Masters were those who achieved the best discipline. Shouting at anybody merely causes resentment, and the best ones took the offenders aside and gave them a severe wigging, but did not scream at them in front of the field.

In the Ledbury country there were a lot of very good 'goers' and an array of beautiful ladies who went like bombs. A day with the Ledbury Ladies pursuing the Ledbury bitches over the Chaceley Flats alongside the Severn, provided some of my happiest hunting memories.

For the first part of this period I had Horatio, my wife's horse. He had been a hunt horse with the Monmouthshire but proved too strong for Teeny after she broke her forearm on him. I am afraid I took him from her and he was a little small for me. He was a horse standing only 16 hands – really a big horse on short legs and I never once brought him home tired. One male groom riding him back to the horsebox after a fairly long day had his arms pulled out. Exhausted, he dismounted to say, 'I have heard of a tiger in the tank – but not two!'

When I was sixty-five I was having a day with the Ledbury and enjoying a nice glass of port with a couple of American friends when the hounds found a fox a mile away. I set off in pursuit. I knew the country well and Madam, whom I was riding, usually jumped better on her own. Unfortunately I went to jump a small post-and-rails and was foolish enough to jump the smallest place as the going looked rather better. In fact it was low because the rail had been broken and there was a piece of wire in its place. Neither of us saw this. She went straight through it and turned right over throwing me on to my head – sixteen stone at thirty miles an hour! Not surprisingly I was dazed and remember little of the next half-hour. The owner of the farm saw what had happened, rode down, picked up my horse and helped me to remount. Apparently, I then set off in pursuit again jumping three gates in a line. I can remember nothing of this at all, but I suddenly realized that I was nowhere near the hounds. It was late in the day so I decided to go back to John Taylor's yard. I appeared to behave quite normally but remember little until later I went to have a bath at the home of Hugh and Veronica Adams. After my bath I recall 'coming to' on the floor. I changed into my dinner-jacket and set off to have dinner with the Manleys at Bacton, half an hour away. Although I stumbled down the steps as I left, the journey went perfectly satisfactorily.

In the middle of dinner I suddenly saw lots of little yellow lights floating from side to side whenever I moved my eyes. I thought, therefore, it was wiser not to go on to the hunt ball for which I was destined, and went home. The lights were still there in the morning so I went off to the Nevill Hall hospital where at least they found there was no fracture to my skull. The delightful specialist passed the remark that my skull was too thick to break, but suggested that I went to see an eye specialist. He sent me immediately to St Woolos Hospital in Newport.

The diagnosis was a hole in my retina which could not be reached by a laser beam, the modern method of treatment, so they had to cut my eyeball, peel it back and insert an instrument which was 83° F below freezing. In this way they were able to reach the hole and create scar tissues between it and the side of my eye.

After a month of convalescence I returned home. Further examinations proved that the operation had gone extremely well and was successful. I have always had astigmatization in my right eye, caused before the war when I had a fall on Bunfight at Cardiff races and my eyeball filled with blood. I was able to wear the same glasses after the operation as I had before. The retina was anchored to the side of my eye and is still fine, but this accident virtually finished my hunting career. How lucky I was to have had so much of it in my lifetime, finishing with three of the best hunters I had ever had.

I now have a thoroughbred mare for guests to ride and a cob called Fiddle, who is a brilliant jumper. I sold Madam but in later seasons rode Jack the Tank and Cathy, following the hounds mostly on the roads and tracks. I still find it great fun even if one is not trying 'to win the hunt'; there is more time to watch the hounds and enjoy their work. Nothing is more thrilling than to see a fox break cover and hear that magic cry of 'Gone Away'.

Had I not had to work for my living for a long period, I could easily have settled down as a Master of Hounds for most of my life and I can think of nothing that can compare with hunting hounds yourself. Breeding also was fascinating and I could have easily become involved as a 'hound' man. I had to fight against that temptation. The ultimate enjoyment for horsemen must surely be riding horses and hunting hounds that they have bred.

This is not a dissertation on foxhunting, but I think that people should be grateful that there are those who dedicate their lives to this activity and show good sport over many years. Not everyone can become a Duke of Beaufort or a Ronnie Wallace but there are many others who have set a wonderful example by their dedication to foxhunting.

I have always resisted appearing on panels defending foxhunting from those who wish to attack it in debate. I believe that the fox 'lives by the sword' and should therefore 'die by the sword'. The fox is a furtive animal and on the defensive every minute of his life. He develops that cunning so necessary for his survival, such as when he travels down-wind when tired, or walks through stream-beds. I am glad that the ritual procedure of 'blooding' people has gone because that gave a quite unnecessary barbaric touch.

The Master, huntsman and a few others realize that hounds must kill foxes so that they know what their function is; but very few people in the field wish to see a fox killed, apart from the farmer whose lambs or chickens the fox has been taking. In fact it is the farmer who will eventually decide whether or not foxhunting will survive. The amount of damage created by a thoughtless field in the latter part of the season, say February or March, can have hounds warned off farms for good.

The only time I had to send someone home was when a senior male member of the hunt swore at the hunt secretary, who had stopped his guest jumping into a new lay on a farm whose owner did not like the hounds to cross his land. I told him not to come out again until he had apologized to the secretary, which he never did.

Having discussed my personal forays into business and farming in the years following the Second World War, I feel that I should devote at least part of a chapter to equestrian administration.

In 1945, when the British Show Jumping Association was located in the basement of 66 Sloane Square, I was asked to be the chairman of a small committee to appoint a secretary-general. We chose Jack Webber, who served the BSJA wonderfully for thirty years. It was largely his organization, and the affection we all felt for him, that put show-jumping on the map under the dominant leadership of Mike Ansell. I am proud that I was chairman of that committee.

One cannot refer to show jumping after the war without drawing attention to the tremendous contribution made by Colonel Sir Mike Ansell, a great leader, referred to as our 'architect of victory'. It was he who fought for having all FEI events opened to civilians. People sometimes forget that before the war only officers could take part in international show jumping competitions, or indeed the three-day-event. It was really Mike, supported by his friends Arnd Franke from Sweden and Ranieri Campbello from Italy, who had the rules changed. We could not have developed an international sport had it not been thrown open to civilians.

When I was in Brussels in the winter of 1944–45, Colonel Taffy Walwyn, one of the trio of great pre-war show jumpers with Malise Graham and Geoffrey Brooke, wrote to me as a steward of the BSJA asking me if I would agree to the appointment of Mike Ansell as chairman. I had not known Mike Ansell at all. I had heard that he had been partially blinded, was marvellous with animals and had persuaded that wonderful race-winning horse, Leopard, to jump a line of swords without 'wings'. I thought that anybody who could do that sort of thing with a horse must be a pretty exceptional person, and of course I was delighted to agree.

After consultation with the other stewards, including Brigadier John Allen, he was put up by Taffy to the committee as having been approved by the stewards, who in those days had more plenary powers than they have now. Mike was appointed – by one vote! That was the beginning of the great team of Mike Ansell and Jack Webber, and they were the people who really carried the burden through all those early years. Mike had great power of industry and he would often put much thought into the future of the BSJA. He was the man who built up not only the BSJA but the two London horse shows and then the British Horse Society itself.

He devoted his life to equestrian matters. No one else could have done that. Apart from his ability, he put in a tremendous amount of work for very little reward. He often said that being blind had certain advantages. In his case his memory had become very much better; his powers of deduction were much improved; he was able to concentrate more deliberately on problems when he set his mind to it.

I think that he is demanding and, to a certain extent a critical and dominant man. He had to be to do the job he did. We had a good relationship and certainly neither he nor I said 'Yes' to each other when we meant 'No' – or vice versa. At times when he used to get a little bit too direct this did not affect me very much because I could just walk out of the room. On the other hand he could equally be very direct with Jack Webber, and I remember Jack two or three times saying, 'Well, I've had this – I'm off.' I used to have to talk to him and say, 'For heaven's sake, don't, because you are really the key man in this and it would be awful if you went.'

I remember on one occasion we rather agreed that Mike was a wonderful chap and we were very lucky to have him but that if we had to analyse our feelings they were 90 per cent admiration and only 10 per cent affection. Eventually we evened things up and became just as much fond of him as we admired him – which was tremendously.

There is no doubt that he was the person mainly responsible for building up this effective governing body. His enthusiasm had a schoolboyish gusto. He was a great winner; he liked *winners* not seconds, and I quite agree with him – I never did either. In that way we were much alike.

I had much to do with the international team although initially I was also involved with the organization. In fact I made out the 'order of battle' plan that was printed in the early rule-books. This chart proved quite valuable when we were throwing off our standing committees; and I was also an original member of their finance committee.

First of all I was captain of the team without a Chef d'Équipe. When this became too much we started appointing Chefs d'Équipe as well as the riders, although I was 'Riding Captain' until I retired from it at the end of 1952. A Chef d'Équipe really has to do an awful lot of work. He has to make the entries, collect the prize money, pay the grooms, arrange the transport, become social secretary and perform many other duties. We now have Ronnie Massarella as Chef d'Équipe; he was appointed during the time I was chairman of the BSJA and he does a wonderful job.

It was through the team that I was chiefly associated with show jumping for over thirty years and later, from 1966 to 1976, I was again chairman of their selection committee. Then in 1966 as chairman of the BSJA I visited America to help open the Morven Riding Academy and also to go to the New York horse shows. In 1968 I was Chef d'Équipe for the team in Mexico when Marion Mould on Stroller won the silver medal in the individual event behind Billy Steinkraus, USA, who won the gold medal. David Broome won the individual bronze medal on Mr Softee. Great Britain were leading after the first round in the Nations Cup but Stroller found himself overfaced so was disqualified in the second round and this put the team out.

I stayed chairman of the International Committee until after the Olympic Games in 1976 when Debbie Johnsey was fourth in the individual but could not get a medal in the team event. This was no doubt largely caused by our best riders having become professional, whilst in other countries most of the best riders remained amateur.

In 1976 General Sir Cecil (Monkey) Blacker then took on the

Selection Committee and has filled the post with all the fire, drive and interest that Mike Ansell showed, possibly because he belonged to the same regiment – the 'Skins'! Monkey is President of the BSJA as well as being our chief selector. Having been the Adjutant General he was second-in-command in the British Army.

There are many robust characters in the BSJA who add flavour and sometimes heat to various debates. These become fast and occasionally furious when the 'Master of Hickstead', Douglas Bunn, George Hobbs, chairman of the Rules Committee, and Trevor Banks, the north-country owner, are all in fighting-trim. But Monkey is tough enough and wise enough to enlist everyone's support, which adds to his enthusiasm in putting new life into the team and international affairs.

Douglas Bunn has made a tremendous contribution since he was seventeen when he was second on Rahin to Kilgeddin in the Victory Cup in 1946. On returning from my visit to Rome in 1947 I wrote, in Ted Lyon's *Horseman's Year* that this country badly needed jumping-grounds such as those in many French watering-places like Deauville, Dinard, La Baule. Duggie has been kind enough to say that this article inspired him to build Hickstead – in the event a far more extensive jumping-ground than any I have seen, with banks and many permanent fences. These include the Trahkener (fences at either end of a lower area with a ditch in it); the 'Tennis Court' (two fences above a raised platform); a water-fence and living-privet hedges.

His enthusiasm in developing Hickstead has been a major factor in preparing the right sort of horse to jump internationally and providing somewhere to stage trials simulating continental conditions. The tremendous drive of Douglas Bunn inspired Wills to sponsor events in this beautiful country arena on the London Road north of Brighton. If it has been a drain on his financial resources, his ability fortunately expressed itself elsewhere and he was able to make a great financial success of a caravan-site on Selsey Bill.

Duggie looks forward, and is most certainly a free-thinker and free talker. Occasionally he offends people by his over-enthusiasm and the strong way in which he makes his points, but the present show-jumping scene in Britain would not be the same without him and we are all very grateful to him for his contribution.

Later, Fred Broome, David's father, developed the Wales and West Show on a site near Chepstow, while Arena North, spurred on by the enthusiasm of Christopher Coldrey, followed the Hickstead example; both have become major shows of international importance.

In the foreword to his book on Nizefela, Hylton Cleaver's analysis of why show jumping 'took off' after the war stresses Mike Ansell's determination resulting in the success of the White City which staged the Royal International Horse Show for many years. Then the advent of television, although not yet in colour, drew attention to this spectacular activity and made a vast public aware of this new international sport.

The winning of gold medals at Helsinki in 1952 drew further attention to a sport in which Great Britain could succeed at a time when it could not really win many other medals, although Miss Jeanette Altweg had earlier won a skating gold medal at the Winter Games.

To quote Hylton Cleaver: 'There have been three instances of television fascination by the public . . . firstly Foxhunter and Harry Llewellyn who were a "perfect partnership." The public gave no more marks to Harry than to the horse; theirs had been an ideal realized. The Englishman revels in the spectacle of comradeship between man and animal.'

Next, Pat Smythe. Cleaver says that he didn't think that 'people minded what horse she rode because there was a glamour with this girl whose gallantry had made her the greatest horsewoman of her age.'

Then he mentions Nizefela and he says, rightly, that 'Nizefela had used his kick-back to attain fame. Everybody was fascinated by seeing him do this on television.' Nizefela was a great jumper and very successful. He had less success on the Continent because he could not cope with the speed, but when it came to Nations Cups he was rightly described as our 'cornerstone' – he always jumped very well.

Bob Dean has now so changed the sponsorship situation that show-jumpers and eventers are jumping for over a million pounds worth of prize money a year. He is responsible for this along with the British Equestrian Promotions Team, which is owned jointly by the British Horse Society, the British Show Jumping Association and Raymond Brooks-Ward, its managing director and another invaluable contributor.

I never particularly wanted to have Mike Ansell's job as president of the British Equestrian Federation; but I suppose having survived and having stayed where I was, and being still interested in the administration, it rather fell into my lap. However, it has been enjoyable, though time-consuming. When I retire at the end of 1980 after my four and a half years at the job, I think I will have done my stint.

When Mike left as president of the Federation he cut clean and has given me a fair run. He put the BEF together; I think he put it together quickly because he had to within his term of office. Since then I have asked him and others their views as to how much more integration there should be between the British Horse Society and the BSJA. I feel strongly that there ought, if only for economic reasons, to be an administrative centre; we should eventually have one office serving the various disciplines. But I believe if we created one body in control of every activity and discipline we would have to appoint standing committees to each section. So why change? Rather than have them appointed as it were from the Federation, let them appoint themselves and the members of the BEF as at present. It works perfectly well that way.

I am lucky indeed in having a super staff officer in General Jack Reynolds my Director General. One must give Mike Ansell the credit for having selected Jack in the first place. Jack has the 'light touch' approach, combined with supreme efficiency; without him this Federation would not operate as effectively as it does. Shan Hackett told me he was the best staff officer he had met and he has proved for me a wise counsellor and warm friend.

I am often asked who was the best rider that I rode against, and who I think is the best rider nowadays.

I consider the best rider in my day, really, was Piero D'Inzeo. He had a marvellous eye in the approach; he sat perfectly in balance and would produce a horse to jump from the optimum place with the minimum of fuss and at the right pace. His father, whom we used to call 'The Maestro', was very helpful to me when I went to Rome in 1947 and I had several lessons from him on the quiet. He brought up both his boys to be first-class riders. Raimondo was the more competitive man. Piero was a great winner too but he was a man who also put a little bit of something different into it all – a gentle rhythm, graceful movement and accuracy.

When it came to sheer aggression I do not think you could ever have beaten the Chevalier D'Orgeix who used to ride Sucre de Pomme and Arlequin D with tremendous dash; he was determined to win, win, win! A good competitor and a good sport – I loved jumping against him. We used to go flat out and it was something special when we had to go against the clock. I used to enjoy it very much.

d'Oriola was less accurate but he was a beautiful rider and went on for a long time after I had stopped. d'Orgeix went off to Indo-China, then to Chad big-game shooting, stock-car racing – every sort of sport; whilst d'Oriola married and lived near the Pyrenees. I think he is still show-jumping as he is not a person to retire.

There were a lot of other good Frenchmen – all of them were taught properly. Captain Max Fresson (now Colonel) used to ride beautifully. His 'silhouette' – in other words, the outline as he rode – was something to copy, but he was not accurate like d'Orgeix. Then there was the French Captain de Fombelle, an active but untidy rider who waved his arms about, but he was very effective like Mancinelli was in his early days. In the early seventies the German, Alwin Schockemohle was another exceptional rider and won the Gold Medal at the 1976 Olympiad in Montreal.

As far as the British were concerned I would not have liked to take on Wilf White anywhere in England under the National Rules, but riding in competitions against the clock came a little bit late in life for him. He was a fine, natural horseman.

Winkler, of course, on Halla, was very steady, accurate and determined to win. Towards the end of Foxhunter's time he was beginning to be rivalled by Halla. She was an exceptional mare. Winkler, who has gone on since and ridden a number of horses, is one of the all time greats.

Of the Spaniards, Paco Goyoaga, in my early days was a hard man to beat. He had a marvellous eye in the approach and used to ride these little Spanish horses brilliantly with great dash.

Then, of course, throughout the whole of my period there was Bill Steinkraus who became a master and who was gradually improving when he came over here with Night Owl. He went on and won the individual Gold Medal for the United States in the 1968 Olympic Games in Mexico.

Amongst present-day riders those at the top are David Broome and Harvey Smith. Both are professionals, ride for their living and are extremely skilful. When it comes to winning the big competition against the clock I would say that David is marginally the better. He always clocks up very quick times over courses because he jumps off a longer stride than Harvey. Harvey is apt to bring them in a bit close and, of course, that takes more time.

On the other hand, if the money is down and it is big enough, Harvey can go like a scalded cat and will upset anybody in the world! If you make Harvey cross he does even better. If somebody drops him out of the team he will then win the next three competitions. He is a wonderful fighter. Where there is money involved they are both fairly keen: they are professionals and they have to be, but it is all done in good humour. Both are great team men and do everything they can to help team members, especially if they have not been chosen themselves.

As far as the ladies are concerned, Pat Smythe must stand out as far as I am concerned as the all time great. She was tremendously determined to win and had a tough, virile approach. I remember once when I beat her in New York by a tenth of a second she stumped away after the competition and never even congratulated me. I mentioned this to her the next day, and she replied, 'I was so cross at being beaten – even by you!' She was a *WINNER*.

Anne Moore, Marion Mould, Alison Westwood and Caroline Bradley rank as top-class international riders, but I think Pat was better than any of them and the best lady rider I have ever seen. Oddly enough, she was more of a hand rider. She had to have a horse taking hold of her in order to ride it. She did not use her legs much but she had a wonderful sense of balance and timing and was a beautiful, natural horsewoman with tremendous guts. What more can I say?

Again, people often ask me how the standard compares nowadays with show jumping in Foxhunter's day. There are now many more good international-class riders than there were, but I really do not believe, with the possible exception of David Broome when his string is in good form, that the best riders today are better than those in the early fifties.

The horses are certainly not as good as they were. Why should they be? The horse was extensively bred for military transport, agricultural and leisure purposes. In this country thousands used to be bred for foxhunting; but our production of middleweight quality horses – those best suited for show jumping – is now minimal. There are plenty of horses to fill events but a large proportion are rejects from racing. As president of the BEF I have striven with Jane Kidd and Jack Reynolds to produce a paper, *The Case for the Riding-Horse* in the hope that many more big quality animals suitable for international competition will be bred. There are now many more shows, and the sport of show jumping has expanded tremendously since civilian riders were allowed to compete.

Even Foxhunter could not go through the card as he sometimes used to do, as there is so much more competition of a high standard. The courses round national shows are larger, but in top-class events and Puissances (power tests) they are essentially no different.

Briefly, there are many more top class riders and national courses are bigger, but the best horses are not as good. Forgive me if I claim that indeed there has never been a horse that was so consistently brilliant over a decade as Foxhunter: *Monseigneur et nonpareil*!

My Home is in Wales

This last decade of my life has proved rewarding in some unexpected ways. I have continued to find new interests, both public and personal.

The Tory Government asked me to become chairman of the Sports Council in October 1971. I accepted and started work immediately although the official term of my three years' appointment did not start until 1 April 1972. I was appointed by the Secretary of State for Wales, Mr Peter Thomas, a member of the Cabinet; I was not appointed by the Department of Environment nor indeed by the Minister for Sport. In fact neither have any remit in respect of our activities at the Sports Council for Wales. When my friend, Denis Howell, visited Wales, he had to get permission from the Secretary of State for Wales who was responsible for guarding Welsh interests. Denis was very resourceful and an active Minister for Sport. I believe that he is a sportsman first and a politician second and I always like to see him, but I made it a condition that he should always stay with me when he visited the Principality.

Once we had been to an international match at Cardiff Arms Park which was followed by a blizzard. Mine was the only car to get home from Cardiff through to Abergavenny that night. Denis had taken over as Minister of Drought the previous year. He was successful in inducing the Rain Gods on the very day he was appointed and, at a later date became the Minister of Floods!

As we arrived home I suggested that he should become the Minister for Snow – by ten o'clock the next morning the Prime Minister, Jim Callaghan, had made the appointment! Denis was the ideal man to deal with national crises of that sort – combining ability and acceptability in the right formula.

I was appointed by the Tories for three years and then by the Socialists for two more terms of three years. Both administrations were guided by the Welsh Office of whom I have the highest opinion.

It is fashionable to run down the Civil Service but I find its members dedicated and helpful. Both administrations gave us a free hand within our remit but their advice was invaluable. They tried their best to get us funds, not always successfully; throughout my nine years there has been a series of money crises.

The Sports Council formed the United Kingdom Affairs Committee; this has since proved invaluable. Being able to coordinate the criteria for administering the grant-aid with which we were entrusted, we were all able to have a voice in United Kingdom and international matters.

I have had a wonderful staff, headed by Harold Oakes, who combines a charming, outgoing personality with great ability as a staff officer. No one can produce a clearer document more quickly. (He has much of the quality of Jodl, the German Chief of Staff who on VE Day sent out the surrender document; he dictated six or seven hundred words without making a single correction.) Born in Lancashire, bred in Yorkshire, Harold Oakes is now basically a Welsh Nationalist!

Through the Sports Council I have met sportsmen from all over the world. I took the opportunity of visiting the Commonwealth Games in Christchurch, New Zealand, and have been abroad on many sporting functions.

The Montreal Games, however, I did not enjoy because everybody seemed to be in such a bad temper, particularly the Quebec Police who made life unbearable for the spectators and many of the competitors. On one occasion the Duke of Edinburgh was stopped by a very bossy Quebec policeman. When Chief Inspector Victor Hagen of Scotland Yard showed his pass, the Quebec policeman said, 'Well, I suppose you can go, but me – I work for Trudeau.' I had enjoyed Montreal on previous visits and have since been to other parts of Canada, having many friends throughout that wonderful country. But few of us who went to those Olympic Games were able to carry away the impression that we would have liked.

The Olympic Games in Munich which I attended in 1972 were, on the other hand, thoroughly enjoyable for everyone, participants and spectators. Endless trouble had been taken for our comfort and convenience. Every sport was extremely efficiently organized. It is sad that the Germans, who wished it to be known that they had become a peaceful nation instead of a warlike one, should have had their Games spoilt by the incident in which fourteen Israeli athletes were shot in the Olympic Village by the Palestinian Liberation Army. No one action brought politics into sport more than this did.

When this happened I had been waiting since six o'clock for the British team to turn up. I knew nothing about the shoot-up until Harvey Smith turned up half an hour later. I asked him why he had been delayed and he nonchalantly replied, 'Oh, there has been a dust-up between the Arabs and Jews – get the horse, Hazel,' and went on with his training. Little did he realize at that time the full horror of what had happened.

I have also seen a tremendous amount more of my own country than I would otherwise have done. Meetings of the Great Britain Sports Council take place in Scotland, Wales and Northern Ireland, so one has had the opportunity of visiting other places of interest and meeting many inspiring and enjoyable people. Having now travelled to all parts of my own country, dare I confess that although I had been to many places abroad, including the far west of Canada, and South Africa, I had never been north of Llandrindod Wells before the war.

I love my own country of Wales. All parts of it have delightful scenery and I feel at home wherever I go, for the Welsh traditionally give everyone a warm welcome. Anyone living in Wales must have at least 10 per cent of his views coloured by Nationalist ideas. I am sorry that I cannot speak the 'language of heaven' but love hearing other people speak it; I understand just a smattering. But forcing it down people's throats does not help the promotion of that language; too much zeal is counter-productive and parents resist their children being compelled to learn Welsh when French, German and Spanish are much more useful and enhance the process of thought just as much as a smattering of Welsh or Latin.

The Sports Council for Wales has to have regard for the wishes of the country's administrators although in fact no one can tell us what to do. Such a devolved body needs no further devolution. But of course the Administration holds the ultimate weapon in that it can both sack you and deny you grant-aid.

When I first rode Silver Step in the local show jumping class I never thought I would become the Welsh Sports boss and I certainly never dreamed that I would become president of the British Equestrian Federation responsible for all equestrian participation on an international scale. I had never coveted either job, neither of which existed in my young days, and which were created at about the same time in the early seventies.

Both jobs have taken up a lot of time. The BEF has been kept busy supporting such matters as the use of butazolidin to alleviate suffering in horses; 'The Case for the Riding Horse' to promote the breeding of competition horses and the withdrawal of our teams from the Moscow Olympic Games.

As chairman of the Sports Council for Wales I try to encourage both young and old, which takes me all over Wales and the rest of the United Kingdom. Apart from flying or going by train, I have motored 40,000 miles a year. The reward for this active life is that I really enjoy it.

Retirement on the 1 April 1981, means that I will have had nine and a half years with the Sports Council. After two-thirds of my term I was rewarded with a Knighthood, which when it came was a surprise. Years ago friends had suggested putting my name forward. I had said that it might be pointless as I was likely to outlive my elder brother who was not well at that time, and who indeed died in 1978 passing on the baronetcy to me. I also said that I did not want to be rewarded for my horsey activities as I had derived so much pleasure from them and the life that I had been able to lead.

When it finally did come up in the pipeline, I was watching flamingoes at Lake Nakuru in Kenya when a man with 'a forked stick' asked me to telephone the High Commissioner, Basil Fringland, who told me that the Prime Minister's secretary had cabled asking if I would accept a Knighthood. I said that I would have to ask my wife. This was on 26 May and the Jubilee Honours were to be published on 11 June so there was not much time. I replied, 'I suppose so.'

He said that was not good enough. He could not telephone Kenneth Strong with that message, so I accepted and said I was delighted.

Another interest that later in life was to prove absorbing was photography. I had always taken photographs on my various trips abroad before the war, and also for the first eighteen months during the war until my camera was brewed-up in Iraq.

Following my Rhodesian shooting-trip in 1932, I had continuously planned to visit Africa to take photographs of the wildlife. When judging in Johannesburg I had been to the Kruger Game Park but it was not until 1973 that I was asked back again and so had the opportunity for which I had longed.

I bought myself a superb M3 Leica and 90-mm lens before leaving London. We flew right into the Okavango Swamps to Xaxaba which was alive with game. Annually, the rains from the mountains in Angola flood internally down the Cubango River, to where it crosses the Caprivi strip before entering Botswana, when it becomes the Okavango. Occasionally, floods are limited. The whole area is unique in appearance, as there are many heavily wooded small islands which are isolated when the floods come but leave large areas of flat land in between, so we were able to move around freely. There were tremendous herds of tssessebe with wonderful trophy heads. On looking at Rowland Ward's *Book of Records* I find that my 1935 world record tssessebe has now been relegated to sixth position because of these Botswana heads. Blast!

Our camp was sited on the side of a stream over which pied kingfishers continually hovered, and it abounded with red lechwe. The bird life was fascinating, with wattle cranes and saddle-bill storks which were plentiful. I am not much of a fisherman these days but rather fancy myself spinning backhand, particularly when the fish so easily surrendered, as they did in our stream. I caught eleven fish out of eleven casts and amongst them were six different varieties, mostly of barbel and bream.

I went with Nico Charter and three Greys from Johannesburg and we had an eventful time. A lechwe bull had been killed a mile from the camp and Lloyd Wilmot had towed the carcass into camp for butchering. As a result the whole area was teaming with hyenas laughing and cackling all night. We slept with our tents well zipped-up as there were many reports of hyenas biting the faces off men when they were asleep. Lion were heard every night near at hand. When I went out in one of the dugout canoes to see a kill I saw the shadow of a tawny shape in a bush fifty yards away. It was enough to send me paddling like mad back to my friends. On another occasion we ran into a pack of wild dog.

Lloyd Wilmot was well known for his familiar approach to wild animals. He was born in the bush. His grandfather was the famous Cronje Wilmot who played such an important part in the anti-tsetse fly game-fences just after the First World War. Lloyd's father is reputed to have shot the world's record crocodile of twenty-one feet, but he was killed by a black mamba shortly before our visit.

When we saw wild dogs, Lloyd leapt out of the jeep and stalked them on his knees. On previous occasions he had got right in amongst them and they had been 'mock charging' him. They fled once he stood up and identified himself as a man.

Lloyd also tried this stunt on lions. There are photographs showing him stalking a lion while another was stalking him! He also had a trick of walking up to an elephant, and based this on the belief that it would only make a mock charge at him. As soon as it stopped he would kick up dust and sticks in its direction which usually discouraged it; but he never invited three such charges from the same animal and so far has survived. I have known many people who feel they have a special understanding of wild animals but regretfully most of them have eventually been killed. I trust Lloyd will survive as he is a brilliant athlete.

On occasions we followed the honey-guide birds which brought us to bees' nests. Whatever the size of the tree or however bare the trunk, Lloyd somehow managed to climb them. Traditionally he left a little honey for the honey-guides to encourage them to help in the future.

This visit to the Okavango fired me with tremendous enthusiasm so on my way home I arranged to spend a week in Kenya. I hired a car and driver and went to the Amboseli and Tsavo Reserves where I saw lion, elephant, buffalo, rhino and hippo, as well as observing two cheetahs kill a wildebeest calf.

Subsequently we spent an hour watching them eat the calf without any other cars or minibuses coming to join us. Suddenly a swarm of them descended upon us so we left, soon to find ourselves marooned, with the engine refusing to start, in the middle of a pride of fifteen lion. The minibuses arrived shortly afterwards and formed a circle round us, while my driver fiddled about and the engine started up again. The lions in this part are so tame that they paid no attention whatsoever to any of us. Meanwhile, I had been snapping away like mad and some of the best pictures I have were taken with my M3 Leica on this trip.

Since then I have visited practically all the game parks in Kenya, Zambia, Malawi, Rhodesia and South Africa, concentrating mostly on the South Luangwa Reserve in Zambia and the Mara in Kenya. Recently I was asked to be the guest host on a pioneer riding-safari just north of the Mara Reserve. Although photography was difficult, this viewing of game added a new dimension. Often we visited places where vehicles could not reach. We felt we were citizen animals and thoroughly enjoyed every minute, including climbing a thousand-foot escarpment on foot and fording the crocodile-infested river Mara. Of all the game-reserves I have been to, visits to Norman Carr's camp at Chibembe up the Luangwa in Zambia, stand out. There was a huge variety of birds and game, including the now rare black rhino.

Photographing wild animals is a distinct art. When one first sees a new species, one takes quick snaps before aiming at producing a 'picture postcard' photograph with a closeup showing the whole animal. Composition ultimately is vital, but unfortunately animals do not pose in the right place at the photographer's request. Having been a competitive person I find competing against myself fascinating. I have to take photographs of every bird or beast that are better than my previous ones.

When I went to the reserves in Zululand in 1976 I started to concentrate more on cine-photography with Super 8 film. When I get home I spend many hours editing films and reliving life out in the bush. I treasure more than anything film records of nyala watering peacefully at Mkuzi in Zululand and at Lengwe in Malawi; a wild dog defending a dead giraffe near Savuti in Botswana as if it were its own kill; two lionesses stalking, killing and devouring a topi in the Mara; birds flying in slow motion (fifty-four slides to the second), including fish eagles, saddle-bill and woolly-necked storks, as well as flocks of flamingo in the Rift valley.

The still photographs of which I am proudest are of the rare pangolin (scaly ant-eater) in Botswana, bongo at the Ark, in Kenya giraffe in front of Kilimanjaro, cheetahs at a kill and various fairly angry elephants.

Since 1976 this has proved an absorbing hobby. For me, taking films is buying happy memories.

Recalling my various experiences I realize that my children have shared comparatively few of them. Dai, Roddy and Anna, however, say I am much more fun away from home and not so bossy. It is three to one – so I must agree. Of course, Teeny and I love having them at home. Dai happens to like living in London. I shall try to avoid doing so until I am very, very old and I know my wife feels the same.

After leaving Eton (with his 'leaving book') Dai went to Milton Abbey to further his studies but having no ambitions in any academic direction went off and found himself a job with Quantas. This he held for a couple of years, earning enough money to enjoy the London life to which apparently he is addicted. I believe he still rides well and enjoys his foxhunting, having a knack for being there at the right time and seldom missing a hunt. So he has the makings of a countryman after all.

247

I later sent him to South Africa and Rhodesia, and he gradually found his way to Sydney before motoring to Perth and taking off for Los Angeles, via Hawaii. During this time he had toughening experiences, earning money quickly, spending it equally quickly and eventually, in Los Angeles, getting himself out of an embarrassing financial position (caused by a venture into the film industry) by selling wigs! He became an expert. He was provided with a Porsche, had tremendous freedom and within three months was out of debt and enjoying himself in New York and Long Island. It might have been better if he had stayed longer as a wig salesman as he was offered a top executive job. Wig making has a guaranteed 'onput' just as undertakers have a guaranteed throughput! He successfully held jobs in London with night-clubs and with Masius Wynn-Williams, the eminent British advertising firm; but after a month or two in each job he was rather apt to tell the Manager what to do. Possibly the independent streak of the Llewellyns sometimes proved unprofitable. Dai has now married Vanessa Hubbard, a delightful and beautiful girl, after having been engaged or semi-engaged to three other charming girls.

Anna was born at Llanvair on 29 May 1956, and was always cheerful and fairly tough. After a local kindergarten she went at the age of eight to Lady Tryon's school at Durnford near Salisbury. Shortly after she asked to see the headmistress, to tell her that she had dreamed that fairies were dancing about on the bottom of her bed. Asked what her reaction had been she replied, 'I just said "Bugger off fairies," and they went!' After a few terms at Millfield, she went to Hatherop – and then to the Schmidt school in Munich to learn German. Later she went to the universities at Tours and Aix-en-Provence to learn French. She loves travel and we have thoroughly enjoyed being on safaris together. After returning from a tour of South America she set off round the world, east to west – following the sun. Now she is studying marine biology near Belize, British Honduras. She has a huge circle of friends and a warm side to her character which endears her to many.

Roddy could not be more charming to his parents. It is no secret in the past there have been periods of friction between him and myself. Fathers plan different careers for their sons from those they choose for themselves.

After leaving Shrewsbury, Roddy went to the university at Aix-en-Provence and came home with a good knowledge of French. After two spells in South Africa and Rhodesia, he agreed to apply for a short service commission. He was interviewed and accepted by Sir John Anderson, Colonel-in-Chief of the 5th Inniskilling Dragoon Guards, of which Mike Ansell was a member and had supported Roddy's application. Roddy then appeared in front of the Royal Armoured Corps Appointments Board. During this interview he was asked why he wanted to join the Army. He replied, 'I do not really want to, but my father thinks it would be good for me.' Not surprisingly, a letter came back saying that at that time Roddy lacked the necessary motivation but possibly should apply at a later date.

He was then accepted by Whitbreads and appeared enthusiastic about entering the brewing industry. He went to the Maltings at Harrogate, liked it and was given an excellent report. At Tennants in Sheffield, an area he did not like so much, he again received an excellent report for his shift-brewing and was put on a good salary. He moved to London to learn brewing at Whitbreads in Chiswell Street. At this stage he suddenly decided not to proceed with a brewing career, to the disappointment of all those involved, including myself. He then spent nearly two years at the College of Arms; he loved the job but the pay was negligible.

After this there was a 'far-out' phase. He drifted to Surrendell Farm in Gloucestershire where a few of his newer friends and he planned to farm on a community basis as practised in many parts of the world, particularly in Russia and Israel. I refused to help finance him for this operation as I felt a collection of mostly unskilled amateurs could not make a success of the farm nor of the restaurant in Bath called the 'Parsenn Sally', in which Roddy had a small investment but was never a director. My wife, much kinder than myself, visited these places, but I never went near either of them.

Roddy is much liked in the neighbourhood where he has many friends. He has a special rapport with Teeny's sister Vicky, who married Tony Llewellen Palmer, one of the four dashing cavalry officer sons of Colonel Pedlar Palmer. He has green fingers and achieved a tremendous amount in our kitchen garden, helping considerably with any minor landscaping problems we had, paying special attention to young trees and shrubberies. In the house he kept a close eye on its condition and if there was a leak in the roof he was on to it in a flash. If leaves were blocking a gutter he was on the spot, if pictures had to be cleaned or removed, he always had good ideas. In other words he was very useful about an establishment such as ours.

When Surrendell folded up and the partners dispersed, Roddy

became associated with Algy Clough, the North Sea Oil king. He was dealing with quite a different type of business and was gradually getting the grip of it, when he set off for India without telling anyone, including Algy Clough. He returned to find that he had lost his job.

Roddy has always helped, with Dai, to organize the Christmas carols at home. He had been head of the choir at Shrewsbury and has a natural, pleasant voice. He could hit a note and sustain it but he never had real volume. He needed training by a professional. I liked his plan to become a singer but I did not approve when I learned that he was not going to have his voice trained. I did not accept the explanation that nowadays one can play about with somebody's voice electronically. If it is slightly off key you turn a switch and if it is not strong enough you press a button. If a note has not been sustained, another button prolongs it.

Most Welshmen are taught to sing from the stomach, look up and have their tongues flat on the bottom of their mouths. Lacking even these basic requirements Roddy was launched on a career as a pop singer. He agrees it is pointless to blame anyone for his failure. Possibly he lacked dedication. Impresarios have succeeded in promoting people with ghastly, croaking voices which come out of their ears. Some untrained voices have won fortunes for their promoters and themselves, but this was not to be in Roddy's case.

Although he sang well enough he did not have enough volume which made it seem all the more extraordinary when, in some of his records, his voice was drowned by the back-up singers. However, he made a little cash out of his exploits and I believe it was fun while this rather light-hearted affair lasted.

My two boys are now well into their thirties, and live their own lives.

18 Looking Back

I am tempted to look back.

On the whole I have been extremely fortunate to have had an enjoyable and full life, with, above all, many wonderful and lasting friendships. Having suffered from ill-health during my school days, I realize how lucky I have been to have enjoyed robust health from then on.

As a child my whole attitude was conditioned by the comfort and warmth of my mother which at the time I felt was overdone. Whereas the breaks from school impeded my scholastic success, and even the desire to achieve it, not being allowed to play games until I was twelve encouraged me to play harder and compete compulsively at every game I subsequently played. Any success with horses in competition – whether racing or show jumping – was the result of this approach to sport.

Thinking back over my life I do not have many regrets. But with the value of hindsight, and knowing how useful the experience would have been, I would have liked to have trained as a chartered accountant, like my friend Peter Lang, as this training qualifies one for so many pursuits and all kinds of industry. I have always been interested in the financial aspect of business, and have been on the finance committees of many bodies at one time or another, when such a training would have helped me.

I have enjoyed nearly everything I have done. I would have liked to have spent more time on artistic interests – pictures, the opera and especially the ballet – but then there was never enough time for everything.

Two final thoughts. Firstly I had the kindest and fairest of mothers and a father who was my guide, mentor and friend. After my father's death early in the war my mother survived for several enjoyable years in her flat at Whitehall Court where she kept her large family of four sons and four daughters very much together. This has resulted in exceedingly close family ties.

Lastly, I cannot express enough my gratitude to Teeny, my wife, for her love and companionship during thirty-five rather hectic years.

Index

257